Hermeneutical Paths to the Sacred Worlds of India

Edited by Katherine K. Young

McGill Studies in Religion

Hermeneutical Paths to the Sacred Worlds of India

McGill Studies in Religion
McGill University

Edited by
Arvind Sharma

Volume 1

HERMENEUTICAL PATHS TO THE SACRED WORLDS OF INDIA

Essays in Honour of Robert W. Stevenson

edited by
Katherine K. Young

Hermeneutical Paths to the Sacred Worlds of India

Essays in Honour of
Robert W. Stevenson

edited by
Katherine K. Young

Scholars Press
Atlanta, Georgia

HERMENEUTICAL PATHS TO THE
SACRED WORLDS OF INDIA
Essays in Honour of
Robert W. Stevenson

edited by
Katherine K. Young

Library of Congress Cataloging-in-Publication Data
Hermeneutical paths to the sacred worlds of India : essays in honour of Robert W. Stevenson / edited by Katherine K. Young.
p. cm. — (McGill University studies in religion ; 1)
Includes bibliographical references.
ISBN 1-55540-952-0
1. India—Religion. 2. Hinduism—Sacred books—Hermeneutics. 3. Philosophy, India. 4. Hermeneutics. I. Stevenson, Robert W. II. Young, Katherine K., 1944- . III. Series.
BL2003.H43 1994
294.5'9—dc20
93-48224
CIP

Printed in the United States of America
on acid-free paper

TO ROBERT W. STEVENSON

Even if I die and pass through seven
births, I shall not forget the good
he has done me.
(A Tamil Proverb)

CONTENTS

PART I: EXPLICATING CONCEPTS BASIC TO THE WORLD OF THE TEXT

PART II: STRATEGIES FOR INTERPRETING INDIAN TEXTS

PREFACE AND ACKNOWLEDGEMENTS

These essays have been written in honour of Robert W. Stevenson (professor of Hinduism and Comparative Religion, McGill University, 1966-1987). The contributors — Katherine K. Young, Richard P. Hayes, Alaka Hejib, Shrinivas Tilak, Nancy Ann Nayar, Leslie C. Orr, Roger Marcaurelle, Julian F. Woods, Tazim Kassam, and Zayn Kassam-Hann — have all been associated with the Faculty of Religious Studies, McGill University, over the past decade. We wish to express our appreciation to the Shastri Indo-Canadian Institute for funding the research of Young, Tilak, Orr, Nayar, T. Kassam, and Marcaurelle at various stages. We also wish to thank Heidi Furcha and Samieun Khan for their efforts in the technical preparation of this manuscript, and to Robert MacKenzie who served as managing editor.

INTRODUCTION

Katherine K. Young

Hermeneutics is about understanding and interpretation. This collection of essays raises questions about hermeneutics in the Indian tradition. How did ancient Indian thinkers understand the nature of a text? Did it have semantic autonomy? Did the author's intention alone define its meaning? Was there an objective meaning if each new reader brought different experiences and awareness to bear on the interpretation? How was scriptural exegesis to be done? Were there rules for legitimate interpretation? Were there levels of meaning in a text? How did ontological and epistemological presuppositions affect the understanding of a text? What role did creativity play in interpretation? Were there systems of interpretation implicit in commentaries? And how did a text relate to the issues of its epoch?

At one time the offspring of Western theology and philology, the emergent discipline of hermeneutics now claims universality. Its claims must be tested, however, in a comparative framework. This volume contributes to this task by: (1) explicating some specific concepts to illustrate the variety of interpretive techniques in the Indian tradition; and (2) discussing some general hermeneutical problems. These essays not only further understanding of notions of karma, time, renunciation, and pervasion in Indian thought, they also shed light on Jaimini's *Mīmāṃsā Sūtras*, Vasubandhu's *Abhidharmakośa-bhāṣya*, Śaṅkara's *Bhagavadgītā-bhāṣya* and *Brahmasūtra-bhāṣya*, Rāmānuja's *Bhagavadgītā-bhāṣya*, Parāśarabhaṭṭar's *Śrīviṣṇusahasranāma-bhāṣya*, Śrīnivāsa's *Yatīndramatadīpikā*, and Pīr Shams' *Brahma Prakāśa*. By extension, they lead us along hermeneutical paths to some sacred "worlds" — Buddhist, Hindu and Islamic — of India.

For modern scholars of ancient texts, interpretation poses some special problems. Researchers must cross many barriers of understanding in order to stand within another world view. They must have expertise in a language such as Sanskrit, Tamil or Hindi (as in the essays in this volume). And they must also be acquainted with Indian methods of interpretation. In the case of orthodox

Sanskrit texts, for example, this ideally involves knowledge of the six limbs (aṅgas) of the Vedas, or scripture par excellence — that is, the "sciences" of correct pronunciation, metre, etymology, grammar, astronomy, and ceremony. Brahmin experts in the Vedas are described, even in the Pali Canon of the Buddhists, as those who know by heart the three Vedas, including the mantras, and the list of difficult words. In addition, experts know ritual, syllables and phonology, exegesis, stories, words, grammar, and lokāyata (*Ambaṭṭha Sutta* 3:18-23). Such learned ones (paṇḍitas) can move about easily within a subject and "carry through" in the sense of knowing and understanding.

Traditionally, the brahmanical tradition placed a premium on the linguistic foundation of culture itself. The word "Sanskrit" (the name of the main religious, philosophical and literary language of India, once the lingua franca), for instance, is from the verbal root saṃskṛ, meaning to form well; to form or arrange according to sacred precept; to adorn, embellish, refine, elaborate, make perfect, especially to form language according to strict rules. To be cultured in classical India was above all to express oneself in elegant Sanskrit studded with jewels of allusion to literary, religious and philosophical works. Cultured people had the mark (lakṣaṇa) of learning.

Even today in India, people perform rituals (pūjā) to their books. They honour and worship those who preserve the texts through exact memory and transmit them with care to sons, students or disciples. Interpreting the texts with technical ingenuity based on the various "sciences" of interpretation, they find the inspiration and guide for right living within them. Indeed, most paths to enlightenment involve devotion to knowledge. Traditional expertise long preserved by the Brahmins still lives on in modern India, though it is becoming rare for a father to transmit this knowledge to his son. Departments of Sanskrit in Indian colleges and universities are taking over the task. Nevertheless, the modern scholar faces an increasingly hermetic textual tradition without the support of traditional oral exegesis. Moreover, mastery of any branch of learning is no small feat, as any student of Pāṇini's *Aṣṭādhyāyī*, which presents the meta-system of Sanskrit grammar, knows only too well.

Principles of interpretation are also embedded in the texts themselves and must be extracted to appreciate the range of exegetical tools ancient Indian thinkers used. One favourite strategy was to arrange all items in a list. This indicated both totality and hierarchy (since the first, final or middle items were most important). But even here, the order of importance was debated and provided exegetes scope to argue different positions. Though there was no manual spelling out these principles, many could be traced to the Mīmāṃsā school. This repertoire of strategies was not confined to intellectual circles; it was part of the larger Indic tradition, embedded in both elite and popular culture. For instance, a principle called "pointing out by way of emphasis" (prādhānyavyapadeśa) was reflected in the tradition of honouring the wife's supremacy as the goddess incarnate on certain ritual occasions even though her traditional position in the home was sometimes subordinate to husband and elders.

Buddhism was not a living tradition of India for many centuries; this means that its theories of text and methods of interpretation must be extracted from the textual record itself or learned from exegetes in other, especially contiguous, Buddhist lands such as Sri Lanka or Tibet.

The Tamil intellectual tradition, too, has its own techniques as can be seen in the *Tolkāppiyam*. By the time of the Bhakti poetry of the Āḻvārs and Nāyaṉmārs, however, the Caṅkam world view reflected in the *Tolkāppiyam* was sufficiently discontinuous, at least in "Hindu" sectarian circles, that such technical expertise was, by and large, preserved only in texts (and rediscovered in the nineteenth century). Meanwhile, the influence of Sanskrit, after the tenth century in South India, meant that understanding the hermeneutical strategies of Sanskrit texts was necessary. Today the scholar of religion, philosophy and text in Tamil Nadu must recover the traditions of both Tamil and Sanskrit interpretation to understand the rich South Indian tradition.

One of the most hermetic Indian traditions has been that of the Ismā^{c}īlīs. On the one hand, this Islamic community was overtly syncretistic. This helped it form alliances with Hindus or convert them. On the other hand, it was covertly Ismā^{c}īlī because the texts (gināns) were ostensibly Hindu. This helped it avoid persecution by other Islamic communities. Because there are no Indian Ismā^{c}īlī texts that make explicit the interpretive methods of the dā^{c}īs or pīrs, the missionaries and leaders of the community who composed the gināns, modern scholars must look for clues in the gināns themselves along with historical and comparative studies.

Western scholars will be familiar with many Indian interpretative methods. They will find striking parallels between Western and Indian discussions about the semantic autonomy of the text, the rules for legitimate interpretation, or the levels of meaning. The articles in this book, however, should stimulate new thinking about some of the claims made in current Western discussions of hermeneutics. In at least one way, Western theories may be more parochial then initially meets the eye. For while their strength lies precisely in understanding the historical context of a text and its interpreters, their weakness lies in the very eclipse of meaning that results from superimposing modern, Western views of epistemology and ontology on non-Western texts. Western-trained interpreters are likely to consider the traditional Hindu approach akin to ahistorical romanticism or the transcendental subjectivism of Husserlian idealism. Contemporary hermeneutics has challenged these approaches in no uncertain terms. Any attempt to extend the discussion of hermeneutics to the Indian tradition will probably meet the same challenge.

Paul Ricoeur writes about the need for a double "distanciation" or distancing: establishing the text's autonomy and projecting oneself into its "being-in-the-world." Appropriation is a response to this "double distanciation." Ricoeur admits that appropriation, in the final analysis, leads to subjectivity and hermeneutics terminates in self-understanding. But for him, understanding can never be isolated radically from the historical moment. It can never be romantic or ahistorical; rather, it is dialectical, oscillating between remoteness and proximity, but always historically rooted. Reality is metamorphosed, moreover, through the "imaginative variations" that literature carries out on the real (Ricoeur 1981, 112). Extrapolating from Ricoeur, we may expand the concept of "being-in-the-world" to embrace a Hindu view of hermeneutics: understanding ahistorical truth contained in "eternal" texts. This expansion, Ricoeur would say, is like the ontological aspects of *play* (Ricoeur 1981, 117). It is open-ended. The self is perpetually changed by it, enlarged continually with new "worlds" presented by new texts. For Ricoeur, literature, with its many "worlds," offers the best texts to ruin the ego's pretension of constituting itself as ultimate origin.

This is put another way by David Tracy. He writes about a "necessary movement in interpretation from otherness, to possibility, to similarity-in-difference," (1987, 21-22) or analogy. One may learn to explore the world manifested in high romantic works. Tracy, however, argues that:

> Our own post-romantic response is not likely to be one of identification with, or great empathy for, the romantic vision. A more wary, ironic, even suspicious response is probably the only one that a postmodernist sensibility can accord the claims for genius, creativity, symbol, and the imagination made by romantics. Insofar as we understand Schleiermacher or Coleridge at all, we understand them differently from how they understood themselves (Tracy 1987, 21).

Tracy and Ricoeur might say the same about the Hindu idealist way of life. They might discover analogies and play, but ultimately they would reject the Indian claim of certainty, mastery and control. "No one can doubt that the use of historical-critical methods has become a central demand in our historically conscious culture. In one sense, we have all become lawyers constantly using such qualifier words as 'allegedly,' 'supposedly,' or, 'it was then believed' whenever we interpret our historical narratives" (Tracy 1987, 35).

Because a historical-critical method is ultimately associated with an epistemology and ontology, it must clash with traditional Hindu claims. The image of play (līlā) also appears in Hindu texts, it is true, but the Self that plays has found Truth. The ego or the ordinary self is destroyed in a moment of illumination, but the real Self now "playing" knows all and has neither need nor desire to "grow" through more "texts":

> One necessary condition for faith in the ultimacy of freedom is the belief that freedom is not only logically possible but *actually* possible, i.e., that at least one route is open which a man can find and travel to complete freedom .... In order to believe that there is a route for any given man, I must presuppose that the notion of a "route" means something; that is, I must believe that certain conditions which are part of the defining characteristics of a "route" can be satisfied. A route is, first, something that a man can be "on." Secondly, it is something which has stages — if only the two stages of "not there yet" and "arrived." If I doubt that a man can ever be "on" a route, then I doubt that freedom is actually possible; the same is true if I doubt that there is any distinction between "not there yet" and "arrived." The experiential counterparts of these intellectualistically expressed doubts are certain fears — the fear that men are never on their way to anything, and the fear that the best there is is what we have already, with all its frustration. Supposing that I am free from such doubts, I must further believe that each and every man is in a position from which he can get himself onto an appropriate route and stay on it .... But the belief in a man's ability to get on and not get off a route presupposes two more beliefs — one is the belief that there is a sufficient condition for getting on and not getting off, and the other the belief that man is free enough from external influences so that he can bring about a sufficient condition for getting on and not getting off his route. The twin doubts pertinent to this set of conditions are, on the one hand, skepticism, the doubt that events are regularly connected and consequently that there is a sufficient condition for getting on and not getting off, and on the other hand, fatalism, the doubt that man is free from a predestined fate determined by impersonal forces independent of his control. The parallel fears are, on the one hand, the fear that nothing one can do can bring about a hoped-for result, and, on the other, the fear that nothing one can do can alter what is about to occur (Potter 1965, 22-23).

So ends the first chapter of Karl Potter's now classic book, *Presuppositions of India's Philosophies*. According to Potter, understanding a text presupposes freedom, a path, and a leap. Speculative philosophy is inextricably connected to freedom, to its conditions, and to self-knowing. Indian philosophy deals with perception, inference, verbal authority, causation, relations, negation and error but all these discussions are to foster understanding and experience of a path to freedom. And because the path enables people to face mortality, it is ultimately a religious one. Because the text reveals a path, it may occasion the "leap" to liberation. Accordingly, philosophy, religion, and text intersect.

It seems, then, that the traditional Hindu world view is remote from that of the post-modern West. So is the Buddhist one. Despite Theravāda Buddhism's doctrine of momentariness and constant flux, its final goal is to "blow out" the self (nirvāṇa), not to expand it. Some schools of Buddhism discuss the "play" of enlightened people. But this, too, is associated with ultimate wisdom, not perpetual growth. Confidence in the reality of the "other world" is a critical point of departure in allowing people to enter and inhabit it. Tracy describes the interpreter as a risk-taker (1987, 22) and realizes that "we can also find ourselves in a radical conflict of interpretations. This conflict can even be internal" (1987, 23). Though he hints that a world view may be fundamentally altered, he has little confidence in the ability of post-modern people to travel down different roads. Any fusion of horizons will be temporary or slightly expansive. By contrast, Indian texts are considered central to the task of enlightenment. Doubt, skepticism, and fatalism characterize current Western discussions of hermeneutics. Calls for play, openness, and risk do not do justice to the traditional Indian confidence in the text as a path to freedom or liberation.

With these general thoughts on hermeneutics in mind, let us turn to the essays found in this volume. We begin with those that analyze particular concepts. Richard P. Hayes' essay, "The Analysis of Karma in Vasubandhu's *Abhidharmakośa-bhāṣya,*" focuses on a key hermeneutical problem: how to understand a concept (in this case, the law of karma) that is central to a particular text and to a world view. He approaches the topic by comparing popular and philosophical notions of karma. The former is represented by several modern Buddhists who resort to moral and natural explanations, the latter by Vasubandhu, an important Buddhist thinker of the Abhidharma school. Hayes examines the ontology of abhidharma in which the ultimately real (atoms or mental properties) is opposed to the conventionally real (a person). He then raises questions regarding the law of karma. If a person is not an ultimate reality who acts but only a composite entity that is constantly changing, what is it that acts? What experiences the consequences of the original action? And in what sense is the agent of the original deed the same as the eventual experiencer of the consequences? How and where are the potential consequences of an action "stored" until they are realized as consequences capable of being experienced?

In the course of his textual analysis, Hayes uses his knowledge of the Abhidharma tradition (ontology, causality, and conditioning factors). More specifically, he uses his knowledge of the Vaibhāṣika school in order to understand not only Vasubandhu's antecedents, but also his originality and refinement regarding the interpretation of karma. The hermeneutical task, accordingly, involves elucidation of a pivotal concept internal not only to the commentary of a particular thinker but also to the historical development of a specific school. Hayes concludes that there are some real difficulties reconciling the law of karma with the Abhidharmic view of ontology. The Abhidharmists themselves came very close to admitting that the law of karma is not real but only a conventional or provisional truth. They did not say so explicitly, thinks Hayes, because they perceived a need to preserve Buddhism as an institution. It is possible, however, that their reluctance to state the implications of their own perspective may, in fact, have been caused by their unwillingness to take a stand that would challenge the words of the Buddha himself (buddha-vācana). In other words, as Shrinivas Tilak suggests in a later essay, there was a tendency in the non-Vedic schools for the author's words to become authoritative. This happened even though the Buddha himself declared that a person's own understanding and experience were ultimately to be the guide to wisdom.

Be that as it may, Hayes' essay demonstrates the intimate relation of religion, philosophy and text in India. On a popular level, of course, the law of karma was linked to religion, for it was about destiny (rebirth or enlightenment). On a technical level, destiny could not be considered apart from right understanding, which introduced philosophy through ontology and epistemology. But even in philosophical arguments, there were continual references to the words of the Buddha or the special characteristics of the arhants (enlightened ones) described in the Canon. This, in fact, was one version of the hermeneutical circle in which the part implies the whole and the whole the part. Philosophy, religion and text (whether scripture, aphorism, or commentary) were integrated in the sacred worlds of India. The word abhi-dharma itself, says Hayes, "can be used figuratively to refer to the wisdom that serves as a necessary condition for nirvāṇa. And by a further extension, this same word can apply to any treatise that, when studied, makes it possible for one to develop wisdom."

Julian F. Woods looks at the brahmanical doctrine of karma in "Karma in the *Bhagavadgītā* according to Śaṅkara and Rāmānuja." He examines karma in three particular senses. First, karma is ignorance (avidyā). This causes the illusion that characterizes human existence and thus causes rebirth (saṃsāra). Second, karma is the action that maintains society and orders it, providing an opportunity to redirect destiny toward enlightenment, and thus prevent rebirth. Third, karma is the discipline of action (karmayoga) leading to liberation. Woods illustrates the relation of scripture (here the *Bhagavadgītā*) to its interpreters (Śaṅkara and Rāmānuja) in the brahmanical tradition. Although both see ignorance as the reason for human bondage — thereby linking philosophy to religion through epistemology — each has a very different understanding of epistemology. This, in turn, is related to their very different understandings of ontology and karmayoga.

Because both commentators claim exegetical fidelity to the text yet emerge with radically different views, the problem of establishing criteria for the authority of a particular interpretation arises. Woods claims that Rāmānuja remains much closer to the spirit of the text than his illustrious predecessor. Śaṅkara is "forced by his theory of illusion (which finds little support in the text) to discount what is, after all, the main purpose of the teaching: to make Arjuna act . . . to restore dharma as an instrument of God's Will." But modern scholars may have different hermeneutical perspectives — with their own epistemology and ontology — that just happen to coincide with Rāmānuja's interpretation of the *Bhagavadgītā*. Many presuppose the historical conditioning of the text; this makes it primarily a product of its age. They also take as the proper scope for interpretation only the text itself, though, in the final analysis, they admit that the text is mediated through the reader's awareness. If we were to "bracket" the historical perspective and entertain the Mīmāṃsā theory of interpretation with its presupposition of the *oneness* of truth contained in *all* Hindu scriptures (and not just a single text), we might be more sympathetic to Śaṅkara's commentary. When many of those Upaniṣadic passages that stress the ultimate reality of Brahman without qualities (nirguṇa) are taken into consideration, Śaṅkara's commentary on the *Bhagavadgītā* certainly makes more sense. Śaṅkara must demonstrate consistency among the Upaniṣads, the *Bhagavadgītā* and the *Brahmasūtras*. He knows full well that epistemology and ontology are central to any search for the "one truth." His interpretation of the *Bhagavadgītā* is consistent if passages such as those that describe Brahman without qualities are thought to dominate the scriptural corpus as a whole, either quantitatively or qualitatively. At the very least, we must understand Śaṅkara's presuppositions.

With the traditional interpretation of Indian texts (be they Hindu or Buddhist), we frequently encounter the idea of two levels of understanding or two levels of reality. We have already encountered the Abhidharma distinction between what is ultimately or substantially real and what is only conventionally real. When we think of Hindu interpretation based on two levels, it is Śaṅkara who comes to mind first owing to his famous analogy of the serpent and the rope. (The serpent is recognized as an illusion once the form is seen as it really is — a rope.) But after studying Śaṅkara's *Brahmasūtra- bhāṣya*, I began to realize that the idea of two levels does injustice to the elegance of Śaṅkara's exegetical system. In point of fact, he implied four levels rather than two. Making illusion (māyā) and superimposition (mithyā) the key concepts leads to a short circuit, so to speak, of the power of Śaṅkara's system to reveal progressively the nature of Brahman. In this sense, Śaṅkara's system functions as a path or sādhana. Each level is presented as real and full. Existential and analytical realization of a level's supposed fullness is followed by instruction on its limitations and preparation for its deconstruction. This leads to awareness of a more inclusive level. Readers move through a series of levels. The last represents a qualitative break with the one before. This is expressed in its radical negation "neti neti" (not this, not this).

Leslie Orr takes up the challenge of this paradigm shift from two levels to four and explores its capacity to elucidate Śaṅkara's concept of time in his *Brahmasūtra-bhāṣya*. Because Brahman is said to be changeless, permanent, immortal, eternal, and limitless — and therefore different from the temporal, phenomenal world — time becomes a pivotal category. But, suggests Orr, instead of there being simply *two* ways of categorizing the temporal status of things or kinds of knowledge — as eternal or temporal — Śaṅkara presented a more complex picture. The levels — characterized as empirical time, transcendental time, time dissolved, and time destroyed — represent: "(a) a world view, a particular understanding of the nature of time and its impact on the individual; (b) a task with respect to the awakening of a certain kind of insight or discrimination; and (c) a particular spiritual goal." This schema helps explain Śaṅkara's concepts of Brahman, the self, the world and liberation. And it shows how Śaṅkara reconciled divergent scriptural texts (śruti or smṛti) and refuted other philosophical systems (darśanas) by switching levels.

Orr warns, though, that Śaṅkara often glossed over differences among the four levels, obscuring their boundaries and points of view. This occurred for several reasons. Śaṅkara realized that the boundaries themselves were somewhat indefinite, making absolute classification impossible. He wanted, moreover, to maintain the validity of different levels of teaching — thereby encouraging the idea of sādhana — rather than the idea that one should supersede another. He presupposed the exegetical principle of unity (tātparya), that is, the single purpose of scripture. He also ignored boundaries to demonstrate such unity. All this had a sociological angle as well. Śaṅkara wanted to create solidarity among the orthodox by stressing similarity rather than difference, thus mounting an intellectual and spiritual offensive against the Buddhists and Jains. Finally, he wanted to establish that unity is the highest truth. This meant that there can be "no gradations of right knowledge and there is but one result of knowledge, that is, liberation." At times, he obscured the levels to make this point.

In "The Basic Types of Renunciation in Hinduism: With Special Reference to Śaṅkara's *Gītā-bhāṣya*," Roger Marcaurelle points out that modern interpreters of Indian texts often cause misunderstanding by not using accurate, systematic and consistent terminology for the concept of renunciation. Using Śaṅkara's commentary on the *Bhagavadgītā* as his example, he makes explicit four categories of renunciation by focusing on what is being renounced. He shows how attention to nuance not only helps avoid ambiguity and inaccurate generalization but also promotes understanding of the commentary itself. Marcaurelle admits that extracting these four types of renunciation may already involve his own act of interpretation. He replies that this is "an unavoidable part of the hermeneutical enterprise, where one is always to intuit the whole by the parts and the parts by the whole, back and forth in an infinitely refining process of understanding."

Zayn Kassam-Hann analyses the concept of pervasion (vibhu) in a late Viśiṣṭādvaita text that purports to summarize the tenets of the school. Brahman, who is viewed theistically in this school, is vibhu by his own form (svarūpa), by his attributive consciousness (dharmabhūtajñāna) and by his special bodies (vigraha). The ensuing examination of pervasion in these three senses illustrates the way philosophical discussion both illumines and shapes religious thought in Hinduism (and vice versa). Skill in interpretation is necessary to hold together ideas such as God's absolute purity, goodness, and knowledge despite his pervasion of cit (souls) and acit (world), which are characterized by impurity, evil and ignorance.

The remaining essays raise more general questions about the nature of hermeneutics in various Indian scriptural traditions. In "The Mīmāṃsā Theory of Text Interpretation," Shrinivas Tilak asks about the nature of a text and of interpretation. He begins by pointing out the origin of the Indian discussion in the Mīmāṃsā school. The Mīmāṃsakas argued that action is the essence of human existence, that the guide to action is contained in the commands (vidhis) of the Vedas, and that the Vedas are authoritative because they are authorless, eternal and inerrant. From a historical perspective, Tilak notes that the Mīmāṃsakas developed their ideas of text and interpretation to meet challenges created by philosophical, political, and social turbulence in the sixth century B.C.E. They wanted to restore the primacy of action over escapism, and ritual action over asceticism. They wanted to maintain the Upaniṣadic ideal of one truth despite the myriad and potentially conflicting ritual commands of the late Brāhmaṇas. And they wanted to establish the authority of the Vedas to counter the Buddhist critique of them as contradictory, superfluous, and therefore hindrances to enlightenment. Tilak discusses the ensuing debate over the nature of the text. It centred on the question of whether scripture can be authoritative or not. He identifies two ideal types: (1) the Vedist (specifically, the Mīmāṃsaka or Vedantic) position; and (2) the non-Vedist (specifically, the Buddhist) position. The former emphasizes the absence of an author and, therefore, the semantic autonomy of the text (apauruṣeya). The latter emphasizes the presence and importance of an author: the Buddha. Tilak sees in these two positions analogues to a contemporary debate in hermeneutics. Does the text itself have objective meaning (therefore semantic autonomy)? Or does the author's intention provide the legitimate meaning? By reconstructing the Indian attacks and counterattacks in this debate, he illumines the theoretical issues.

The French Indologist Madeleine Biardeau is acutely aware of the conflict between historical and ahistorical approaches to the text. This is discussed by Julian Woods in his essay "Hinduism and the Structural Approach of Madeleine Biardeau." Biardeau presupposes that Hindu mythology is consistent, for the mental environment of symbolic meanings is a product of the brahmanical mindset. She argues that the world view of Hinduism, its "essence" or comprehensive vision, can be explained in myth, because myth is a "privileged medium" that raises fundamental questions and governs values. This is best done by examining the Purāṇas as the logical starting point for cosmology, eschatology, and macrocosmic time. But that may involve searching for antecedents in earlier texts such as the Vedas, Brāhmaṇas and Upaniṣads. Only with all this in mind can the *Mahābhārata*, with its focus on cosmic time and individual destiny, be studied adequately.

By taking the mythic corpus as a whole and using the structural methods of Dumézil and Lévi-Strauss, Biardeau's ahistorical approach may, in fact, elucidate the approach of past Brahmin thinkers. These Brahmins, as mentioned previously, presupposed the unity and consistency of all scriptures. At the highest level, they acknowledged an ahistorical vision of reality. According to Biardeau, "whatever the historical truth of these events, the account of them is given in myth and a mythical necessity drives the account, not the other way around." Leaving aside Biardeau's structural analysis of the *Mahābhārata*, which Woods presents in this essay, let it suffice to say that, with Biardeau, we return to an emphasis on the text itself to provide criteria for interpretation. We find ourselves in a mythic realm that has its affinities with an ahistorical world view. This calls into question the appropriateness of a *primary* emphasis on history, in a civilization such as India's. Indeed, the Brahmins obscured change through myths, thereby giving an ahistorical dimension to much of the historical record. (This understanding need not exclude modern historical studies but highlights the brahmanical approach to scriptural texts.)

Like modern scholars, traditional thinkers mediated one world of meaning and another. This was especially true in Tamil Nadu, where Dravidian and Sanskritic traditions were undergoing contact and change. Śrīvaiṣṇava Brahmin Ācaryas, for instance, developed the interpretive category ubhāya-vedānta (both vedāntas) to acknowledge their scriptures in Tamil and Sanskrit, their dual religious heritage. From the thirteenth century C.E., Ācaryas accepted the idea that earlier teachers were knowledgeable of both the Sanskrit religious texts and the Tamil hymns of the Āḻvārs. In their commentaries they noted parallels between the two scriptures and created various links to integrate the texts into a unified world view. This approach was dramatically challenged in the 1960's by the textual analysis of an American scholar, Robert Lester. He observed, through his historical-critical method, a lack of references in the Sanskrit works of the first three Ācaryas (Nāthamuni, Yāmuna and Rāmānuja) to the Āḻvārs, their Tamil poetic corpus, and their most important ideas. Accordingly, he concluded that these Ācaryas had nothing to do with the Tamil tradition, indeed, cannot even be considered Ācaryas of the temple tradition despite the sect's claim to the contrary. Rather, their writings — especially those of Rāmānuja — were merely appropriated by the Śrīvaiṣṇava community to legitimate the Tamil temple tradition through association with prestigious Sanskrit learning and Rāmānuja's philosophy of qualified non-dualism (viśiṣṭādvaita).

In "The Tamilizing of a Sacred Text: The Devotional Mood of Rāmānuja's *Bhagavadgītā-bhāṣya* and Āḻvār Spirituality," Nancy Anne Nayar reassesses the findings of modern textual analysis regarding the discontinuity between Rāmānuja and the Āḻvārs. She reviews the explicit links between them made in such Śrīvaiṣṇava texts as the *Irāmānujanūṟṟantāti*, the taṉiyaṉs, the three major hagiographies, and the stotras. Returning to Rāmānuja's commentary on the

Bhagavadgītā, she searches for clues to this problem. She focuses her analysis on the concept of God's untaintedness (nirmalatvam/ amalatvam) and on the devotee's inability to find sustenance for the soul in separation from God. Nayar finds evidence for the influence of Āḻvār spirituality in Rāmānuja's commentary on the *Bhagavadgītā* and connects it to specific Āḻvār poems. These findings substantiate my own argument that although Rāmānuja nowhere refers explicitly to the image-incarnation (arcāvatāra) so important in the Āḻvār poems and later Śrīvaiṣṇava thought, he nonetheless provides a blueprint for this idea in his commentary on *Bhagavadgītā* 4:7-11. Nayar herself, in another study, comes to much the same position about the concept of surrender (prapatti).

Taking all these studies together for evidence, it may be concluded that reliance on the explicit meaning of a text, especially as captured in key terms, can do great injustice to its interpretation and even to the larger tradition. Superficial use of textual criticism can create misunderstanding rather than understanding, especially when this involves a claim to superior truth by virtue of an "objective" method. An author may quite intentionally play with overt and covert meanings knowing full well that those outside the immediate sect will focus on the overt while those within the community will recognize the covert. This still leaves the problem of how Rāmānuja's use of overt and covert meanings is to be understood. Why does he offer only an elusive blueprint for certain ideas so important for Tamil Vaiṣṇava spirituality? To explain this, it is necessary to look beyond the text to the aims of the author, the community, and the age. There are limitations, in other words, to the idea of textual autonomy.

My joint essay with Alaka Hejib — "Etymology as a Bridge between Text and Sectarian Context: A Case Study of Parāśarabhaṭṭar's Commentary on *Śrīviṣṇusahasranāma*" — is about the role of "etymology" in understanding and interpreting the text. We apply the discussion of etymology as a "science" of interpretation (according to Yāska's *Nirukta* and Durga's commentary) to Parāśarabhaṭṭar's commentary on the one thousand names of Viṣṇu. To link these names to basic principles of Viśiṣṭādvaita, Parāśarabhaṭṭar used etymologies. He generally observed the rules for deriving etymologies formulated by Yāska. On occasion, however, he was creative. But even his creativity was prefigured in Yāska's admission that etymology may be derived in accordance with the desired effect. In other words, Yāska had already legitimated an author's creativity.

Tazim Kassam may have had the most difficult interpretive task of all in her study of the *Satpanthī Khojās* (Indian Ismā^{c}īlīs). This sect has remained hermetic throughout its history, has spanned intellectual and folk traditions, and has embraced Hindu symbols to facilitate the conversion of Hindus to Islam. Moreover, its script has been secret and its texts have contained all the linguistic difficulties of Indian vernacular literatures. The sect has even appropriated the texts of other religious groups and attributed their authorship to famous Ismā^{c}īlī religious leaders of earlier centuries. Today the sect is undergoing a process of Islamization in part because its scriptures (the ginān̄s) contain much Hindu content.

With such obstacles, understanding a text such as *Brahma Prakāśa* is a major challenge. Was it written by an Ismā[c]īlī or not? Could that author really have been Pīr Shams, a figure thought to have lived in the twelfth century C.E.? The language of this text and many of its allusions, after all, are characteristic of the sixteenth century. Is it simply a hodgepodge of Hindu and Islamic elements? Or is there a subtle integration of the two, showing signs of intellectual design and well-crafted poetry? Did it facilitate conversion of Hindus to the Ismā[c]īlī sect? Or was it sufficiently Hindu that Hindus considered it just another Hindu work? Kassam argues persuasively for the genius of an author who subtly created a double reading: one Hindu and one Islamic. This can be grasped best through the analogy of a "figure-ground" diagram where the "figure" may be either Hindu or Islamic (depending on who is reading the text) or first one and then the other (as in the case of some converts or intellectuals who perceive the double message). That its final verses focus on the Imām who has come in this age to save everyone, though, suggests that the author was an Ismā[c]īlī, probably a pīr, whose goal was conversion of Hindus.

The study of hermeneutics in the rich textual traditions of India is just beginning. Because of differing approaches to epistemology and ontology, not to mention the "art" of interpretation itself, it is best to proceed cautiously by the case study method. In this manner, some hermeneutical paths may be cut through the underbrush and markers left to guide others on their journeys deep into India's sacred worlds. We hope this volume will be a significant step on the way.

BIBLIOGRAPHY

Auerbach, Erich. 1953. *Mimesis: The Representation of Reality in Western Literature*. Princeton: Princeton University Press.

Bedekar, V.M. 1969. "Principles of Mahābhārata Textual Criticism: The Need for Restatement." *Purāṇa* 11:210-228.

Biardeau, Madeleine. 1968. "Some More Considerations about Textual Criticism." *Purāṇa* 10:115-123.

Gachter, Othmar. 1983. *Hermeneutics and Language in Pūrvamīmāṃsā: A Study in Śabara Bhāṣya*. Delhi: Motilal Banarsidass.

Gupta, Ananda Swarupa. 1970. "A Problem of Purānic Text-Reconstruction." *Purāṇa* 12:304-321.

Kantawala, S.G. 1986. "Purānas and Textual Criticism." *Purāṇa* 28:34-44.

Lewis, David. 1986. *On the Plurality of Worlds*. Oxford: Basil Blackwell.

Monier-Williams, Monier. [1899] 1970. *A Sanskrit-English Dictionary*. Reprint. Oxford: Clarendon Press, 1970.

O'Flaherty, Wendy Doniger. 1979. *The Critical Study of Sacred Texts*. Berkeley Religious Studies Series. Berkeley: The Graduate Theological Union.

Palmer, Richard E. 1969. *Hermeneutics*. Evanston: Northwestern University Press.

Potter, Karl H. 1965. *Presuppositions of India's Philosophies*. New Delhi: Prentice-Hall.

Ricoeur, Paul. 1974. *The Conflict of Interpretations: Essays in Hermeneutics*. Evanston: Northwestern University Press.

—. 1981. *Hermeneutics and the Human Sciences: Essays on Language, Action and Interpretation*. Ed. and trans. John B. Thompson. Cambridge: Cambridge University Press.

Timm, Jeffrey R. 1992. *Traditional Hermeneutics in South Asia*. SUNY Press.

Tracy, David. 1987. *Plurality and Ambiguity: Hermeneutics, Religion, Hope*. San Francisco: Harper and Row.

PART I

EXPLICATING CONCEPTS BASIC TO THE WORLD OF THE TEXT

THE ANALYSIS OF KARMA IN VASUBANDHU'S ABHIDHARMAKOŚA-BHĀṢYA

Richard P. Hayes

As a popular teaching, the Buddhist doctrine of karmic fruition (karma-vipāka) is relatively easy to understand and poses few problems. In the popular Buddhist view, the law of karma is a principle of nature, according to which a person who acts in a certain way must later experience consequences that are pleasant or unpleasant, depending upon the nature of the action itself. Geshe Ngawang Dhargyey, a modern Tibetan author, thus explains the law of karma as a special case of the general law of cause and effect. "Karmic seeds," he writes, "inevitably ripen in accordance with their cause, i.e., virtue leads to joy, and non-virtue to sorrow" (Dhargyey 1974, 71). Another modern Tibetan author, Geshe Rabten, states the matter even more forcefully: "Just as a seed cannot grow into a plant of a different type, so our actions can only produce actions of their own type. An unvirtuous action can only give rise to suffering, and a positive action can only give rise to happiness. This order can never be mixed up" (Rabten 1984, 114).

Expanding on this basic principle, Geshe Dhargyey explains that the effects of the fruition of an action are of three kinds. The first and principal kind of effect is rebirth in an appropriate realm; taking life, for example, is said to lead to rebirth in hell or in the form of an animal or hungry ghost. The second kind of effect is the formation of a habit or tendency to commit similar kinds of actions in the future; thus, one who delights in taking life in one human birth will be more likely to take life again in future human births. And the third kind of effect is what Geshe Dhargyey calls general "environmental" effect, such that, for example, nourishment and medicines that would normally be effective tend to fail to produce healthy effects in a person who has a history of vicious conduct (Dhargyey 1974, 87-88).

In some versions of the doctrine of karmic fruition, the principle of karma is not restricted to individuals but is also manifested in the living circumstances in which collections of people such as families, peoples and nations find themselves. A nation that has been warlike, for example, is likely to suffer the ill consequences of its collective acts of aggression in future generations. Such a nation is said to be especially prone to poverty, invasion by foreign powers and other forms of misery. When an individual is born in a nation that is going through evil times, it is regarded as the natural consequence of the individual's having acted in such a way that he or she deserves to be born in such circumstances. Thus, the karmic makeup of a set of circumstances is seen as an intricate network of collective and individual factors. The law of karma is said to manifest itself even in those areas of life that one might not intuitively take as being morally determined, as can be seen by the assertion of Geshe Rabten that "every detail, such as the colour in a peacock's tail, has its karmic cause" (Rabten 1984, 114).

But whether karma is considered individually or collectively, what remains constant is the principle that no circumstance arises by chance or fate or luck; rather, every circumstance is the natural fruition of actions performed in the past. There is, therefore, no injustice in a universe that has as an essential part of its structure a natural moral dimension. This moral dimension is, in the Buddhist view, as much an invariable part of the natural universe as are such physical dimensions as the law of gravity and the laws of thermodynamics.

Some authors, such as Walpola Rahula, emphasize the law of karmic fruition as a purely natural law to such an extent that they deny that it is a moral law at all. Rahula writes:

> The theory of karma should not be confused with so-called 'moral justice' or 'reward and punishment.' The idea of moral justice, or reward and punishment, arises out of the conception of a supreme being, a God, who sits in judgment, who is a law-giver and who decides what is right or wrong. The term 'justice' is ambiguous and dangerous, and in its name more harm than good is done to humanity. The theory of karma is the theory of cause and effect, of action and reaction; it is a natural law, which has nothing to do with the idea of justice or reward and punishment. Every volitional action produces its effects or results. If a good action produces good effects and a bad action bad effects, it is not justice, or reward, or punishment meted out by anybody or any power sitting in judgment on your action, but this is in virtue of its own nature, its own law (Rahula 1967, 32).

For reasons that will be outlined below, Ven. Walpola Rahula's claim that the Buddhist law of karmic fruition has nothing to do with notions of justice is one that must be examined more carefully. But whether or not one agrees with him, his statement is representative of how the law of karmic fruition is regarded by many Buddhist authors.

The popular version of the law of karma as presented above by various modern Buddhist writers is evidently well suited as a metaphysical foundation for the traditionally eudaemonic ethical guidelines of Buddhism. This doctrine gives the appearance, on the surface at least, of being well grounded in ordinary experience. Wrongdoing does, in the experience of most people, give rise to such unpleasant mental states as remorse and feelings of guilt, and these unpleasant mental states do seem to be as much a natural consequence of wrongdoing as becoming overweight seems to be a natural consequence of eating more than necessary. But how does the law of karma fare under the constraints of the more precise and rigorous presentations of Buddhist theory known as abhidharma?

While the talks of Gautama the Buddha were generally delivered to ordinary people in ordinary language and so adhered to the relatively loose linguistic and conceptual conventions of society at large, the purpose of abhidharma is to convey the teachings of the Buddha in a more exact and systematic way that is, ideally at least, as free as possible of figurative expressions and other kinds of conceptual shortcuts. The purpose of this essay is to examine the discussion of karma as found in the *Abhidharmakośa* of the fourth century C.E. Indian abhidharma specialist Vasubandhu.

Ideally, any abhidharmic account of experience should refer only to things that are ultimately real, as opposed to things that are established only in virtue of the agreement of society. The principal criterion of being ultimately real, as opposed to being a convenient social fiction, is stated by Vasubandhu to be simplicity or irreducibility. That which cannot be broken down, either physically or conceptually, into more primitive constituents is said to be ultimately or substantially real (paramārtha- or dravya- sat); on the other hand, that which can be physically broken or analysed into more simple concepts is said to be only conventionally real (saṃvṛti-sat) (*Abhidharmakośa* 6:4). A piece of pottery, for example, can be broken into shards, and those shards can, in turn, be broken down further, in principle at least, until one finally arrives at individual atoms that are not further divisible. The pottery is therefore considered real only in virtue of a social convention that arises because the pottery serves the practical needs of the community that puts it to some specific use. To state the matter another way, a pot is a pot only insofar as it is perceived as serving the needs of people who make use of it as a vessel for storage, cooking, carrying and so forth. Once these needs no longer exist, or once the item called a pot no longer serves those needs, the word "pot" either falls into disuse altogether or ceases to be applicable to that item. A configuration of atoms that serves no specific function to society has no specific name and therefore does not have any conventional existence as a separate object; such a configuration of atoms simply remains an indistinct part of the perceptual background. The individual atoms, on the other hand, exist independently of any social conventions. Moreover, they are the ultimate building blocks from which all other physical objects are made. And so the atoms, unlike the objects that are composed of them, are, according to Vasubandhu's criterion, ultimately real.

Applying Vasubandhu's criterion of what is ultimately real to the realm of human behaviour leads to the abhidharmic analysis of the complex object, known conventionally as a person, into constituent parts that are themselves not susceptible to further analysis. This analysis is familiar to every student of Buddhism, so there is no need to give more than the bare outlines here. What is conventionally called a person is analysed by abhidharma first into two broad sets of components, namely, the physical body (rūpa) and the collection of mental properties (nāma). The physical body is analysed into the primary principles of solidity, cohesion, motion and heat, which are conventionally called the primary elements of earth, water, wind and fire. In the body of a living being, these elements are arranged into organic components such as the sense faculties, sensible properties, and reproductive organs; since these features are composed of the primary elements, they are said to be derivative material properties.

The mental aspect of the person, on the other hand, is analysed into four categories: (1) vedanā, which is the capacity to sense physical pleasure and pain; (2) samjñā, which is the capacity to recognize patterns; (3) six vijñānas, which are the six types of sensory awareness corresponding to the five external sense faculties and the intellect; and (4) a large number of saṃskāras, which are the various habits and abilities that collectively define personality or character. A great deal of abhidharmic literature is devoted to giving precise definitions of these constituent parts and accounting coherently for how they interact.

When one looks at the doctrine of karma from an abhidharmic perspective, a number of questions naturally arise. According to the popular version of the doctrine, for example, whatever action a person performs has a consequence that that same person will eventually experience. But according to abhidharma, the person is not an ultimate reality. So the first challenge facing the abhidharma analyst is to describe exactly what it is that acts; this amounts to giving an account of which of the various ultimately real components that make up a person is the agent of a deed. The next challenge is to describe exactly what it is that experiences the consequences of the original action; this amounts to giving an account of which of the various ultimately real components that make up a person is the experiencer of the consequences of the deed. A third challenge is to give some account of the sense in which the agent of the original deed is the same as the eventual experiencer of the consequences. And a fourth challenge is to explain how and where the potential consequences of an action are "stored" until such time as they are realized as consequences that are capable of being experienced.

To illustrate some of the above-mentioned challenges facing the abhidharma analyst, let us take the example given above by Geshe Dhargyey of the person who deliberately takes life and then is reborn as, say, a peacock, in some future birth. What the abhidharma analyst must be able to explain is where this "seed," which has been sown when a human being with a human mind kills a living being, is stored until it naturally ripens into the consequence of a peacock's body being born with a peacock's mind. Is it to be supposed that the atoms that once made up the human being's body somehow bear the imprint of this murderous misconduct in such a way that they reformulate later into a peacock's body? And if so, how? Or is it to be supposed that the karmic imprint is borne by one of the mental properties that makes up the human being's character in such a way that the human being's character is eventually transformed into a peacock's character? If so, then which of the ultimately real mental properties is so imprinted? And how does the imprinting govern the loss of attendant mental properties, such as intellect, suitable to a human being and the subsequent acquisition of mental properties suitable to a peacock? Bearing these questions in mind, let us turn now to Vasubandhu's abhidharmic analysis of the theory of karma.

The fruition of karma, as was said above, is a special case of the general law of cause and effect. So before we can come to terms with the special laws of karmic causality, it will be necessary to review some general principles of causality as treated in Vasubandhu's system of abhidharma and to review what exactly abhidharma is.

The word abhidharma is explained by Vasubandhu as referring literally to the supreme (abhi) property (dharma), that is, to nirvāṇa, which is the property that every Buddhist strives to acquire as his or her ultimate goal. Nirvāṇa can be attained by no other means than by eliminating erroneous views as to which physical and mental properties are healthy (kuśala) and which are unhealthy (akuśala). This capacity to discern the healthy from the unhealthy is called wisdom (prajñā). Wisdom, therefore, is the *sine qua non* of attaining nirvāṇa. By metonymy, the substitution of the name of a cause for the name of an effect or vice versa, the word abhidharma can be used figuratively to refer to the wisdom that serves as a necessary condition for nirvāṇa. And by a further extension, this same word can apply to any treatise that when studied makes it possible for one to develop wisdom (*Abhidharmakośa-bhāṣya* ad 1:1-2).

The proper subject matter of an abhidharma treatise is the entire set of properties or dharmas that are the ultimate constituents of experience. These properties fall into natural groups according to shared features. One such natural classification is the five groups (skandha) of properties that make up what is called a person: (1) the group of material properties (rūpa-skandha) found in the physical body; (2) the group of physical sensations (vedanā-skandha); (3) the group of ideas (saṃyñā-skandha); (4) the group of conditioning characteristics (saṃskāra- skandha); and (5) the group of types of specific sensory awareness (vijñāna-skandha). All the properties that fall into one of these five natural groups are composite (samskṛta); that is, they are made (kṛta) from a plurality of causes that have assembled (sametya) to produce an effect. Here we have the first principle of causality: no composite thing whatsoever arises from a single cause (*Abhidharmakośa-bhāṣya* ad 1:7).

Closely related to the principle that all composite properties arise from a plurality of causes is the principle that whatever is composite is innately unstable and liable to change; that is, every composite property has an innate potential to decompose. From the principle that whatever is composite has an innate potential to decompose, Vasubandhu derives the principle of radical momentariness. This principle states that whatever is composite must decompose in the very moment that it arises. This principle is not one that can be derived from empirical observation, for indeed it appears to the senses that physical bodies and so forth endure through time. That composite things must decompose in the very moment that they arise is a principle that can be derived only by reflecting upon what it means to say of a thing that it has an innate potential to do something (*Abhidharmakośa-bhāṣya* ad 4:2-3).

When we say that a thing has an innate potential to act in a certain way, we are saying that nothing outside that thing is necessary to prompt it into acting in that specified way. If we say, for example, that fire has an innate capacity to give off heat, we are saying that fire in and of itself gives off heat quite independently of any other factors. If fire has an innate capacity to give off heat, then it is not the case that the fire burns as its principal action and that its giving off heat is a further action that may arise or not, depending on whether or not some further condition separate from the fire comes along to prompt it to give off heat. This principle becomes more clear if we contrast an innate potential with an accidental or extrinsic potential. A book placed on a shelf has a potential to fall to the floor. But in order for this potential to be actualized, something outside the book, a force of some kind, is necessary to make the book fall. The book's potential to fall is therefore not an innate potential but rather is an accidental potential. So when we say that a composite thing has an innate potential to decompose, we are saying that no further factor is necessary to prompt it into decomposition. Rather, composite things decompose entirely on their own.

If we now pursue this notion of innate potential to its logical conclusion, it can be shown to follow that whatever has an innate potential to act in a certain way must act in that way in each moment of its existence. Fire, for example, if it has an innate potential to give off heat must give off heat in each moment that it exists as fire. For if it were not the case that fire realized this potential in each moment of existence, we should have to find some explanation for why it realized its potential in some moments of its existence and not in others. If it were the case that fire sometimes gave off heat and at other times did not, this variation in its behaviour would have to be due to some factor outside the fire that was acting upon the fire to enable it to give off heat in some moments but not in other moments. But if this were the case, then the potential to give off heat would be accidental to fire and not innate. Applying this line of reasoning to a composite property, it can be seen that if a composite property has an innate potential to decompose, then it must decompose in every moment of its existence. But when a composite thing decomposes, it ceases to exist as a composite thing. Therefore, a composite thing must cease to exist in every moment that it exists. In other words, a composite thing exists for only one moment.

Vasubandhu's conclusion that no composite thing exists for more than a single moment is evidently in harmony with the general Buddhist tenet that there is no enduring self (ātman) or person (pudgala), and that any belief in an enduring self is therefore a delusion. But this conclusion also raises a number of difficult problems for the doctrine of karma. For example, if an action perishes in the very moment that it is performed, how can it have any consequences in the future? And even if this problem can be solved, the question still remains how can it be said that the composite "person" who performed the action in the first place and also decomposed immediately is the same "person" who experiences the consequences of that action at some future moment?

The problem of how an action that perishes in the very moment that it is performed can have any effects in the future is a special case of the general problem of how any composite property can have an effect in any moment after its single moment of existence. According to Vasubandhu, all composite properties have an innate potential to decompose, but some composite properties also have an innate potential to cause another property to arise in the immediately subsequent moment either in exactly the same place or in an immediately adjacent place. There are, however, various constraints on what kinds of properties can give rise to what kinds of immediate successors. These constraints are outlined in Vasubandhu's discussion of the various types of cause (*Abhidharmakośa-bhāṣya* ad 2:49-57).

The system of abhidharma that Vasubandhu endorses recognizes six basic types of cause. The first and most general type of cause is a productive cause (kāraṇa-hetu, or jānaka-hetu). In general, insofar as no property obstructs the coming into being of any other property, every property is regarded as a productive cause of every property other than itself. But, more specifically, a productive cause is one that gives rise immediately to its proper effect; thus, for example, the eye, attentiveness and colour are jointly the productive causes of vision, for vision arises if and only if all three of these factors are present in the immediately preceding moment.

The second type of cause is called an interdependent cause (sahabhū-hetu); two properties are said to be interdependent in case each is the cause of the other (*Abhidharmakośa* 2:50). This kind of causal relationship is said to exist among the four elementary principles of matter, namely, solidity, cohesion, motion and heat, for none of them can exist without the presence of the other three. Similarly, a relationship of causal interdependence exists between thought (citta) and the various properties that accompany thought (caittas), for there can be no thought in the absence of these other factors, nor can these other factors arise in the absence of thought. Not all properties that exist in the same moment are interdependent, but all interdependent properties are simultaneous.

The third type of cause is called a like cause (sabhāga-hetu), because it gives rise to an effect that is similar to it with respect to its being healthy, unhealthy or indeterminate; that is, a healthy (kuśala) property always engenders a healthy successor, and so on (*Abhidharmakośa* 2:52). The effect that resembles its causes in healthiness is called a resultant effect (niṣyanda-phala), and it always arises immediately after the like cause that engendered it (*Abhidharmakośa* 2:57-59). A healthy cause is defined as one that gives rise to a desired result (iṣṭa- phala) and therefore makes one immune to suffering for a period of time ranging in length from one moment to forever; the immunity from suffering forever, of course, is said to be possible only for those who have completely eradicated the false belief in an enduring self and the desires and animosities grounded in that false belief (*Abhidharmakośa-bhāṣya* 4:45). An unhealthy cause is one that leads to some result other than what one desired and therefore causes temporary suffering.

The only kinds of properties that are capable of being healthy or unhealthy are premeditated bodily and verbal actions, thoughts and acts of awareness that accompany those thoughts. An act of visual awareness, for example, that is accompanied by a lustful thought is unhealthy due to the unhealthiness of lust, but an act of visual awareness that is accompanied by equanimity and modesty is healthy due to the healthiness of equanimity and modesty. Thus, it is not the case that some sight, such as that of a beautiful woman, is in and of itself healthy or unhealthy; what makes the sight of a beautiful woman healthy or unhealthy is the mental disposition of the person who sees her. All visible properties and all sounds aside from deliberate actions are said to be ethically indeterminate (avyākṛta), as are the four primary elements of matter, the five physical senses, and all odours, tastes and tangible properties (*Abhidharmakośa* 4:46).

The fourth type of cause is called an associated cause (samprayukta-hetu), and this type of causal relation occurs only between acts of awareness and their associated mental states. Lust, for example, is an associated cause of a lustful act of visual awareness (*Abhidharmakośa* 2:51).

The fifth type of cause is called a universal cause, and it applies to a set of ten properties that are supposed to be invariably present with every moment of awareness. According to Vasubandhu, every moment of awareness is accompanied by some physical sensation (vedanā), intention (cetanā), the recognition of patterns (samjñā), a desire to act (chanda), contact (sparśa) between a sense-organ and a sensible property, the ability to discern properties from one another (mati), attentiveness (smṛti), mental effort (manaskāra), some degree of reflection (adhimukti) and some degree of mental focus (samādhi). Since these properties accompany every moment of thought, they are not in themselves either healthy or unhealthy (*Abhidharmakośa* 2:54).

The sixth type of cause is called the cause of fruition (vipāka-hetu). It is regarded as the cause that gives rise to the final result of a causal sequence initiated by an action or karma in the past. This final fruition is the experience of happiness or frustration that naturally results from a healthy or an unhealthy action. Being a final result, the fruition itself is indeterminate, for it does not give rise to any further healthy or unhealthy properties, but it is invariably caused by an antecedent healthy or unhealthy action. One further point concerning this fruition is that only certain kinds of actions have a fruition at all. Unhealthy actions are said always to have a corresponding fruition. But only some kinds of healthy actions have karmic consequences, namely, those that are accompanied by what the Buddhists call contaminations (āsrava). The four contaminations enumerated by the Buddhists are sensual desire (kāma), craving for further existence (bhava), misconception (avidyā) and opinions (dṛṣṭi). According to all systems of abhidharma, which here follow a long-standing traditional teaching of Buddhism, a person who has eradicated sensual desire, has no longing for continued existence, is free of erroneous views and has no trace of opinions never again produces karma. In other words, a person who has fully developed wisdom (prajñā) may continue to perform actions, but these actions are not regarded as karma. Since a wise person's actions are not karma, she or he never has to be reborn in order to experience the consequences of actions performed in this life (*Abhidharmakośa* 2:57).

Closely associated with the notions of fruition-cause (vipāka-hetu) and contamination (āsrava) is the doctrine of the three realms or spheres (dhātu) of existence. The lowest of these realms is that of sensual desire (kāma-dhātu), which is so called because in this realm desire for the objects of the five external senses of vision, hearing, tasting, smelling and touch play a leading role in one's experience (*Abhidharmakośa-bhāṣya* ad 2:12). In this realm the factors of the noble eight-fold path are said to be absent in their purest form (*Abhidharmakośa* 6:73).

The second realm is that of pure form (rūpa), which one enters by entering into one of the stages of meditation (dhyāna) in which the elements of deliberation and sustained thought (vitarka and vicāra) are replaced by dispassion (upekṣa) or indifference to objects of sense. In the first stage of meditation there may be either pleasant or neutral sensation associated with awareness of sights, sounds and bodily feelings. In this first stage there may also be either happiness or indifference associated with the internal faculty of awareness, which is called mind (manas). The second and third stages of meditation are defined as those stages in which there are no physical sensations of any type. And so in these stages the only sensations are the mental sensations of either happiness or indifference. The fourth stage of meditation is defined as that in which there is only a mental sensation of indifference (*Abhidharmakośa* 8:12).

The third realm of experience is called the formless sphere (arūpa-dhātu), which one enters by practising the types of meditation in which the mind is dissociated entirely from the senses (*Abhidharmakośa-bhāṣya* ad 2:12).

It was noted above that not all kinds of healthy action produce karmic fruition, for it is only karma that is accompanied by a false belief in an enduring self that produces consequences. The Buddhists have a special name for people who have not yet recognized that all things are complex and therefore impermanent; such people are called the immature or foolish (bala) masses (putthujjana in Pali, pṛthagjana in Sanskrit). The immature masses are those who lack wisdom and therefore act out of desire for personal rewards (*Abhidharmakośa-bhāṣya* ad 3:28). It is only those people who lack wisdom who perform healthy actions that are motivated by a desire to experience pleasure in the realm of desire in the future. The healthy action that such people perform is called meritorious action (puṇya-karman), and it can take the form of making donations of land to the monastic community, or giving food, medicine or clothing to monks. All meritorious action is healthy, and therefore eventually results in temporary happiness, but not all healthy action is meritorious. People who practice meditation and cultivate wisdom, for example, perform healthy actions, but they do not generate merit, for merit is the exclusive possession of those who lack wisdom.

Given this outline of the types of cause recognized in Vasubandhu's system of abhidharma, we can begin to see how the abhidharma analyst accounts for how an action that immediately perishes still manages to give rise at some time in the future to an effect in the form of an experience of contentment or frustration. The initial healthy or unhealthy action immediately gives rise to an effect of the same type, and this, in turn, gives rise to another effect of the same type. This series of contiguous moments continues until finally an experience of morally indeterminate pleasure or pain arises. But the question still remains, what is it that keeps this causal chain of contiguous moments associated with the same "person?" For it must be borne in mind that the karmic chain is only one of many causal chains that together constitute what we call a person. At the same time that the karmic sequence is continuing itself through a series of moments, there are also causal sequences of elemental and derived physical properties, acts of awareness, attitudes and so forth. What is it that keeps all these sequences bound together in the complex of sequences that we intuitively take to be an individual person?

It is in his treatment of this question that Vasubandhu distinguishes himself from some abhidharma theorists who preceded him. The *Abhidharmakośa* is a work that comprises a set of verses along with Vasubandhu's own prose commentary to each of the verses. The verse portion of the work is said to present the abhidharma system of the Vaibhāṣika or Sarvāstivāda school of Buddhism, but in his prose commentary Vasubandhu takes the liberty of criticizing the Vaibhāṣika position on a number of points. In the area of the theory of karma, Vasubandhu departs from the Vaibhāṣikas on two important issues. The first of these issues concerns what it is that binds many causal sequences together into one complex known as a person. The second issue concerns how and where a karmic potential is "stored" until its consequence is experienced at some time in the future. In the paragraphs that follow we shall first examine the Vaibhāṣika views on these issues, and then we shall examine Vasubandhu's criticism of these views, followed finally by a presentation of his own theory of karma.

The Vaibhāṣika school of abhidharma recognized within the broad group of conditioning characteristics (saṃskāra-skandha) a special subcategory of fourteen properties that were said to be dissociated from thought (citta-viprayukta). Generally speaking, thought becomes healthy or unhealthy depending upon the characteristics with which it is associated (samprayukta); characteristics that do not influence the health of thought are therefore said by the Vaibhāṣikas to be dissociated from thought. This miscellany of fourteen properties dissociated from thought was supposed to account for a variety of experiences that could not be easily explained within classical systems of abhidharma. Among them, for example, were three properties that enabled people to understand the individual syllables, words and sentences of human speech. Closely related to speech is the idea of an objectively real similarity among individual things, which accounts for our ability to recognize patterns and therefore give names to things in the first place; this principle of similarity, rather like the universals of Platonic philosophy, was counted by the Vaibhāṣikas as one of the fourteen dissociated conditioning characteristics. Also among these fourteen were four secondary properties, that is, universal characteristics of properties (dharma-lakṣaṇa). All properties, said the Vaibhāṣikas, have the characteristics of coming into being, enduring, decaying and perishing; these four characteristics belong to all properties of every type and therefore do not influence the state of health of the mind.

Also included by the Vaibhāṣikas among these fourteen special conditioning characteristics was a property that had the peculiar function of collecting other properties together into an integrated complex known in abhidharma as a continuum of consciousness (citta-santāna). This continuum of consciousness corresponds to what is known in ordinary conversation as an individual person. This continuum was said to be held together by a special conditioning characteristic known as acquisition (prāpti), which worked in conjunction with a second conditioning characteristic known as non-acquisition or prevention (aprāpti), whose function was to exclude some types of properties from a particular consciousness continuum. Acquisition, according to the Vaibhāṣikas, served to help a continuum acquire new properties and hold on to them in such a way that the continuum could be recognized over the course of time as the "same" person. It was this property known as acquisition that was also supposed to determine the states in which beings found themselves; some living beings, for example, are in the state of being arhants who are purified of all delusion and other contaminations, while other living beings are in the state of being deluded worldly beings. It is the property known as acquisition that ensures that the arhant's properties are those pure properties that are suitable to an arhant, while the worldly being's properties are those impure properties that are appropriate for a worldy being (*Abhidharmakośa* 2:35-36).

It is apparent that this special property known as acquisition was included by the Vaibhāṣikas in response to the need to be able to point to some ultimately real property capable of accounting for the intuition, regarded by Buddhists as a fundamental delusion, that people have more or less stable personalities despite their being made up of sequences of momentary properties that are constantly perishing. But in addition to that, a need was evidently felt to secure the doctrine that once one enters the noble path (ārya-mārga), by first abandoning belief in a real self and attachments to rites and rituals, one is no longer liable to fall back into the essentially "worldly" (laukika) preoccupations with gaining profit, comfort, good reputation and praise and avoiding material loss, discomfort, notoriety and blame. Thus, once one enters the noble path, the property known as acquisition is supposed to ensure that one acquire noble properties in the future, while the property known as non-acquisition is supposed to ensure that one avoid acquiring certain worldly properties in the future. Similarly, as one enters into further stages of the noble path, ending with entering the final state of an arhant, one's security from falling back into lower stages of the path is ensured, according to the Vaibhāṣikas, by the combined forces of acquisition and non-acquisition.

In addition to acquisition and non-acquisition, the two special conditioning characteristics dissociated from thought, the Vaibhāṣikas recognized a special form of matter belonging to the group of material properties (rūpa-skandha) that, unlike all other forms of matter, was invisible and intangible and therefore imperceptible. This unmanifested or non-phenomenal matter (avijñapti-rūpa) also played a key role in the Vaibhāṣika theory of karma. According to this theory, when a person performs a bodily action or a vocal action, the action itself is sensible as a visible or audible property. Because an action can be sensed by the eye or the ear, it follows that the action belongs to the group of material properties (rūpa-skandha) and is composed of the primary elements. This primary action, like all complex properties, immediately and spontaneously perishes. Therefore, a moment after it has been performed an action is no longer sensible. Moreover, some time may elapse between the time when the sensible action was performed and the time when its consequences become manifest, and during this interval between sensible action and sensible fruition, neither the action itself nor its eventual sensible consequences are perceived. Therefore, argue the Vaibhāṣikas, there must exist a continuum of imperceptible causes and effects that link the original sensible action with its eventual sensible consequences. Thus, they say, a sensible material action causes a non-phenomenal material property to arise in the immediately following moment, which, in turn, causes another non-phenomenal material property to arise in the moment immediately following that, and so on until one of these non-phenomenal material properties causes a phenomenal material property to arise, which can legitimately be regarded as the natural ultimate fruition of the original action.

Obviously, since non-phenomenal matter is by definition beyond the range of the senses, it can never be directly experienced but must be established by reason. The Vaibhāṣikas offer a series of arguments designed to prove that non-phenomenal matter must exist (*Abhidharmakośa-bhāṣya* ad 4:4).

The first argument that the Vaibhāṣikas offer is that the Buddha himself said that there are three types of matter. There is, he said, matter that is both visible and resistant; being resistant means that it prevents any other matter from occupying the same place at the same time. Secondly, there is matter that is resistant but invisible. And finally there is matter that is neither visible nor resistant. Now it is easy to find an example of resistant visible matter in earth, water or fire. And the fourth material element of wind is resistant but invisible. But what sort of matter is neither visible nor resistant? In speaking of this third category of matter, say the Vaibhāṣikas, the Buddha must have been alluding to this non-phenomenal matter.

The second argument for non-phenomenal matter is that the Buddha declared "The merit of a faithful son or daughter of good family who is endowed with the seven material articles of meritorious action, constantly and incessantly increases, whether he or she is moving, sleeping, standing or awake; the merit does indeed grow." This passage is usually interpreted to mean that a layperson who gives material gifts to the order of monks can expect to generate merit that increases more rapidly than merit produced by acts of kindness performed for ordinary people. But there is, say the Vaibhāṣikas, no way to account for this constant increase of merit in a person who is sleeping or who begins thinking of something other than meritorious action, unless one accepts that there is a non-phenomenal causal sequence at work "behind the scenes" while the person sleeps or engages in some activity other than that of deliberately increasing his or her merit.

A third consideration that the Vaibhāṣikas put forward is that a person may have his or her intentions carried out by a second party. A son may, for example, wish the death of his own mother, but, not wanting to perform a matricide by his own hand, he may command a servant or hire an assassin to perform the deed. In this case, neither the assassin nor the person who hired the assassin would actually be killing his own mother and so apparently neither would incur the especially grave consequences of matricide, which according to the Buddhists is the most heinous of acts and one that therefore has the most horrible consequences for the one who commits it. But surely, argue the Vaibhāṣikas, the law of karma cannot have such an egregious "loophole" that would allow a person to avoid serious consequences by merely having someone else actually perform a harmful act. Therefore, they say, the assassin's action of killing the mother must cause some non-phenomenal effect to arise in the continuum of the son who hired the assassin, whereby the son eventually experiences the consequences of matricide as if he himself had performed the murder.

A fourth argument advanced by the Vaibhāṣikas is that when a monk takes monastic vows, the power of these vows is said to remain binding for the remainder of the monk's career, that is, until he formally renounces his status as a Buddhist monk and declares himself free of further monastic restraint. Thus, a person who has taken monastic vows remains a monk even during those times when he is not engaged in meditation or any other especially monkish activity, is not explicitly thinking of himself as a monk and is not wearing robes or bearing any of the other visible signs of being a monk. A monk cannot, for example, simply decide for an evening to dress as a layperson and thereby take a temporary vacation from the monastic rules against taking alcohol, engaging in sexual practices and so forth. What keeps the monk bound to his vows and protects him from misconduct, say the Vaibhāṣikas, is an invisible and intangible property that he acquires upon taking the vows. This invisible property is the same non-phenomenal matter (avijñapti-rūpa) that operates in any person who has performed a sensible action whose sensible consequences have not yet arisen.

Another consideration that makes it necessary to posit a positive property that binds the monk to his vows, say the Vaibhāṣikas, is that the vows are essentially negative in nature. That is, the monk takes a vow to desist from all future killing, stealing, lying and so forth. Honouring these vows consists only in the absence of wrongdoing. But absence is not a real thing and can therefore have no real consequences. Consequently, if the taking of monastic vows is to have any positive effect, there must be some real property generated by taking them, namely, the property of non-phenomenal matter.

Vasubandhu rejects both the Vaibhāṣikas' theory of non-phenomenal matter and their theory of acquisition and non-acquisition. Let us consider first his replies to the four arguments that the Vaibhāṣikas advanced in favour of accepting non-phenomenal matter. The first Vaibhāṣika argument was that the Buddha's reference to matter that is neither visible nor resistant must have been an allusion to the non-phenomenal matter that is supposed to be the result of sensible actions. But this is not the only possible explanation of the Buddha's statement, says Vasubandhu. It could equally well refer to the essentially subjective sights and sounds that one experiences in certain types of meditation. Vasubandhu points out that it is generally accepted by Buddhists that every experience has some objective content, that is, that there is some external object that is grasped by the perceiving subject. But it is also accepted that people who are practicing meditation have experiences of sights and sounds that are not publicly observable. In cases such as these, what is the nature of the external object that is grasped by the perceiving subject? According to the Yogācāra system of abhidharma, such external objects are made up of a special kind of subtle matter that is produced by the act of meditation itself. This special subtle matter is said to be different from ordinary matter in that it is not publicly visible, and since it does not prevent other matter from occupying the same space at the same time, it is also not resistant. The Buddha's reference to invisible and non-resistant matter could have been to this special subtle matter produced by meditation rather than to the nonphenomenal matter endorsed by the Vaibhāṣikas. So unless further evidence can be produced to prove that the Buddha was referring to the type of subtle matter accepted by the Vaibhāṣikas and not to that accepted by the Yogācāras, this first Vaibhāṣika appeal to the words of the Buddha is not conclusive.

The second Vaibhāṣika argument was that non-phenomenal matter is necessary to account for the growth of merit in one who has given gifts to the community of monks. Once again, Vasubandhu argues that the increase of merit can be accounted for in other ways than by appealing to special subtle matter. The traditional explanation given by other Buddhist teachers was that it is simply the special virtues of the recipient of a favour that multiplies the good effects of that favour in the person who bestowed it. A monk who accepts alms, for example, uses the nourishment from his food in especially productive ways, using his energy for such things as cultivating universal love and kindness. It is because the monk cultivates love towards all beings that the food given to him has the ultimate effect of producing much good in the world, and therefore whoever offered the gift of food is indirectly responsible for doing great good to the world at large. Since the monk continues to cultivate love even when the layperson who gave alms has gone to sleep or has otherwise forgotten all about giving the alms, the benefits of the alms-giving grows no matter what the layperson may be doing. There is no need to posit the existence of a special property in the donor to account for the increase in his merit, since the increase in merit can be explained fully by the special virtues of the recipient.

The third Vaibhāṣika argument was that non-phenomenal matter is necessary to account for karmic consequences being experienced by a person who has another act on his behalf. Vasubandhu replies to this argument by saying that all that is necessary to account for a son's suffering ill consequences from the murder of his mother is the son's wish to see his mother killed. It is surely just this wish for the death of his own mother that serves to transform the son for the worse. The son will surely not experience any less guilt or shame if he has an assassin kill his mother than he would feel if he were to kill his mother by his own hand. Moreover, he will not suffer less guilt or shame if he orders the killing of his mother and the assassin somehow fails to carry out the execution than he would experience if the assassination were successful. Therefore, it is the wish to see one's mother die and not the actual carrying out of that wish by oneself or by another that sets the karmic chain in motion. And this karmic sequence can be explained, as we shall see below, without having recourse to the theory of non-phenomenal matter. And since a more simple explanation can be found, there is no point in adopting the unnecessarily complicated theory that when an action is actually performed by a person instigated to do it, the continuum of the instigator of the action acquires an invisible property that it did not have until the instigated action was successfully carried out.

The fourth Vaibhāṣika argument was that non-phenomenal matter is necessary to account for the presence of monastic restraint even in a monk who is not consciously thinking of being a monk and is not otherwise bearing the physical signs of being a monk. Here Vasubandhu claims that all that is necessary is to admit that there is a transformation in the continuum (santāna-pariṇāma) of the person who has a positive intention to avoid wrongdoing. It is this intention to avoid wrongdoing, rather than the actual taking of vows, that transforms a person for the better and enables him or her to avoid mischief, in much the same way that it is the intention or wish to see one's mother dead that transforms an offspring for the worse. But this intention is, like all other properties, impermanent and may eventually be replaced by other kinds of intention. It is only because the monk habitually recalls and renews his original intention to avoid wrongdoing that he succeeds in avoiding misconduct. It is the fact that intentions are impermanent, says Vasubandhu, that accounts for the fact that a monk does occasionally violate his vows quite deliberately. If the taking of vows produced a special property, such as the non-phenomenal matter that the Vaibhāṣikas posit, that protected the monk from the time of vow-taking onwards, then it would be difficult to explain how a monk who had once taken vows could later deliberately break them.

In Vasubandhu's arguments against the Vaibhāṣika theory of non-phenomenal matter, we have seen that he makes reference to what he calls a transformation in the personal continuum (santāna-pariṇāma) of one who deliberately undertakes a certain kind of action. It is to this concept of a transformation in the continuum that Vasubandhu also appeals in his rejection of the Vaibhāṣika doctrine that there are special conditioning characteristics known as acquisition and non- acquisition. It appears to be Vasubandhu's feeling that to say that there are ultimately real properties known as acquisition and non-acquisition which lie behind the deluded notion of a stable self comes dangerously close to admitting that the notion of an enduring self is not entirely delusory after all. But if the idea of a person is to be regarded as no more than a popular convention that is superimposed upon the reality of constantly perishing complex properties, then the properties of acquisition and non-acquisition must also be purely conventional ideas rather than ultimately real properties. In fact, the idea of these properties is arguably as much derived from the idea of a stable person as the idea of a stable person is derived from the idea of these properties. If we did not have the idea of a stable personality in the first place, there would be no need to explain how a given type of "person" consistently acquires the same kinds of mental properties. Therefore, Vasubandhu remains content to allow all talk of stability to be relegated for the most part to the realm of popular discourse rather than to the more rigorous realm of abhidharmic discourse.

On the other hand, the problem still remains that if all talk of persons is relegated to the realm of popular discourse, the whole doctrine of karma, according to which a person experiences the consequences of his or her own former actions, would have to be seen as nothing more than a popular teaching that had no place in the more scientific realm of abhidharma. Vasubandhu is not quite willing to regard the doctrine of karma as a purely conventional teaching, for he tries to show that an account of karma can be given within a system of abhidharma without having to add special properties to the list of ultimately real things.

The view of the Vaibhāṣikas was that the special property of acquisition served to ensure that a person who had attained the state of a noble person by abandoning the belief in a real self would acquire those properties that are appropriate to a noble person and that another special property of non-acquisition would ensure that the noble person would not acquire properties suitable to an ordinary worldly person. The view of Vasubandhu, on the other hand, is that once a person has abandoned the belief in a real self, his or her causal continuum simply becomes devoid of the causes of further worldly properties. If a lamp runs out of fuel, it is not necessary to say that the running out of fuel then produces a special property in the lamp that keeps a flame from burning in it; rather, all that is necessary is to say that a lamp without fuel no longer contains the conditions necessary for flame to burn in it. Flamelessness is not a property in itself that arises because of a special condition that prevents flame, but rather it is simply that flame no longer occurs owing to the absence of fuel. Similarly, when a continuum of thoughts becomes exhausted of false beliefs, it is not necessary to say that the exhaustion of false beliefs then produces a special property in the person that keeps certain kinds of wrongful motivations at bay. Rather, it is enough to say simply that wrongful motivations no longer arise owing to the absence of false beliefs. The depletion of the causes of certain kinds of effects in a thing can be called a transformation of that thing. The idea of a person is a conventional designation that is superimposed upon the reality of five groups of properties. When those five groups of properties no longer include worldly properties, then we can say conventionally that the person has undergone a transformation of character. But in saying such a thing there is no need, in the final analysis, to speak of more than the properties themselves and the causal relations among them (*Abhidharmakośa-bhāṣya* ad 2:36).

Let us now recapitulate Vasubandhu's account of karma in the light of the four challenges that were outlined towards the beginning of this essay. The first challenge facing the abhidharma analyst is to describe exactly what it is that acts if there is no stable and enduring person. According to Vasubandhu, the primary action is always an intention (cetanā) to do something, which is an action of the mind (manas-karman). This intention is a mental property (caitta-dharma) that belongs to the group of conditioning characteristics (saṃskāra-skandha). Since every act of awareness is necessarily accompanied by an intention to act, the intention to act in and of itself is not considered either pure (anāsrava) or impure (sāsrava). What makes an intention pure or impure is the fact that it occurs together with other conditioning characteristics that are either pure or impure. An intention to act that is not associated with wisdom, for example, is bound to be associated with the impurity of belief in a continuing self and therefore becomes an impure intention, whereas an intention that is accompanied by wisdom, that is, the realization that all things are impermanent, becomes a pure intention. An impure intention is bound to be accompanied by such conditioning characteristics as selfish desire or anger, and it becomes either an unhealthy intention, in case it is accompanied by a desire to bring harm to another, or a healthy intention, in case it is accompanied by a desire to bring benefit to another. Therefore, an impure intention becomes healthy or unhealthy owing to its association with healthy or unhealthy conditioning characteristics.

A pure intention to act gives rise to an actual bodily or vocal action; that is, one either does something or says something. And since the pure intention is by definition one that is accompanied by wisdom, the physical or vocal action that follows it can be motivated only by a wish to bring benefit to others, for wisdom can never be accompanied by a desire to do harm. Moreover, an act that is motivated by wisdom can never be accompanied by a desire for continued existence, for wisdom is the very realization that nothing endures. In the absence of a desire for continued existence, the root cause for continued existence does not exist, and therefore an act that stems from a pure motivation does not have the consequence of continued existence. In other words, a bodily or vocal action that is performed as a result of a pure intention is not a karma and therefore does not lead to karmic fruition (karma- vipāka) in the future. The causal sequence set into motion with a pure intention to act ends when the intention is carried out. Once the intention is carried out, it is completely exhausted and does not give rise to further intentions.

An impure intention, on the other hand, is an intention that is accompanied by a belief in and desire for the continued existence of the agent, and this desire acts as the cause of future properties to arise in the causal continuum. When this impure intention gives rise to a bodily or verbal action, it gives rise not only to the action itself but also to its own successors, that is, to further impure intentions. Moreover, the bodily or vocal action performed as a result of the impure intention brings about a subtle physical change in the heart, which is defined as the physical organ that serves as the seat (āśraya) of thought.

We have then two causal chains set in motion by an impure intention. The first is the formation of a habit, that is, a tendency to want to repeat the intention, which transforms the group of conditioning characteristics (saṃskāra-skandha). And the second is a physical change in the heart, which transforms the group of physical properties (rūpa-skandha). When the heart, the seat of thought, is transformed by an action of the body or the speech, it becomes inclined by this change to act as a support of the same kinds of intentions it has had in the past. Thus, when one acts in anger, for example, the heart becomes just a little more physically hardened, and this hardening of the heart makes it more difficult for both kind thoughts and contentment to occur in it in the future. But when one acts out of kindness, the heart becomes a little more physically pliant, and this pliancy makes it more easy for both kind thoughts and contentment to occur in it in the future. According to Vasubandhu, this physical change in the heart takes two forms. One is an immediate change, which determines the kinds of experiences that are likely to arise in the heart for the remainder of the current life. The other is called a projection (ākṣepa). It is this projection that determines the form of life that the heart will enter into in future births. About this more will be said later.

The second challenge facing the abhidharma analyst is to describe what it is that experiences the consequences of the original karma. Vasubandhu's answer to this is that it is the awareness of the mind (mano-vijñāna), which has the form of an awareness of either mental contentment (saumanasya) or discontent (daurmanasya), which are respectively the natural consequences of intending to help and to harm others. The physical seat of this awareness of the mind is the heart, which, as was described above, has undergone physical changes in accordance with the accumulation of past healthy and unhealthy intentions.

The third challenge to the abhidharma analyst is to give an account of the sense in which the agent of the original deed is the same as the eventual experiencer of the consequences of the deed. According to Vasubandhu, the heart, like all other complex things, is a causal continuum of momentary properties, and the properties that it has at any given moment is the cumulative effect of previous karma. So it is just the fact that the heart is a causal continuum, an unbroken chain of momentary causes giving rise immediately to subsequent effects, that makes it in a sense the same heart when it serves as the seat of resultant contentment or discontent as it was when it served as the seat of the original healthy or unhealthy intentions.

As to the fourth challenge, which is to explain how and where the potential consequences of an action are stored until they reach fruition, Vasubandhu's answer is that karma is not really stored anywhere at all. Rather than karma being somehow stored up for future fruition, it is more a matter, as we have seen above, of the physical heart being altered in such a way that it becomes capable of being the seat of only certain kinds of experiences. A "hardened" heart, as we have seen, is much less likely to be able to be the seat of contentment than a pliant heart, and so one who has had ill intentions in the past is much less likely to be happy than one who has had benevolent intentions. It is really only in this sense that karma appears to be stored until such time as it comes to fruition.

One rather difficult problem still remains to be dealt with in Vasubandhu's account of karma. In his system of abhidharma, it is the physical body that plays the leading role in determining the kinds of experiences that one has. The physical body is the seat of awareness, both in the sense that no awareness occurs without the five external physical sense faculties and in the sense that neither thought nor awareness nor mental properties can occur without their physical seat in the heart. This poses no great problem so long as one is considering karma and its fruition within a single lifetime, where the continuum of the physical body is more obvious. But it is somewhat difficult to see how Vasubandhu might account for the commonly accepted Buddhist notion of rebirth. Since awareness cannot occur without a physical seat, according to Vasubandhu, it is impossible for him to accept the theory, accepted by some Buddhists, that consciousness leaves one physical body at death and travels in a disembodied state until it enters the womb of its mother in the next life.

Vasubandhu thus rejects the theory, well-known to those who are familiar with the so-called *Tibetan Book of the Dead*, of an intermediate disembodied existence (antarbhava) between one incarnation and another. Rather, he is committed to the view that the continuum of physical properties known as the heart, which like all other physical things is composed of atoms, becomes dissociated from one large material body and "travels" until it finds a suitable womb. Given, of course, that everything is momentary, it is not really the case that the heart travels, for motion must be regarded as a fiction; strictly speaking, the heart perishes in each moment only to be replaced in immediately subsequent moments in immediately adjacent locations by its effects. In any case, at the moment when an egg is fertilized in a womb, the heart from a previous life-continuum joins with the newly fertilized egg to form a new life, and as the new foetus evolves it gradually acquires the kinds of external sense organs and other physical characteristics appropriate for the species of life-form that the mother is capable of producing in her womb. Thus, a heart that once belonged to a human being might find itself in the womb of a cat, where it becomes associated with the kinds of sense organs and bodily traits that only cats have.

The type of egg or womb that a heart enters into is, according to Vasubandhu, determined by the quality of a special kind of karma, which is called projection, produced in previous lives. Acts accompanied by great stupidity or delusion, for example, are said to project the heart into the wombs of dumb birds or animals in future lives; acts accompanied by strong greed or desire are said to project the heart into the wombs of hungry ghosts; and especially malicious acts are said to project the heart into the wombs of beings born in one of the many hells or purgatories. Acts accompanied by more benevolent motivations, on the other hand, project the heart into human mothers or into mothers residing in one of the paradises.

From all that has been described so far, it can be seen that Vasubandhu provides answers from an abhidharma perspective to all the questions concerning karma that were raised at the outset of this essay. Whether or not these answers are satisfactory to a critical inquirer is another matter. Although I do not intend in the present essay to subject Vasubandhu's theories to a detailed critique, I should like to end by pointing out in general some ways in which any Buddhist account of karma and rebirth fails to provide philosophical satisfaction.

Let me begin by returning to the statement of Ven. Walpola Rahula quoted near the beginning of this essay. It will be recalled that it was his contention that the Buddhist theory of karmic fruition is a purely natural law, "which has nothing to do with the idea of justice or reward and punishment." It must be admitted that Rahula is correct in saying that the Buddhist theory of karma has no connection with the notion of God or any other law-giver who rewards those who obey his rules and punishes those who disobey. Indeed, as Rahula has pointed out, the Buddhist philosophers were consistent in their explicit rejection of all theories of cosmic justice being meted out or administered in any way by a divine superintendent. But to say, as Rahula does, that the idea of moral justice is necessarily associated with a belief in a supreme God is to take, in my opinion, an unnecessarily narrow view of moral justice.

To suggest that the law of karma as understood by Buddhists is a purely natural law, almost like a law of physics or biology, is to overlook the undeniable fact that the universe is always presented by Buddhists as having an inescapably moral structure, whereby noble intentions are invariably followed by contentment and ignoble intentions are invariably followed by discontent. No modern natural scientist to my knowledge would feel comfortable with the assertion that it is a law of nature that happiness is an invariable consequence of wishing well for the world at large and that misery is an invariable consequence of wishing harm to others. Whereas one does not experience exceptions to the physical law of gravity, for example, one does experience exceptions rather frequently to the law of karma as stated in popular Buddhist teachings; for there do seem to be people who act rather badly in this life without apparently being bothered by guilt and other forms of anxiety, and there are also people who suffer apparently undeserved misfortunes. This so-called "law" of karma is a pious hope, not a scientific discovery, and the failure of some Buddhists to recognize this can only serve to make their claims seem rather silly to those who do not share their religious sentiments.

That the Buddhist law of karma as traditionally presented is different in kind from natural scientific laws can be seen by considering the fact that it is not regarded as a truly universal law. As we have seen, it is not the case that all deliberate actions qualify as karma in the Buddhist view. Arhants, for example, are said not to produce karma when they act deliberately. The deliberate actions of arhants, unlike the actions of ordinary beings, are said not to set in motion a causal sequence that results eventually in karmic fruition. But it is only the law of karma, and not ordinary physical laws, from which arhants are said to be exempt. If, for example, an arhant steps off a platform he falls to the ground in exactly the same way that any other being would fall to the ground. The law that governs falling to the ground is universal in that it applies uniformly to all beings that have physical mass.

Now why should it be the case that an arhant's deliberate actions do not produce the same karmic consequences as do the deliberate actions of all other beings? The answer to this can only be found in the Buddhist dogma that arhants, unlike other beings, are free from future rebirth. If an arhant's deliberate actions necessarily resulted in fruition, then, since no one, not even arhants, can avoid deliberate action right up to the last moment of life, it would follow that arhants would have to be reborn in order to experience the fruitions of actions performed towards the end of life. And if arhants had to be reborn, there would, of course, be no liberation as traditionally described within Buddhism, and the very purpose of following the Buddhist path in the first place would turn out to be an unattainable goal. Moreover, the basic dogmas of Buddhism require that only arhants be exempt from the law of karma, for if it were admitted that no beings really generate karma that requires them to be reborn to experience the fruitions of their wrongful actions, then it would also have to be admitted that beings could behave rather badly during the last years of their lives without having to suffer all the unhappiness that bad actions are supposed to engender. Making a distinction between the deliberate actions of arhants and the deliberate actions of ordinary beings is fundamental to providing the necessary psychological incentive for following the rigours of the Buddhist way of life. Without an incentive based on this distinction, it would seem to most people rather foolish to undertake the difficult discipline and the denial of immediate gratification that most forms of Buddhist practice entail.

But that a given dogma is necessary as an incentive to undertake any particular religious path does not, of course, make the dogma true. Because it is so firmly rooted in the fundamental Buddhist dogma that liberation from suffering is possible, the law of karma is different from truly natural laws, which are held to be valid independent of all considerations of psychological need and motivation. The law of gravity, for example, is not a law for which people have a psychological need as an incentive to keep them from the wrongful action of jumping out of the windows of tall buildings; the law of gravity is simply true, whether one likes it or not. The same cannot be said for the Buddhist "law" of karma, which can only be said to appear to be true to people who are attached to thinking that they live in a moral universe.

Perhaps the most elegant way to avoid the many difficulties inherent in reconciling the popular Buddhist teaching of karmic fruition and rebirth with the more rigorous system of abhidharma would be simply to declare both these teachings as conventional truth. As can be seen by a study of the Vaibhāṣika system of abhidharma, these doctrines can be preserved only by introducing a number of essentially ad hoc principles into the abhidharma system. But once one has admitted that the arhant does not produce karma because he is free of the notion of an enduring person, which is a notion that does not bear up under close scrutiny, one has virtually admitted also that the very notion of karma is as incapable of bearing up under close scrutiny as is the notion of an enduring person. The abhidharma theorists argued that meritorious action belongs only to those who have a desire for personal rewards but ceases to exist in people who have no desire for such rewards. But in arguing that the desire for personal rewards is based upon a fundamental delusion, they also are saying in effect that the notion of merit, which is based on a wish for personal rewards, is also ultimately based on a fundamental delusion. And this is coming very close to saying that merit and demerit are ultimately delusions.

What is particularly intriguing is that the abhidharma theorists come very close to admitting that the notions of karma, rebirth and merit are ultimately delusions but that they restrain themselves from actually saying it. That they do not actually say so is, I suspect, not so much a result of their failing to see the obvious implications of their other statements as it was a matter of their not daring to say explicitly that such notions as karma and merit are, in the final analysis, unwarranted. And their not daring to say that these notions are unwarranted is a function, I suspect, of the perceived need to preserve Buddhism as an institution. Without the notion that a lay person stores up merit by giving material requisites to monks, the whole monastic institution would undoubtedly soon crumble, for people would see no other incentive to support it. And so the reticence of abhidharmists to state the conclusions that their initial premises entail is, I would argue, one of the many instances that one can see in the history of religions of philosophical rigour and integrity being compromised by the perceived need to preserve a social institution.

BIBLIOGRAPHY

Dhargyey, Geshe Ngawang. 1974. *Tibetan Tradition of Mental Development: Oral Teachings of a Tibetan Lama*. Dharamsala: Library of Tibetan Works and Archives.

Rabten, Feshe. 1974. *The Essential Nectar: Meditations on the Buddhist Path*. London: Wisdom Publications.

Rahula, Walpola. 1967. *What the Buddha Taught*. Bedford, England: Gordon Fraser.

Vasubandhu. [1967] 1975. *Abhidharmakośa-bhāṣya of Vasubandhu*. 2d rev. ed. Ed. P. Pradhan; rev. Aruna Haldar. Patna: K.P. Jayaswaz Research Institute.

KARMA IN THE BHAGAVADGĪTĀ ACCORDING TO ŚAṄKARA AND RĀMĀNUJA

Julian Woods

The task of this essay is to examine the views of two major commentators on the *Bhagavadgītā* (*BG*),[1] Śaṅkara and Rāmānuja, with respect to action (karma), and in particular with respect to those teachings described in this Hindu text as karmayoga, the path of action. In this connection we will focus on *BG* chapters 2-6, and 18 (which summarizes much of the doctrine outlined in the previous chapters). Other textual references will be used to highlight differences of concept where appropriate. We begin by outlining briefly the major epistemological, ontological and ethical differences between these two thinkers that have a bearing on their respective approaches to the text. The major part of the essay will be devoted to the commentators' interpretations of Kṛṣṇa's actual words about karma. A concluding section will evaluate the merits of both approaches.

The Basic Misunderstanding

The karmayoga of the *BG* is clearly based on a particular epistemology, but its exact nature has long been subject to debate. Different exegetical traditions (sampradāyas) have proposed widely divergent views on the matter. All agree that the existential condition of the individual — bondage to the cycle of birth and death known as saṃsāra — is due to a basic misunderstanding about the self (the microcosm) and about reality as a whole (the macrocosm). However, this is about as far as agreement goes.

Śaṅkara (in the prologue to his *Brahmasūtra-bhāṣya*) characterizes reality or the self (ātman) as pure, non-dual (advitīya) consciousness, which is also transcendent as the apophatic (nirguṇa) Brahman. The basic misunderstanding regarding the self, according to him, is due to superimposition of the not-self on the self. This superimposition is a product of cosmic illusion (māyā). Thus, through the veiling and projecting power of māyā, the non-dual consciousness becomes differentiated into the subject-object world of name and form, which the individual perceives as the macrocosm and experiences as the microcosm, the limited embodied soul (jīva). This is the crux of Arjuna's problem in the *BG* (cf. *SGB* 13.26).

For Rāmānuja, on the other hand, Arjuna's confusion about his dharma (*BG* 2.7) is complicated by a threefold delusion arising out of the triple reality of Viśiṣṭādvaita: (1) sentient nature, that is, cit (the individual souls); (2) insentient nature, that is, acit (the material realm); and (3) God (Īśvara). Arjuna does not understand his true sentient nature (cit), since he mistakenly identifies himself (i.e. his particular ātman) with his own insentient (acit) body. Further, he does not realize that all sentient and insentient beings and things make up the body of God who is also the inner Self of all creation (including Arjuna himself). Finally, he fails to comprehend that his own duty as a warrior is a legitimate means of liberation when performed in a spirit of service to God, abandoning all sense of agency, action and attachment to the results of action (*RGB* 2.9). Only at *BG* 18.73 is Arjuna released from this triple source of error.

Ontological Differences

These different interpretations of Arjuna's dilemma are, in turn, related to conflicting views regarding the ontological status of human experience. For Śaṅkara, on the one hand, the problem of the self is endemic to human experience since it goes back to the illusion of subject and object. Reality is neither subject nor object but the ground (simultaneously immanent and transcendent) of all possible experience. In this view, human beings (jīvas) are fictional self-identities performing unreal activities out of attachment to objects, emotional states and ideas about a world that does not really exist (*SGB* 15.7). Everyday consciousness, accordingly, is mithyā or illusory in this scheme of things.

For Rāmānuja, on the other hand, the individual and the things of the world are fully real. The source of human misunderstanding is not in objective reality as such (since the souls and the world are real) but in understanding the relations among the three entities involved, namely, the individual souls (ātman; cit), the bodies and objects derived from matter (prakṛti; acit), and God (Īśvara). A person or any other living being is a real composite of soul (ātman) and body (śarīra, deha, piṇḍa) trapped in a real cycle of change (saṃsāra) based on real modifications of nature (prakṛti). Fortunately, however, "the same prakṛti, through its own modifications ... becomes the cause of salvation (of the ātman)" (*RGB* 13.19).

Epistemological Differences

While reality is accessible through knowledge (jñāna) for both Śaṅkara and Rāmānuja, the epistemological recovery of reality is governed by contrasting views with respect to the nature of this knowledge. For Śaṅkara, "when knowledge of the true nature of the Self has been attained, neither organs of knowledge nor objects of knowledge present themselves to consciousness any longer" (*SGB* 2.69). True knowledge is thus the pure, non-dual consciousness itself reached by negation of the phenomenal world characterized by ignorance (avidyā). Only knowledge can remove ignorance just as:

> in the case of a rope (mistaken for a serpent), as soon as the light of the lamp removes the darkness which caused the error, the rope is no longer mistaken for a serpent. The result of illumination culminates, indeed, in the liberation of the rope, in freeing the rope from the various mistaken notions of serpent etc., which then cease altogether. So, too, as regards self-knowledge (*SGB* 18.66).

But for Rāmānuja, jñāna is always knowledge of an object by a subject. He defines it as "the positive conclusion about an object with the help of the senses, inference, the scriptures and Yoga" (*RGB* 15.15). This object always represents reality in some form or other, whether this is a modification of prakṛti (such as the body), the ātman or Īśvara himself (the Supreme Object). The subject is also the ātman which, like the sun, can illuminate both itself and other objects (*RGB* 5.16). However, this light is darkened by impurities in the embodied state including, for example, unconscious drives (vāsanas) arising from actions undertaken in the past.

Differences in the Concept of Karma

These ontological and epistemological differences lead, in turn, to differences regarding karmayoga (the path of action) and to the role of karmayoga in the economy of salvation. Śaṅkara's views are clear enough. Karma is a product of ignorance (avidyā), since it is found in the pluralistic world of individual actors and instruments of action which are themselves the product of avidyā. "Before the dawn of wisdom, avidyā presents itself in various forms as actions, means and results, is regarded as authoritative, and becomes the source of all actions" (*SGB* 2.69). It is inconceivable that ignorance can be a means of liberation from ignorance. Knowledge (jñāna) alone is that means and "it is not possible to imagine even in a dream that the man who knows the Self can have anything to do with karmayoga, [it being] so opposed to right knowledge and entirely based on illusory knowledge" (*SGB* 5. Introduction).

Śaṅkara acknowledges, however, that while appropriate for one who sees the truth, such an attitude is not suitable for a mind:

> deluded by ahaṃkāra, identifying the body and the senses with the ātman i.e. who ascribes to himself all the attributes of the body and the senses and thus thoroughly identifies with them — he by nescience, sees action in himself; as regards every action he thinks, 'I am the doer' (*SGB* 3.27).

Under these circumstances, says Śaṅkara, Kṛṣṇa finds it necessary to teach a twofold dharma of renunciation of action (nivṛtti) and performance of action (pravṛtti) geared to the needs of two distinct classes of aspirant. In the *BG* these are: (1) the Sāṃkhyas who are devoted to knowledge (jñānaniṣṭhā) of the (non-active) ātman first described in *BG* 2. 11-30; and (2) the Yogins who believe in a plurality of actors and enjoyers and who are devoted to action (karmaniṣṭhā). Karmayoga (first introduced at *BG* 2.40-53) is useful and, indeed, necessary for members of the latter group to purify and pacify a turbulent mind prior to removal of its objective content.

The nature and role of karma and karmayoga is regarded very differently by Rāmānuja. There is no question for him about the reality of the acts and the resulting states and conditions of existence in the real realms of transmigration (saṃsāra). In the first place karma is the principal cause of all differentiation and inequality in the universe (*RGB* 4.14). Īśvara always creates according to the respective karmas (i.e. the vāsanas) of the souls, which are individually responsible for the condition of embodiment in the saṃsāric chain of beings from Brahmā, the creator, to a clump of grass (*RGB* 4.13). In this respect, sentient beings create themselves by their own activities performed through countless cycles of existence.

In addition to this self-creative aspect, according to Rāmānuja, karma makes it difficult for an embodied being to cut away the roots of bondage and to realize its own true nature and freedom (*RGB* 5.15). The result is "ahaṃkāra, the feeling of 'I' in regard to the prakṛti which is not the thing denoted by 'I'" (*RGB* 3.27). It is also the appropriation of sense objects in the form "this is mine" (mamatā). Desire, aversion and other delusory states of bondage to prakṛti follow, prompting action leading to new forms of attachment to bodies, objects and so on.

For Rāmānuja, there are important additional aspects of karma. What an individual has done by karma can also be undone by a change in attitude based on self-knowledge (ātmajñāna). All that is needed is a change of the mind's attention and attachment from prakṛti (the habitual extroversion of the mind through the senses to their objects) to the ātman itself (*RGB* 2.13). It is this latter type of karma, performed in the right spirit as a yoga of liberation, which is the subject of Kṛṣṇa's advice to Arjuna in the *BG* and the selected topic for this essay.

Kṛṣṇa's Teaching With Respect To Karma

(a) *BG* Chapter 2

Kṛṣṇa begins (*BG* 2.39) by making a distinction between the sāṃkhye buddhi and the yoge buddhi. Śaṅkara regards these as the two important teachings of the *BG*, and puts great emphasis on *BG* 2.11-30, which deals with the sāṃkhye buddhi. He glosses sāṃkhye as knowledge with respect to the identity of the highest Reality (sāṃkhye = paramārthavastuviveka). In other words, the teaching of *BG* 2.11-30 points to the pure, undifferentiated consciousness (the ātman) and liberation (mokṣa). The yoge buddhi of 2.40-53 is of secondary truth-value, since it relates only to the *means* leading to knowledge (jñāna), not directly to liberation.

Rāmānuja sees this distinction in a quite different light. Arjuna's despondency and his confused babbling (*BG* 1.25-47) point directly to the source of the problem: his misplaced identification with that part of himself that derives from the prakṛtic element, viz. the body (rather than the ātman). This leads Arjuna to regard his duty as a warrior (kṣatriyadharma) — originally embarked upon to secure the worldly fruits of enjoyment of kingdom and power (bhogaiśvārya) — as an unmitigated disaster.

In order to set Arjuna straight, according to Rāmānuja, Kṛṣṇa must lead his disciple through two major stages of awakening: (1) his own self-awakening (to his own nature as the ātman free from prakṛtic entanglement); and (2) his awakening to God who has the universe for his body and who is the inner Self of all beings. The first task alone is difficult enough, since it requires a radical transformation of Arjuna's sense of himself and of his being-in-the-world. Kṛṣṇa can only do this, thought Rāmānuja, by means of a dual approach. The first deals with knowledge of the ātman. The second deals with action, in this case with turning the karma of war from being a source of bondage into its being a means (sādhana, yoga) of liberation. It is this dual approach that is the source of the distinction drawn by Kṛṣṇa (at *BG* 2.39) between the sāṃkhye buddhi and the yoge buddhi.

Rāmānuja comments that the sāṃkhye buddhi is concerned with the basic facts about the ātman (ātmatattva). Buddhi is the intellectual knowledge of this (ātmajñāna). Yoga, on the other hand, is concerned with method, specifically with the ways and means of converting the abstract truths of ātmajñāna into the living reality of direct vision (ātmāvalokana) and experience (ātmānubhava).

By their very nature as means to ends, observes Rāmānuja, these yogas are concerned with action or karma. They also include, however, an element of knowledge (jñāna), voluntary action being inconceivable without some knowledge of both means and ends. Hence, even the yoga of action itself (karmayoga) contains an element of knowledge. Rāmānuja himself maintains that karmayoga is jñānayogākāratā. It also incorporates elements of the more sophisticated yoga of knowledge within it (*RGB* 4, Introduction). In effect, Rāmānuja, unlike Śaṅkara, sets great store by karma as a yoga.

Given the nature of the task at hand, thinks Rāmānuja, it is therefore quite appropriate that Kṛṣṇa preface his remarks on karmayoga (introduced at *BG* 2.39) with the necessary knowledge (jñāna) about the nature of: (1) the body, which is subject to change and destruction; and (2) the indestructible soul (ātman), which migrates successively from body to body. This discussion has nothing to do with the supreme reality as Śaṅkara would have it. God can only be attained through a special form of karma known as Bhakti. This second part of the teaching is not introduced for serious discussion before *BG* chapter 7. It should be remembered, however, that ātmajñāna, the goal of this introductory section (which is *BG* 2.12-30 in Rāmānuja's opinion), is simply an abstract form of self-understanding.

The main thrust of Kṛṣṇa's teaching in this chapter is yoga, the different steps that must be taken to transform these abstract ideas into concrete reality, knowledge into vision, bondage and grief into freedom and bliss. This is a complex spiritual journey, which is divided by Rāmānuja into a number of stages:

> Karmayoga, which is preceded by ātmajñāna based on the śāstras, leads to devotion to knowledge (jñānaniṣṭhā) known as the state of steady understanding (sthitaprajñatā) and the state of steady understanding which is in the form of devotion to knowledge, brings about the vision of the self (ātmāvalokana) known as yoga (*RGB* 2.53).

Karma, performed as a yoga, leads naturally to introspection and meditation (jñānayoga), and on to knowledge and vision. In effect, the two disciplines are one, and Rāmānuja can combine them or separate them as demanded by the text. However, before discussing the means, we will briefly examine the goal itself and the conditions for its attainment.

The goal of this progressive transformation of action into realization is characterized by Kṛṣṇa (*BG* 2.72) as brahmanirvāṇa (equated by Rāmānuja with ātmāvalokana), a state of being or experience combining three main features. In the first place, it is a state of bliss (sukha) (*RGB* 2.72). It is also peace of mind, described successively as prasāda (*BG* 2.65) and śānti (*BG* 2.66;2.71). Third, and perhaps most important, it is a state free of identification of the ātman with the body (the not-self) and the desire to possess (mamatā). Significantly, this state is also one of knowledge in which the ātman is seen (*RGB* 2.71).

The necessary condition for attaining brahmanirvāṇa (or ātmāvalokana) is, according to Rāmānuja, a state of steady understanding or sthitaprajñatā, characterized by tranquillity (samātva), based on complete control of the senses. This is contrasted with the turbulent mind of saṃsāra in which knowledge (prajñā) is carried away like a ship before the wind (*BG* 2.67). A tranquil mind, in turn, is the necessary condition for meditation on the ātman, i.e. for jñānayoga. This state is thus also known as jñānaniṣṭhā or devotion to knowledge of the ātman. According to Rāmānuja, there are four levels of sthitaprajñatā, described in descending order at *BG* 2.55-58. One has reached the first stage who can withdraw the senses from their objects like a tortoise who withdraws its limbs into its body (*BG* 2.58). This is only negative control, since it excludes the sense objects. At the highest level one is satisfied in oneself with oneself (ātmanyevātmanā tuṣṭa), in whom all desires can enter as the waters enter the ocean (*BG* 2.70).

Control of the senses, continues Rāmānuja, can only be achieved once the natural tendency of the mind to "fall" into the various states of saṃsāra described in *BG* 2.62-63 is reversed. This can be done by burning away "impurities" (mala, kalmaṣa), that is, the subtle traces of past action in the unconscious known as the vāsanas, which obscure knowledge of the ātman and lead it into the embrace of prakṛti with its various modifications and states. This is no simple matter (*RGB* 2.60). Any attempt to repress these vāsanas is quite futile, even for a wise man (*BG* 2.60). The only hope is to redirect the energies involved (the guṇas) in such a manner that the old vāsanas become exhausted without being replaced by new ones. This is the task of both karmayoga and of jñānayoga, whether regarded as separate disciplines or as two aspects of the various techniques for seeing the self. Titles are irrelevant. By the very fact of life itself, as Kṛṣṇa suggests (*BG* 3.8), they involve action.

According to Rāmānuja, the transformation of action that would ordinarily lead to bondage into a means of liberation from bondage involves a major change of course, followed by faithful adherence to the words of the teacher (guru) and the scripture (śāstra). The key step is to wake up to the vanity of the world and to abandon all goals but that of liberation. Those who delight in the Vedic formulae (vedavādaratha) for securing worldly things for themselves (bhogaiśvārya) are to be censured (*BG* 2.42). Kṛṣṇa uses this example to exhort Arjuna to be free of the realm of prakṛti and its guṇas, free of the play of the opposites (dvandva), and free of the desire to have and to hold (yogakṣema). He is to seek the ātman alone with all his actions! (*BG* 2.45)

This advice is not as self-seeking as it may appear. For Rāmānuja, what is sought is not the ego (ahaṃkāra), the person identified with the body and with the perquisites and powers of kingship. Quite the contrary. The goal is the destruction of egoity (ahaṃkāra) and all sense of possession (mamatā) that goes with it. This is done by progressively shedding the illusory identity with body, emotions, senses and their objects. These modifications of prakṛti are owned by God alone (as his body), not by any separate self.

Having made this decision, argues Rāmānuja, the actual practice of karmayoga can begin in earnest. For once Arjuna has accepted mokṣa alone as the goal of life, all worldly ties to action (such as war) will tend to weaken by themselves. He will be less inclined to fret about who lives and who dies, who wins and who loses. This shift of goals will automatically bring a shift of attitude to the conduct and outcome of the war. However, since desire in any form (even the desire for liberation) is a form of bondage, Kṛṣṇa quickly brings the point home by warning: "To work alone is your right, never to the fruits" (*BG* 2.47). In other words, although on the stage of life he has no choice but to play his pre-ordained role (determined by his own past acts), he can play it in one of two ways. He can identify himself with it completely and fear the outcome. This is a recipe for bondage. Or he can play it as he is in reality, the ātman free of involvement with the role. This is the way of knowledge and freedom from bondage. While he has no true understanding of himself as yet and hence no freedom to follow this advice completely, the very attempt to do so is a means (sādhana) of exhausting his stock of vāsanas and of preventing others from accumulating. This leads to the removal of the cause of his present state of ignorance about himself.

However, Rāmānuja thinks that this will not happen to Arjuna by his own volition. Additional assistance is needed. Kṛṣṇa advises Arjuna on several occasions (*BG* 2.61; 2.64; 2.66; 2.68) to invoke his help in meditation. Taking his cue from these passages and from subsequent pronouncements of Kṛṣṇa (*BG* 3.30), Rāmānuja introduces his important thesis that all activities enjoined in the Vedas should be performed day after day until death "as a form of My Worship" (*RGB* 2.47). He has little faith in the ability of the human species to pull itself up by its own bootstraps. In the final analysis, the sublimation of these energies into knowledge is the work of the Lord. He comments: "one who strives to conquer the senses, relying on the weight of his own exertions and without fixing his mind on Me in this manner, becomes lost" (*RGB* 2.61). The net result is that the "Paramapuruṣa, pleased by sacrifices and other such works, bestows on him the undisturbed vision of the self, after eradicating the vāsanas of the actions of the person which have continued from time immemorial" (*RGB* 3.9).

The second part of *BG* 2.47, in which Kṛṣṇa advises Arjuna ("Be not the cause of action or its fruit. Neither be attached to inaction") has important implications for Rāmānuja's understanding of abandonment (saṃnyāsa; tyāga) and for the techniques of karmayoga to which this understanding leads. As will be made clear at *BG* 3.5, 3.27-29 and elsewhere, Kṛṣṇa points to prakṛti as the source of the individual's desire to act in saṃsāra. This is the natural result of identifying with it. However, since prakṛti really belongs to the transcendent God who owns it as his body, the ultimate seat and source of all action must be the Lord alone (who is also the inner self and controller of all beings). Thus, in performing all action, says Rāmānuja, "it is necessary to meditate on yourself ... not being the agent." He adds: "Later on, it will be taught that both these (i.e. the agency of action and the bringing about of the fruits) ought to be considered as belonging either to the guṇas or to Me who am the Lord of all. So work thinking thus" (*RGB* 2.47).

In effect, in Rāmānuja's view, Kṛṣṇa is teaching a sādhana based on abandonment of three important causes of bondage: (1) the sense of agency involved in the action (kartṛtva); (2) the action itself (karma); and (3) its results (karmaphala). The first part of the teaching is designed to eradicate the sense of doership ("I do") in the action by attributing all agency to the guṇas or to their Ruler (*RGB* 14.19, 18.14). The second part is designed to eliminate the sense of ownership (mamatā) in something that can only belong to God. Finally, abandonment of the result or fruit (phala) should involve the notion that the "results of action such as heaven and so forth should not be mine" (*RGB* 18.4). The phala must clearly also belong to God.

(b) *BG* Chapter 3

The interpretation given to the terms sāṃkhye buddhi and yoge buddhi is important for what follows through most of the next four chapters and, indeed, in the *BG* as a whole. Arjuna himself is puzzled by what Kṛṣṇa has in mind and chapter 3 opens with his question on the matter. Kṛṣṇa begins his response by affirming the existence of these two practices (niṣṭhā). However, he confines himself almost exclusively to talk about action and its importance to spiritual progress (*BG* 3.4), to embodied life (*BG* 3.5), to the gods (*BG* 3.10-13), and to the cycle of nature (*BG* 3.14-16). He promotes the cause of action over inaction (*BG* 3.8) and the conduct of the karmayogin over the pious fraud (mithyācāra). Even the ātmarati (*BG* 3.17), one who no longer finds any purpose in action or inaction, should act for the common good (lokasaṃgraha). Kṛṣṇa also provides further insight into the sources of human motivation (*BG* 3.27-29; 3.33-34; 3.37-43). He encourages Arjuna once again to prefer his own dharma to that of another (*BG* 3. 35) and to fight in a spirit of non-attachment by deferring all actions to him (*BG* 3.30). This is a further extension of his teaching on karmayoga. Finally, Kṛṣṇa introduces important new terms such as naiśkarmya (*BG* 3.4), karma (*BG* 3.8), brahman (*BG* 3.15) and para (*BG* 3.43), which become food for much divergent interpretation.

This emphasis on action is read quite differently by the two commentators. Action is important for Śaṅkara only in comparison with the kind of false renunciation of action described in *BG* 3.4 as "mere renunciation" and at *BG* 3.8 as non-action (akarma). A more detailed review of tamasic and rajasic renunciation is given at *BG* 18.7 and *BG* 18.8. We may recall that Arjuna himself had toyed with the possibility of mere renunciation (*BG* 2.5). Action of any kind is better than this, thinks Śaṅkara, provided it is not expressly prohibited by the Veda. However, even karmayoga cannot lead to mokṣa directly, since "mokṣa, being no effect of an act, no action will be of any use to a mumukṣu" (one desirous of liberation; *SGB* 3 Introduction). Only the highest form of non-action — the renunciation of all action by the saṃnyāsin qualified by his state of mental equilibrium (samātva) to meditate on the supreme truth (paramārthika satya) of non-duality — is equal to this task.

Śaṅkara observes that Kṛṣṇa had already indicated that this highest path of renunciation (nivṛttimārga) is open only to the Sāṃkhyas, "to those possessed of clear knowledge of the ātman and that which is not the ātman, who have renounced the world from the brahmacarya order, who have determined the nature of things in the light of Vedāntic wisdom and who belong to the highest class of saṃnyāsins known as the paramahaṃsas, whose thought ever dwelt on Brahman alone" (*SGB* 3.3). He realizes only too well that to require an action-oriented person such as Arjuna to renounce all action would provoke disaster. He therefore loses no time in warning his disciple that "not by abstaining from action does one win naiṣkarmya nor by mere renunciation does [one] attain perfection" (*BG* 3.4).

While Śaṅkara, unlike Rāmānuja, is not willing to admit any overlap of disciplines, he does accept the possibility of a transition from one discipline to the other (*SGB* 3.3). In effect, thinks Śaṅkara, Kṛṣṇa is warning Arjuna that any misplaced abandonment such as resorting to beggary would not qualify him for jñānayoga. Naiṣkarmya is the meditative state preparatory to knowledge. Śaṅkara glosses naiṣkarmya as karmaśunyatā, an actionless void, which is the essential form of the immutable ātman (niṣkriyātmasvarūpa). According to Śaṅkara, Kṛṣṇa only emphasizes the need for action in order to lead Arjuna from the inaction of illusion (mithyā) to the true inaction of knowledge (vidyā), from the dualistic path of karmayoga to the one and only true path of jñānayoga.

In contrast to Śaṅkara, Rāmānuja wishes to demonstrate exactly the reverse, namely the superiority of the practice of karmayoga (for the realization of the individual ātman), even for those who are qualified to practise jñānayoga (*RGB* 3.8). Rāmānuja's position on this subject, progressively developed through his commentary on the next three chapters, is based on Kṛṣṇa's words about yajña (*BG* 3.9-19). Yajña or sacrifice was instituted by the all-merciful Prajāpati at the time of creation for all beings caught in the cycle of embodiment as a result of karma. It acts for the mutual support and sustenance of all things in the universe, including human beings, and when performed in the right spirit it also becomes a means of redemption (*RGB* 3.9). Furthermore, when joined to the idea of gratitude for the bounties of nature provided by the gods, yajña becomes a form of worship of the Lord himself. Just as yajña is the source and sustenance of all life, so it also becomes its end when this attitude is realized in performance.

The importance of yajña in the economy of salvation is such that Rāmānuja takes the reading of *BG* 3.8 in the sense that karma, now assimilated to the idea of yajña, "is superior to what is other than work (akarma), that is, even to the discipline of jñāna" (*RGB* 3.8). This gives an entirely different twist to the meanings of karma and akarma, compared with the sense of these same words in the reading of Śaṅkara. Karma is not just work but ritualistic duty and akarma is no longer some kind of misplaced abandonment but the more difficult route to self-realization not recommended by Kṛṣṇa.

Śaṅkara, on the other hand, thinks that since the karmakāṇḍa portion of the Veda is only a guide for the perplexed in the tradition of non-dualism (advaita), Kṛṣṇa introduces this discussion of yajña only to show why the yogi, the ordinary man with no knowledge of the ātman, should act rather than enter upon a premature abandonment of action (*SGB* 3.16). In addition to purification of the mind through the worship of Īśvara (*BG* 3.9), these reasons include gratitude to the gods (*BG* 3.10-12), freedom from involuntary sin (*BG* 3.13), and keeping the good order of the world (*BG* 3.14-16).

The superiority of jñānayoga is vindicated for Śaṅkara by the distinction that Kṛṣṇa draws between: (1) the person who delights in the senses (indriyārāma) and must be guided by injunction (vidhi); and (2) the one who delights only in the self (ātmarati), has nothing to accomplish in the world, and thus has no purpose whatsoever in action (*BG* 3.16). However, Kṛṣṇa goes on to explain that while He himself may be truly self-satisfied (ātmani saṃtuṣṭa), the man of wisdom must nevertheless have regard for the results of previous actions (prārabdhakarma) that brought him into the world. The man of wisdom must continue to work untiringly in the world, like the Lord himself, for the welfare of the world (lokasaṃgraha). And he must also set an example for the masses (*BG* 3.17-26). In effect, while the purpose of life in the form of mokṣa has been achieved for such a man as an individual, there yet remains a kind of supra-individual purpose for him to fulfill while his body is still seen to act in the world by those people who are governed by the actions of the guṇas.

The merits of jñānayoga are further confirmed for Śaṅkara by what Kṛṣṇa has to say about the deluding effects of prakṛti. So powerful is the belief in one's own personality (which is nothing but the result of prārabdhakarma in the present birth) that even the man of knowledge (jñānavān) is forced to follow the dictates of the saṃskāras (= vāsanas). He has also to confront his two enemies of love and hatred (rāgadveṣau). In a rather extraordinary comment on *BG* 3.33,

Śaṅkara suggests that even Kṛṣṇa himself might have difficulty in this regard: "In other words, whether for me [i.e. for Kṛṣṇa] or for anyone else, the prakṛti is difficult to control." This implies for Śaṅkara that the only scope for personal exertion (puruṣakāra) lies in the capacity for knowledge, for "when a person restrains these feelings by means of their enemy (jñāna), then he will become mindful of the teaching only, no longer subject to his own nature" (*SGB* 3.34).

As we have seen, Rāmānuja is able to invoke the Lord of the universe to shower his grace on the sincere devotee (Īśvara is only a helpful fiction for Śaṅkara at *SGB* 4.11). His preference for karmayoga is, therefore, part and parcel of the development of the idea of worship and reward embodied in the practice of yajña, which finds its fulfilment in the practice of karmayoga and ultimately of bhaktiyoga. While the vision of the Self (ātmāvalokana) is the product of jñāna, this can be realized only in the meditative states of a pure mind granted by the Lord as a reward for the practice of more active forms of karmayoga. On this basis, Rāmānuja builds his understanding of Kṛṣṇa's words in this chapter as follows:

> Thus, after having stated [in *BG* 3.3-3.7] that for an aspirant for mokṣa who is qualified for karmayoga, karmayoga alone is what should be followed, on account of [his] unfitness for jñānayoga, it was [then] pointed out with reasons [in *BG* 3.8-3.19] that even to one qualified for jñānayoga, karmayoga indeed is better than jñānayoga. Now [in *BG* 3.20-3.26] it is said that karmayoga is in every way what should be performed by one who is distinguished in wisdom (*RGB* 3.20).

This being established:

> He (Śri Kṛṣṇa) teaches [in *BG* 3.27-30] the manner in which the ātman is to be thought of as not being the agent, as a required element of karmayoga, after pointing out the distinction between the wise and the unwise among those practicing karmayoga (*RGB* 3.26).

Finally in *BG* 3.31-32:

> He (Śri Kṛṣṇa) says that this (teaching about karmayoga independent of jñānayoga) indeed is the meaning which actually forms the essential element of the Upaniṣads (*RGB* 3.30).

And that:

> in the remaining portion of this chapter, the liability of jñānayoga to mistakes, on account of its difficulty of performance, is taught (*RGB* 3.32).

Rāmānuja thinks that the scope of practice for karmayoga is enlarged considerably during the course of Kṛṣṇa's instruction. In *BG* 2.47, the seeker was advised to regard himself as not being the agent of his actions. In *BG* 3.27-29, Kṛṣṇa explains where the agency lies, viz. in the guṇas. These operate according to the personality, according to the manner in which the vāsanas direct the organs of action into certain lines of activity. All desire-prompted activities derive from the prakṛtic element. The wise person will therefore work at all times thinking: "the guṇas act among the guṇas" (guṇa guṇeṣu vartanta iti) (cf. also *RGB* 3.29).

However, this is only a first step, according to Rāmānuja. The prakṛti acts, but the prakṛti belongs to the Lord. It is the Lord as his body. This leads to the understanding that it is the Lord himself who acts or rather who allows action to take place, even the desire-prompted action conducive to bondage for the ātman. In order to escape this bondage, the one desirous of liberation (mumukṣu) must develop the habit of switching allegiance from prakṛti and its desires arising out of a misplaced ego-identity (ahaṃkāra) to the Lord by "making over all actions to [him]" (*BG* 3.30). This is understood by Rāmānuja to be a meditation of the form:

> Therefore, make over to Me, who am the Supreme Person, all activities, regarding them as being done by Me, by meditating on the ātman as being of such a nature as to be set into activity by Me only, on account of its being My Body. And perform them, looking upon them merely as services to Me (*RGB* 3.30).

This meditation on the ātman as the body of God must be distinguished from the meditation on the Lord himself as having the ātman for his body, which is an aspect of bhaktiyoga leading to God-realization (rather than to self-realization which is the purpose here).

Interestingly enough, Rāmānuja does not take advantage of the statement of *BG* 3.15 (karma brahmodbhava) to make the above point. He interprets Brahman as the body rather than as Vasudeva, since it better suits the development of his argument. As for Śaṅkara, he interprets Brahman as the Veda because he could hardly admit that action proceeded from the Immutable One. (He reads yajña as apūrva in the same verse.) The word para also falls victim to the contrasting valuations of the two yogas. For Śaṅkara it is the ātman that will be known and experienced on the elimination of desire. For Rāmānuja, it is the enemy of the ātman or desire itself that must be destroyed by means of karmayoga (*BG* 3.43).

(c) *BG* Chapter 4

The contrasting perspectives of the two men become increasingly evident in the fourth chapter of the *BG*. The claim to pedigree with which the chapter opens (*BG* 4.1-3) is regarded by Śaṅkara as Kṛṣṇa's concluding remarks on the doctrine of the two yogas revealed in chapters 2 and 3. Rāmānuja regards it as the introduction to the idea that karmayoga contains within it those elements of jñāna on which the discipline itself is based (jñānayogākāratā.). In his view, this issue of karma as a form of jñāna goes back to *BG* 2.47, which implied the need for constant meditation on the nature of the ātman as distinct from prakṛti. The idea that the ātman is not the agent of actions is made more explicit at *BG* 3.27-30. These developments enable Rāmānuja to answer the question raised at *BG* 4.16 (kiṃ karma kimakarmeti?) by explaining that:

> Karma is a form of worship of the Lord without attachment to the fruits; akarma is regarded as knowledge (jñāna) about the truth of the ātman of the one who performs the action (*RGB* 4.16).

Rāmānuja points out that Kṛṣṇa progressively reveals the specific kinds of information incorporated in the discipline of karmayoga in the verses that follow. In addition to knowledge of the self (ātmajñāna) on which the practice of karmayoga must be based, knowledge is also necessary for the performance of the various nitya-, naimittika- and kāmya-karmas (vikarma), as well as for jñānayoga (=akarma) (*RGB* 4.17). Only when a man understands the intimate connection between karma and jñāna is he fulfilled in his life's work as a kṛtsnakarmakṛt. He becomes an integrated personality (yukta) who sees the truth of the ātman in all he does (sees non-action in action) and sees all action in the light of knowledge (sees action in non-action) (*RGB* 4.18). The importance of the element of knowledge is further revealed when Kṛṣṇa teaches that:

> all work that is being done by the aspirant for mokṣa is of the form of knowledge (jñānākāra), because it is associated with meditation on its having the Supreme Brahman for its soul (parabrahmātmaka). It is a direct means for seeing the self, and not through the interposition of the discipline of knowledge (*RGB* 4.24).

The second sentence shows why karmayoga may be preferred even by one who is qualified for jñānayoga.

Following the description of the numerous options available for the performance of karmayoga, Kṛṣṇa makes the statement in *BG* 4.33 "that the sacrifice of knowledge is superior to the sacrifice of material objects." This, of course, is a particularly significant statement for Śaṅkara. What this means for Rāmānuja, however, is that: "In karma (i.e. karmayoga), which has a dual aspect, the element consisting of knowledge is superior to the element consisting of material objects" (*RGB* 4.33). In the remaining verses of this chapter (*BG* 4.34-42), says Rāmānuja, Kṛṣṇa "speaks of the characteristic of the knowledge about the nature of the self when it has the form of direct vision (śakṣātkṛtātmasvarūpa)" (*RGB* 4.34). The reference to "one who has given up all action through knowledge" in *BG* 4.41 is glossed by Rāmānuja as one "whose work has assumed the form of knowledge (jñānākāratāpannakarmāṇa)," i.e. it has nothing to do with renunciation of action.

Not surprisingly, the message of this chapter is seen in an entirely different light by Śaṅkara. From his point of view, the emphasis on action in chapter 3 is needed to lead Arjuna away from premature abandonment of his responsibilities. As a warrior and a yogi, Arjunas's duty and need are for action to prepare him for jñāna, a knowledge that can arise only in a pure and tranquil mind. Thinking that he has made this clear to his student, Kṛṣṇa expands on his answer to Arjuna's question (*BG* 4.4) to reveal (prematurely as it turns out) the true nature of action and inaction from the standpoint of one who is established in the highest truth (paramārthikasatya).

Kṛṣṇa introduces this topic at *BG* 4.16 by raising the issue of karma and akarma. However, akarma is not jñānayoga, says Śaṅkara, but simply the cessation of physical and mental activities which, like karma, "is falsely attributed to the Ātman and causes the feeling of egoism as expressed in the words, 'quiet and doing nothing, I sit happily'" (*SGB* 4.18). In reality, the Immutable One is beyond all notions of agency. The truly wise man, continues Śaṅkara, is he who sees inaction in action, i.e. who sees that the actions commonly attributed to the ātman are prompted by the guṇas, not the ātman. He also sees action in inaction, since the vulgar notion of inaction is really only a form of this same action (*SGB* 4.18). From the absolute standpoint of Brahman (with whom the wise man is identified), "he" does nothing at all (*SGB* 4.20), incurs no sin (*SGB* 4.21) and is not bound (*SGB* 4.22), since everything he does simply melts away (*SGB* 4.23).

Śaṅkara says that in order to accentuate the sense of otherness in these verses, Kṛṣṇa proceeds to contrast what he calls the knowledge-sacrifice (jñānayajña) of *BG* 4.24 with the kind of sacrificial action traditionally sanctioned by the Vedas (karmakaṇḍa). Karmakaṇḍa is born of action (karmaja), that is, "born of the not-Self — of action in deed, speech and thought, for the Self is actionless" (*SGB* 4.32). And Kṛṣṇa then makes his point even more strongly with the all-important statement that "superior is the sacrifice of knowledge to the sacrifice of material objects" (*BG* 4.33). Śaṅkara says that it is superior, because "jñāna, which is the means to mokṣa, comprehends all action" (*SGB* 4.33). This is, of course, exactly the reverse of what Rāmānuja would have us understand in this same text.

According to Śaṅkara, Kṛṣṇa's compelling portrait of the man of true vision (drawn by eighteen evocative strokes at *BG* 4.18-23) shows him in two modes, as it were. He is the contemplative sage who renounces action, doing only what is needed for the bare maintenance of the body. He is also the sage who lives an active life, either to offer an example to the world or to avoid giving offence to the orthodox. Whether he appears to us to act or to renounce all actions, he is a true saṃnyāsin (from his own absolute point of view), in whose wisdom-fire all actions are reduced to ashes (*BG* 4.37). Here, Śaṅkara explains that from the mundane point of view the actions of the body must still continue, since "the actions by which this body has been brought into existence will come to an end only when their effects will have been fully worked out; for those actions have already commenced their effects" (*SGB* 4.37).

(d) *BG* Chapter 5

Arjuna temporarily loses the thread of the argument once again at this point. He understands fully that conduct has little to do with worldly effects (which in the case of war can be disastrous). It is instead related to the transformative effects on the inner life. Indeed, action must be taken precisely to free the personality from its slavish attachment to these worldly effects that belong to God, not to the ego (ahaṃkāra). But he fails to understand that the choice of a life of action or of renunciation (or the yoga of knowledge) is not given primarily by the circumstances of time or place but by the record of the past (vāsanas) manifested in the spiritual status (adhikāra) of the seeker himself. In this there is no personal choice.

Because of this, Arjuna has trouble reconciling why Kṛṣṇa should first extol the merits of the knowledge sacrifice (*BG* 4.33-4.39) and of renunciation (*BG* 4.41) and then exhort him to "get up [and fight]" (*BG* 4.42). He sees an apparent contradiction between the merits of karmasaṃnyāsa — literally, abandonment of action — and yoga, the performance of action in one form or another. Which one is the better of the two? His question echoes a similar concern raised earlier (*BG* 3.1).

Rāmānuja's line of thinking fits very well with Kṛṣṇa's reply that karmayoga is the better of the two . It confirms his thesis that karmayoga, whatever the spiritual status of the seeker, is to be preferred to the more austere and more difficult practice of jñānayoga (which is, of course, how he glosses the term karmasaṃnyāsa). In addition to the reasons already given, this is because karmayoga:

> is quicker in securing results than the discipline of jñāna as a means for the realisation of the ātman (*BG* 4.2-7). Then is taught the manner of

> meditation [on the ātman] as not being an agent, which is included in karmayoga (*BG* 4.8-15). This knowledge which has its roots in [i.e. arises from or is caused by] that karmayoga is then investigated (*BG* 4.16-19); (*RGB* 5 Introduction).

Śaṅkara, on the other hand, has to explain why a practice that cannot lead directly to mokṣa is better than karmasaṃnyāsa based on knowledge (as discussed in chapter 4). As usual, he solves the problem by building a hierarchy of meanings for the term karmasaṃnyāsa (renunciation of action), depending on whether it is based on ignorance or on knowledge. Total abstention from action is impossible in saṃsāra (cf. *BG* 3.5), and any premature withdrawal from worldly duties can only lead to greater bondage and confusion. Escapism of this kind will be described by Kṛṣṇa later on as tamasic (cf. *BG* 18.7) and rajasic (*BG* 18.8) abandonment. Kṛṣṇa has already said that under these conditions "karma is superior to akarma" (cf. *BG* 3.8). The most that the ordinary, ignorant yogi is capable of doing, in Śaṅkara's view, is to perform his duties in a spirit of renunciation of the worldly fruits. Kṛṣṇa will call this type of abandonment sattvic (cf. *BG* 18.9). Only a highly integrated personality (yukta) with complete mastery of his mental and physical energies (guṇātīta), he believes, can take directly to the path of renunciation and knowledge. (Even this Sāṃkhya personality should act, according to need, for the welfare of the world.) Where is one to place Arjuna's use of the term here? This is the challenge for Śaṅkara.

Comparison with the term yoga suggests that whatever Arjuna had in mind by karmasaṃnyāsa, it is neither the sattvic renunciation integral to the discipline of karmayoga nor the renunciation of the sage that takes place as a result of knowledge. It is clearly a sādhana of some kind which, as we know, must be a product of ignorance and not knowledge (vidyā) (because it is based on the notion of agency). This forces Śaṅkara to distinguish yet another form of renunciation based on the practice of asceticism (tapas), which he calls kevalasaṃnyāsa (mere renunciation) unaccompanied by knowledge:

> This saṃnyāsa, which consists in renouncing a few actions only while yet there is an idea of agency, is different from the one already spoken of, from the renunciation of all actions, which is resorted to by the man who has realized the Self. The former becomes very difficult of performance as it is further associated with 'yama' and 'niyama' and the like (which are the various forms of self-control). Karmayoga is comparatively easier of performance and is therefore spoken of as the better of the two (*SGB* 5 Introduction).

By this hermeneutic device, Śaṅkara can safely explain why Kṛṣṇa would say karmayoga is better than karmasaṃnyāsa without compromising the key tenet of Advaita: that true karmasaṃnyāsa — the renunciation of the Sāṃkhya which he calls supreme renunciation (paramārthasaṃnyāsa) — is the only valid way to enter the realm of knowledge. In fact, through comparison of Sāṃkhya and Yoga of *BG* 5.4, Kṛṣṇa himself brings the subject back to the true paramārthasaṃnyāsa in *BG* 5.6. Here Sāṃkhyas are seekers qualified to renounce the world out of devotion to knowledge (jñānaniṣṭhā). This provides Śaṅkara with the opening he needs to explain that:

> the Lord, without leaving these (i.e. the notion of 'mere saṃnyāsa' and 'mere karmayoga') has added to them some conceptions of His own and has answered the question speaking of them under other names, sāṃkhya and yoga. In the opinion of the Lord, (mere) saṃnyāsa and (mere) karmayoga are themselves termed 'sāṃkhya' and 'yoga' when knowledge of the Self (ātmajñāna) and equanimity (samabuddhitva) are added to them respectively (*SGB* 5.4).

The fact that Kṛṣṇa equates these two terms in the sense that the end-state (sthāna) is the same for both is no obstacle, since Śaṅkara can simply point to the fact that the path of karmayoga is an indirect one and must eventually lead into true karmasaṃnyāsa.

Śaṅkara concludes his rather tortured line of argument as follows:

> It is mere karmasaṃnyāsa (i.e. tapas) and mere karmayoga with reference to "which you have asked me which one is the better of the two?" In accordance with the question, My answer has been given — without having regard to knowledge — that karmayoga is superior to karmasaṃnyāsa. But that saṃnyāsa which is based upon knowledge is regarded by Me as Sāṃkhya, and Sāṃkhya itself is the true (paramārtha) Yoga. It is only by a figure of speech that the yoga through Vedic rites is called 'yoga' or 'saṃnyāsa,' inasmuch as it conduces to the true (paramārtha) Yoga or Saṃnyāsa (*SGB* 5.5).

This refers to the fact that Kṛṣṇa habitually designates karmayogins as saṃnyāsins (e.g. at *BG* 5.3 and at *BG* 6.1). In his introduction to chapter 6, Śaṅkara comments that this is only "by way of praise (stuti)."

By way of these circuitous explanations, Śaṅkara is able to explain why Kṛṣṇa says that for an ego-centred personality such as Arjuna karmayoga is more appropriate than either a yoga based on denial (such as the various forms of tapas) or on any vain attempt to abandon the I-sense (paramārthasaṃnyāsa) which is "hard to attain without yoga (duḥkhamāptumayogata)" (*BG* 5.6). The common man, says Śaṅkara, is not qualified for the sudden leap into awareness and must proceed by stages: "first purity of mind; then attainment of knowledge; then renunciation of all actions; and finally, devotion to knowledge" (*SGB* 5.12). "Renouncing all actions by thought," he can rest happily in the nine-gated city of the body, "neither acting nor causing to act" (*BG* 5.13). He is "established in Brahman ... that is, he does no action, he has renounced all action" (*SGB* 5.20).

Rāmānuja profits from the same text but reaches an opposite conclusion. "The meaning [of *BG* 5.4] is that they are not possessed of true wisdom who say that karmayoga brings about only jñānayoga, that jñānayoga alone brings about the vision of the self and that the two are thus different on account of difference in their fruits" (*RGB* 5.4). And the knowledge of the sage who can say "I do nothing at all [for] the senses move among the objects of the senses" (*BG* 5.8-9) involves no denial of reality to actions or even abandonment of them in a physical sense. It simply involves dissociation of the ātman from its prakṛtic embodiment. All that happens is that "the embodied self makes over all works to the city of nine gateways with the help of the mind which has judged that the agency of the self in respect of works is due to association with the body as a result of ancient karmas and not to its own nature" (*RGB* 5.13). Svabhāva is the cause of action (*BG* 5.14), but once "established in brahman" (glossed as ātman), all bondage in saṃsāra is broken. He attains brahmabhūta (*BG* 5.24), which Rāmānuja glosses as the bliss of self-experience (ātmānubhavasukha).

(e) *BG* Chapter 6

The sixth chapter of the *BG* is regarded by Rāmānuja as the culmination (śira) of all that has been discussed of karmayoga and jñānayoga in chapters 2-5. It is Kṛṣṇa's instruction for meditation that leads to the final awakening to one's own true freedom as the ātman liberated from the bonds of prakṛti. This final awakening is characterized by him as ātmāvalokanarūpayoga, the yoga that is of the nature of the vision of the self. It should be remembered that for him this is really only the starting point for Bhakti (a form of karma not discussed in this essay), which leads to the much greater awakening to the Lord of creation, who has the universe for his body and dwells in the hearts of all (bhaktiyoga is first introduced at *BG* 6.47).

Both Rāmānuja and Śaṅkara have to deal with Kṛṣṇa's eclectic use of terms, in particular with the terms saṃnyāsa and yoga. Saṃnyāsa, as we have seen, has a variety of meanings. The word yoga can refer to both a means (sādhana) and an end-state of some kind. While Kṛṣṇa clearly wishes to produce a synthesis of disciplines culminating in this meditation, he leaves ample room for speculation by making a distinction (*BG* 6.1) that places the saṃnyāsins together with the yogins in the category of those engaged in action for its own sake, against those who are not eligible to perform Vedic rites (akriya). The second verse equates the two disciplines. He links them further in the third verse by saying that karma is the means for a sage (muni) who seeks to ascend to yoga (as an end-state), whereas śama (tranquillity) is the means for one who has already ascended to yoga (yogārūḍha).

Rāmānuja takes the word saṃnyāsa, applied by Kṛṣṇa to one who performs works, as a reference to the knowledge element in karmayoga. The akriya are those who follow only jñānayoga. (Why these latter are characterized by Kṛṣṇa as *not* being saṃnyāsins is unclear.) This element of knowledge involves the abandonment of saṃkalpa, glossed as the delusive identification of the ātman with the prakṛti (*RGB* 6.2). This is in agreement with Rāmānuja's original use of the term at *BG* 4.19. (He uses it again without gloss at *RGB* 6.4 and *RGB* 6.24.) Rāmānuja then glosses śama in the next verse as cessation of works (karmanivṛtti). "The meaning is that works ought to be performed until there is the attainment of mokṣa in the form of the vision of the self" (*RGB* 6.3). Normally, however, works are performed day after day until death finally liberates the ātman for all time.

Rāmānuja, in contrast to Śaṅkara, does not consider the meditation taught here as a cessation of activity but as part of karmayoga. While it is true that the activity of the mind comes to an end as a result of this yoga (*BG* 6.25), meditation is considered a daily practice (an activity) designed to elevate the mind through the four stages described at *BG* 6.29-6.32 to the final vision of the ātman.

Śaṅkara has much more difficulty with the use of the term saṃnyāsin in *BG* 6.1-4. He must first of all explain the order to extol it, based on a perceived identity between the abandonment of action itself and the abandonment of the fruits of action. Both involve the abandonment of thoughts (saṃkalpa), the first with regard to action as a whole, the second with respect to the fruits alone. He then interprets śama, the path of the yogārūḍha (*BG* 6.3.), as abstaining from all actions (sarvakarmabhyo nivṛtti). "The more thoroughly he abstains from action, the more free he is from trouble" (*SGB* 6.3). And the expression sarvasaṃkalpasaṃnyāsa (*BG* 6.4) also implies that all desires and actions are abandoned, "for on surrendering all thoughts, one cannot move at all" (*SGB* 6.4). Śaṅkara is quite radical on this score. Thus, in contrast to Rāmānuja, "no action forms a necessary duty throughout life" (*SGB* 6 Introduction).

Throughout his commentary, Śaṅkara tacitly, and sometimes explicitly as here, ties the notion of paramārthasaṃnyāsa to the fourth stage of life, that is, saṃnyāsa or renunciation (which may be entered upon at any time of life, cf. Introduction to chapter 3). Thus, the yoga described by Kṛṣṇa at *BG* 6.10 and following, is explicitly reserved for saṃnyāsins only, not for the house-holder (gṛhastha). When the mind is restrained by the practice of this yoga of right vision (saṃyagdarśanalakṣaṇayoga):

> the yogin sees the Self, the Supreme Intelligence (caitanya) and All-resplendent Light, by means of the self (antaḥkaraṇa), by the mind which has been purified by samādhi, and attains satisfaction in the Self (*SGB* 6.20).

Conclusion

When attempting to understand any text, we would do well to recall the words of Gadamer:

> Every time will have to understand a text handed down to it in its own way, for it is subject to the whole of the tradition in which it has a material interest, and in which it seeks to understand itself.... The meaning of the text surpasses its author not occasionally, but always (Gadamer 1960, 280).

A text is never a static entity but moves and speaks to us in its presentations like a work of art or a game. It is never dependent on its creator alone or on its interpreters in the sense that through one or the other of these we may grasp the essential meaning or message in itself. This is perhaps especially true of the *BG* which, after all, is an attempt to transform or rather to create the necessary conditions for a human being to be transformed.

However, a number of observations may be made. In the first place, there is little doubt, even for Śaṅkara, about the *BG*'s call to action through the discourse as a whole. Arjuna cannot exchange the battlefield of his life for a mendicant existence without incurring great danger. "Better one's own duty though deficient, than the duty of another well-performed" (*BG* 3.35 and 18.47). The choice of *what* to do in life is rather narrowly defined by one's own existential situation, first and foremost by one's tasks and responsibilities, which have been created through the actions of one's own past. As a man of action and a warrior, Arjuna must first "get up" and fight (uttiṣṭha bhārata).

Beyond the problem of what to do in life, however, lies the *how* and the *why*, the ethical choices of means and ends. Arjuna quickly decides in favour of mokṣa as the highest good (śreyas) but is confused about the best means to get there. Kṛṣṇa tells him little about mokṣa. He has much to say, however, about the two bases (niṣṭhā) for it: jñānayoga and karmayoga. He is cautious about jñānayoga. He does say that all action is comprehended in knowledge (*BG* 4.33) and that the knower (jñānī) is his very Self (*BG* 7.18). He also makes it quite clear that karmayoga is superior (*BG* 5.2), and that the yogi is superior to the saṃnyāsins (*BG* 6.46). Karmayoga is also easier and quicker than jñānayoga (*BG* 5.6). Greater difficulty (kleśa) is given to those who take the path of the unmanifest (avyakta) (*BG* 12.5), whether this be jñānayoga (Rāmānuja's reading) or the nirguṇabrahman, brahman without qualities (Śaṅkara's reading).

More importantly, Kṛṣṇa strongly urges Arjuna to take up karmayoga on at least nine separate occasions (*BG* 2.48,50; 3.8,9, 20,30,43; 4.15, 42), since he is born to it and bound to it by his own nature (svabhāva) (*BG* 18.60). The spirit of the text certainly supports Rāmānuja on this score. Rāmānuja has problems mainly with respect to his particular notion of self-identity and must stretch the meaning of saṃkalpa (particularly at *BG* 4.19 and 6.2) in order to accommodate his point of view. Śaṅkara, on the other hand, has great difficulty explaining how action can be superior to non-action. Why Kṛṣṇa would confuse his student with so many nuances about the word saṃnyāsa is unfathomable. (Rāmānuja himself is guilty of this, although his reading of the threefold saṃnyāsa of *BG* 18.4 does have some support in earlier sections of the text.)

Both men agree that the rationale for karmayoga is control of the mind and the senses by way of purification (ātmaśuddhi). He who is master of himself (vijitātmā) acts not only for the welfare of the world (lokasaṃgraha), rather than in his own interests (bhogaiśvarya), but also becomes qualified for meditation on the truth of the ātman (according to their very different conceptions of this). Rāmānuja regards meditation, however, as an integral part of karma, which, with the Lord's grace, becomes a self-sufficient way to liberation. This is the experience of the self, mokṣa or ātmānubhava. Śaṅkara cannot accept this view, although there is little support in the text for his theory of superimposition and illusion.

Rāmānuja goes much further than Śaṅkara in developing a content for karmayoga. With some creative use of the text, he proposes a graduated series of techniques for behaviour modification based on the knowledge aspect of karmayoga. This is designed to break the identity of the ātman with the ego (ahaṃkāra) by attributing actions, the agency behind them, and the fruits to other entities. Action and agency belong to the guṇas and ultimately to the Lord who permits them. The fruits of all actions belong exclusively to the Lord. The techniques themselves, in the form of suggestive meditations, introduced at *BG* 2.47 and *BG* 3.27-29 (cf. also *BG* 13.29), attribute agency to the guṇas. Action is attributed to the Lord, the initiator (pravartayitṛ) of all actions, at *BG* 3. 30 and *BG* 18.14. Ultimately, agency, too, must be ascribed to the Supreme Person (*BG* 18.13-15). The ātman is never the agent, though it is held accountable for all actions undertaken in the composite form of the embodied self (jīvātman) (*RGB* 14.20 quoting *Vedāntasūtra* II.3.33). Other practices include meditations on the Lord to elicit grace (e.g. *BG* 2.61; 2.66) and the practice of virtue, the conscious attempt to refine oneself in the form of the virtues ascribed to men of realization, such as the sthitaprajña of chapter 2, the guṇātīta of chapter 14 and those of the daivisaṃpad of chapter 16.

Śaṅkara also accepts the practice of action. "For everywhere in spiritual science (adhyātmaśāstra), the very characteristic attributes of the successful yogin are taught as the means [of attaining that stage], since they are to be attained by effort (yatna)" (*SGB* 2.54). However, he clearly has much less interest in any sādhana based on karma. He merely suggests that actions should be surrendered "with the wise thought that I, the agent, do this for Īśvara's sake as his servitor (bhṛtya)" (*SGB* 3.30 2.48 and 5.10). The yogin must also think of himself as the witness (sākṣin) of all he does (*SGB* 18.17).

In conclusion, Rāmānuja remains, by and large, much closer to the spirit of the text than his illustrious predecessor. His interest in sādhana (which, of course, includes the all-important bhaktiyoga) forces him into a procrustean bed from time to time, but he generally emerges none the worse for wear. Śaṅkara, on the other hand, is forced by his theory of illusion (which finds little support in the text) to discount what is, after all, the main purpose of the teaching. This is to make Arjuna act in his own best interest and in the interest of the world (more specifically, to restore dharma as an instrument of God's will). It is surely inconceivable that Kṛṣṇa would also teach Arjuna a doctrine he is not yet ready for. For these reasons, we find ourselves in agreement with the assessment of T.G. Mainkar that Rāmānuja is "definitely more faithful to the *Bhagavadgītā* than Śaṅkara" (Mainkar 1969, 33).

NOTES

1. Quotations marked *BG* are taken from the Sanskrit text of the *Bhagavadgītā* in *The Mahābhārata* (Sukthankar et al., eds., 1947). Quotations marked *SGB* and *RGB* refer to the relevant commentaries of Śaṅkara and Rāmānuja. I have quoted from the translations of Sastri and Sampatkumaran respectively but have used the original Sanskrit to recover the technical vocabulary.

BIBLIOGRAPHY

Gadamer, H.G. 1960. *Wahrheit und Methode: Grundzuge einer philosophischen Hermeneutik*. Tübingen: Mohr.

Gokhale, Dinkar Vishnu, ed. 1950. *The Bhagavad-Gītā with the Commentary of Śrī Śaṅkarācārya*. 2d rev. ed. Poona: Oriental Book Agency.

Mainkar, T.G. 1969. *A Comparative Study of the Commentaries on the Bhagavadgītā*. Delhi: Motilal Banarsidass.

Sampatkumaran, M.R., trans. 1969. *The Gītābhāṣhya of Rāmānuja*. Madras: Prof. M. Rangacharya Memorial Trust.

Śastri, A. Mahādeva, trans. 1972. *The Bhagavad-Gītā with the Commentary of Śrī Śaṅkarāchārya*. Madras: V. Ramaswamy Sastrulu and Sons.

Sukthankar, Vishnu S., S.K. Belvaklar, et al, eds. 1947. *The Mahābhārata*. Poona: Bhandarkar Oriental Research Institute.

THE CONCEPT OF TIME IN ŚAṄKARA'S BRAHMASŪTRA-BHĀṢYA

Leslie C. Orr

Introduction

As a foundation text for the system of Advaita Vedānta, Śaṅkara's commentary on the *Brahmasūtras* is focused on explaining the nature of Brahman, the singular and absolute essence of the universe. Central to the conception of Brahman is its character in relation to time: Brahman, because it is changeless, permanent, immortal, eternal, and limitless, is different from the temporal, phenomenal world. Śaṅkara, in his task of explication, must inevitably treat concepts of time. My examination of the ways in which Śaṅkara approaches this problem in the *Brahmasūtra-bhāṣya* has revealed various formulations of transience, continuity, change and immortality. Instead of there being simply *two* ways of categorizing the temporal status — as eternal or not — Śaṅkara presents a more complex picture of time.

This essay proposes a four-fold typology of the kinds of time Śaṅkara deals with in his *Brahmasūtra-bhāṣya*:[1] (1) empirical time; (2) transcendental time; (3) time dissolved; and (4) time destroyed. This is not necessarily a hierarchical ontological scheme, showing levels of existence each "more real" than the last, culminating in absolute Reality. Instead, each level represents several kinds of concerns: (a) a world view, a particular understanding of the nature of time and its impact on the individual; (b) a task, with respect to the awakening of a certain kind of insight or discrimination; and (c) a particular spiritual goal.[2] The framework for the organization of this study will be an analysis of these three categories of concern at each of the four levels of time.

By using this typology of four levels of time, we are able to see how Śaṅkara has constructed a *series* of coherent systems of understanding and teaching. Within each level, too, we may see tensions or limitations that have the potential to evoke in the student an insight that would bring about a "paradigm shift" into the next of the four levels. If we see the four levels in terms of such a progression, we appreciate Śaṅkara's *Brahmasūtra-bhāṣya* in terms of its didactic purpose in furthering the discipline (sādhana) that leads to the spiritual goal of the system of Vedānta. But each of the four levels is also meaningful in its own right, representing reality in its own terms, and is not only a stepping stone toward a final truth.

Advaita Vedānta is very often described as a system of "two truths" — the lower, everyday, commonsense truth of the experience of diversity and multiplicity and the transcendent, ultimate, absolute truth of the knowledge of the unity of Brahman.[3] This black-and-white, all-or-nothing view of the system does not, however, reflect the subtlety and sophistication of Śaṅkara's explanation of concepts of time in the *Brahmasūtra-bhāṣya*. But why is it necessary for Śaṅkara to present *several* viewpoints — at the four levels I have identified — if there is indeed but one ultimate truth (paramārtha), as he himself insists (II.1.14 P, 20; II.1.11 P, 16)?

I have already pointed out the potential of the four levels in terms of their usefulness in a progressive sādhana, one which perhaps mitigates the drastic discontinuity of "two truths," providing a bridge by means of which the finite human bound in time may reach the infinite and timeless truth he or she seeks. Śaṅkara addresses directly the issue of practice, of the means of attaining liberating knowledge.

There are two other aspects of Śaṅkara's task in the *Brahmasūtra-bhāṣya* that are served by his multi-layered presentation of truth. First, he must reconcile the various and contradictory statements of the Upaniṣads that relate to the issue of time. According to Śaṅkara, śruti, the revealed and eternal Vedic texts including the Upaniṣads, is the sole source of knowledge and authority with respect to understanding the nature of Brahman and thereby realizing liberation (mokṣa); in fact, the sole purport of the Upaniṣads is the explanation of the nature of Brahman (I. 1.2-4). Śaṅkara's task of reconciling texts and traditions is further complicated by the intellectual developments that have occurred in the period of time — more than a millennium — between the era of the Upaniṣads and his own era. His exposition of Vedānta must be consistent with an established philosophical system, and it must make sense of the *Brahmasūtras* upon which his bhāṣya is a commentary. He must also come to terms with widely-accepted philosophical, cosmological, and theological concepts — some of which are quite foreign to the Upaniṣads — as they are expressed in smṛti (the Epic and Purānic scriptures that have come to be accepted as authoritative). A second concern of Śaṅkara's is the refutation of the contentions of other religio-philosophical systems. The possibility of drawing on several levels of understanding both to reconcile various authoritative texts and to demonstrate the weaknesses of his opponents' positions enhances considerably his power of argumentation.

Let us examine each of the four levels of time.

1. Level One: Empirical Time

The first level of time is that defined in terms of human experience — empirical time. Our primary apprehension of time is in terms of change, the passage of time embodied in the transformation and the destruction of things, in the alternation of day and night, in the rotation of the seasons, and in human life, in birth, aging and death. Many of these forms of change, notably those that most intimately affect people, are directional, irreversible, proceeding in a particular order. Empirical existence is defined in terms of the three times — past, present, and future — which, because of our notion of the unidirectional arrow of time, seem each to have a unique character. Conventional expressions of action, causation, and change depend on the notion of all the three times. Our very experience of change is based on our sense that we exist not only in time but through time; we have the feeling of the continuity of our existence. Empirical time, characterized by both the sense of change and the sense of continuity, is the first level of time.

Level One World View: Personal Continuity and Persistence after Death

Śaṅkara offers several explanations for the sense of personal continuity in empirical time. Our physical being is clearly subject to change, but our psychological or intellectual being provides us with a sense of permanence. Indeed, says Śaṅkara, the mind (manas) does transcend the momentary present:

> The mind functions in all the three times and with respect to all objects but is singular (though with) many functions (vṛtti); and according to its (various) ways of functioning is classified as mind (manas), intellect (buddhi), egoity (ahaṃkāra) or thought (citta) (II. 4.6 B, 634).[4]

Śaṅkara treats some of these mental functions in detail. He describes intellect (buddhi) as having various qualities (guṇas) such as desire, aversion, happiness and sorrow. He maintains that "these qualities of intellect are the essential factors in the association of the self (ātman) with the condition of transmigration," since they act as qualifications (upādhis) defining the self as an agent (kartṛ) and experiencer (bhoktṛ). Although the embodied self (jīva) is not identical with the intellect, to talk of a distinction between the self and the intellect is like talking about the difference between a grindstone and the grindstone's body (II.3. 29 B, 610). And "for as long as the self is in contact with buddhi, so long will that self be transmigratory (saṃsārin)" (II.3.30 B, 611).

The idea of the continuity of the individual as identified with mind or intellect thus has two aspects. One is the notion of change — alteration of states through time, modality with respect to qualities or functions. The other is the idea of permanence, a constancy with respect to the three times or even with respect to death and rebirth in the cycle of saṃsāra.

The mind (manas) is considered to be one of the organs. It is, therefore, surprising to find Śaṅkara suggesting that mental functions may survive death, serving even to condition rebirth.[5] In life, the mind, like the other organs and the body itself, is dependent on prāṇa (life force) for its continuance (II.4.11 C, 539). Freedom from death is, on the level of empirical time, associated with prāṇa. Prāṇa is considered as the foremost (śreṣṭha) among the sensory and mental organs since "it alone is beyond the grasp of Death ... whereas the others are within Death's reach" (22.4.19 C, 546). How, then, can the mental functions of the individual endure beyond death? In what sense is prāṇa immortal?

Śaṅkara, basing himself on the accounts of the Upaniṣads, describes the way in which the psychological self persists. At the time of death the functions (vṛttis) of the sense organs undergo absorption (pralaya) into the mind (manas). Mental functioning is absorbed, in turn, by prāṇa. And then prāṇa merges with the vijñānātman (the "awareness-self") or the self constituted by awareness (vijñānamaya), which is qualified by ignorance (avidyā), action (karma) and remembrance (pūrvaprajñā) (IV.2.2-4 B, 967-9).[6] In this conscious condition, delimited by a particular "personality" born of past behaviour and experience, the individual soul acquires a subtle body and moves toward the rebirth or future existence that corresponds to its particular character (IV.2.5ff). The transmigrating self is thus eternally present *through* time, but exists in a changeful manner, conditioned by factors operating *in* time.

The term "vijñāna" is used in the Upaniṣads to refer to the transmigrating soul. In interpreting *Bṛhadāraṇyaka Upaniṣad* 4.3.7, Śaṅkara identifies vijñāna with intellect (buddhi) (II.3.30 B, 611), one of the mental functions characterized as changeful.[7] But in reference to a parallel passage in *Bṛhadāraṇyaka Upaniṣad* 4.4.22, Śaṅkara says that vijñāna is equivalent to consciousness (caitanya) (I.3.29 B, 609).

Consciousness (caitanya) is represented by Śaṅkara as something rather more than a faculty of mind. It is, in fact, the very nature (rūpa) of the self. Like the various aspects of mental functioning, it is an important indicator of the continuity of the self through time. Despite the apparent character of consciousness as intermittent (kādācitka) — seemingly lost in such states as sleeping, fainting and possession — it is eternal (nitya). This fact is established, Śaṅkara says, both by śruti — textual references drawn from the Upaniṣads — and by the experience of continuity of knowledge, the ongoing awareness or recognition (vijñāna), "I know this" (II.3.18 B, 604). Here caitanya is identified with vijñāna, and the aspects of knowledge and remembrance seem to be central. Further on, Śaṅkara again relates caitanya to vijñāna — linking these elements also to intellect (buddhi) and intelligence (prajñā) — this time in the context of a discussion of sensory awareness. And here again he reiterates that caitanya is the self's very nature, as heat and light are the nature of fire (II.3.27-9 B, 608-9). Caitanya, thus, seems to be a term Śaṅkara uses to draw together a number of different factors of consciousness that are mentioned in the Upaniṣads — sentience, intelligence, knowledge, recognition — and that relate to the continuity of the individual through time. In contrast to his characterization of buddhi and vijñāna, Śaṅkara de-emphasizes the modality of caitanya or its dependence on specific time and space in terms of its content or function. Does caitanya represent a more transcendent, more eternal aspect of the self?

Memory (anusmṛti) is another aspect of individual psychological being that Śaṅkara seems to consider especially important in terms of establishing the permanence of the self. For instance, he uses the fact of memory to argue against the Buddhist doctrine of anātman (II.2.31 C, 412-4). The ordinary experiences of remembrance (smṛti) and recollection (pratisaṃdhāna) are for Śaṅkara strong proofs of the reality of the continuity of the self through the three times of past, present and future (II.2.31 P, 75). Śaṅkara discusses memory — and forgetting — in the context of sleeping and reawakening in order to show the continuity of the self (ātman). In deep sleep, the individual self merges with Brahman, the Supreme Self. But, having reawakened, this experience is forgotten. Yet our waking self recognizes itself as the same one that it was before sleep through the action of memory: "I saw this on the previous day … I am that very person" (III.2.7-9 C 602-4).

Memory, therefore, indicates the continuity of the individual through time in this life. Śaṅkara in at least one context considers time as a function (vṛtti) of mind (II.4.12 C, 540). Perhaps, like other psychological functions, memory is merged into the vijñānātman, the transmigrating self, and thus persists beyond this life, beyond even death.[8] In fact, remembrance (pūrvaprajñā) is one of the qualifications (upādhis) of this transmigrating self, which play a role in determining its destiny. Pūrvaprajñā is, in this context, not simply a capacity for memory but is remembrance with a specific content. Its changeful character and particularity with respect to time and space are, indeed, the means by which it fulfils its role in qualifying the transmigrating self.

Continuity through time, both in life and after death, is associated not only with mental functions and psychological factors but also with action (karma). In the description of the condition of the transmigrating soul just referred to, for instance, Śaṅkara says that action, remembrance, and ignorance are the three qualifications (upādhis) delimiting the self that condition rebirth (IV. 2.4 B, 969). When he considers the continuity of the self through sleep, he emphasizes that the identity of the self before sleep and after sleep is established not only by memory (anusmṛti), but also by action, by the statements of śruti, and by the injunctions (vidhi) found in śruti. Here, Śaṅkara shows how action is an indicator of the continuity of the individual in that after awakening, unfinished work is resumed. The injunctions of the Vedic texts to perform various rites and meditations for specific purposes would be pointless unless the same individual being who performed these actions survived to enjoy their fruits (III.2.9 C, 604-5).

If śruti is meaningful, in terms of its association of the individual person with the results of that person's actions, then one must conclude, says Śaṅkara, that the individual self has no origin or dissolution (II. 3.16 B, 600). In treating the issue of action and its consequences, Śaṅkara must make a systematic presentation of the fate of the self after death, reconciling the Upaniṣadic passages that variously describe the courses of transmigrating souls. Among the paths the souls may take after death are: (1) the path of the ancestors (pitṛyāna) to the lunar world (candramaṇḍalam), which is attained through meritorious action (karma); and (2) the path of the gods (devayāna) to the realm of Brahmā, achieved through understanding (vidyā) (III.1.17 C, 577-8; IV.3.1-8 C, 870-80). Those who follow the pitṛyāna are, after a heavenly sojourn, reborn in various conditions according to their former actions; those who follow the devayāna do not return, according to the Upaniṣads (III.1.7-8; IV.3. 9).

The cause and effect process — in which action in one time yields consequences at a later time — demonstrates the eternality of the self, yet action itself takes place in the context of a particular space, time, and cause (deśakālanimitta) (II.3.37 B, 614). And although action as such seems to have a continuous existence in carrying through time its potential for producing consequences, these karmic fruits "ripen" only when there is the occurrence of a particular space, time and cause (III.4.51 B, 924).

Śaṅkara refers in several different contexts to the problem of how action can persist through time. Karma, he says, is not destroyed, except through the realization of its fruits or expiation (prāyaścitta), or through the seeing of truth (samyagdarśana) (III.1.8 B, 669-70). Residual karma (anuśaya or śeṣakarma), that karma whose fruits remain unrealized at death, has real and continuous existence (sadbhāva). It survives the individual's death, and even heavenly existences, to exert its influence on future rebirths (III.1.8 B, 670). But elsewhere, Śaṅkara states that action in and of itself cannot persist: it is illogical to accept that the consequences of action in the future are produced by action which itself exists only in the moment (III.2.38 C, 640-1).[9] Śaṅkara considers the alternative that momentary action produces some other potency that can persist through time. He seems to accept the Mīmāṃsaka concept of apūrva ("without precedent," i.e. a consequence not immediately preceded by its cause) to explain how the performance of sacrificial rites may result in heavenly reward (III.1.6 C, 562).[10]

At times, Śaṅkara uses the term apūrva interchangeably with the term adṛṣṭa ("unseen" potentiality) to refer not only to sacrificial karma but to action in general. He affirms that adṛṣṭa produces the experience (bhoga) of the fruits of action (II.2.12 P, 57; III.1.8 B, 669).

In the end, Śaṅkara rejects the view that either action or apūrva/adṛṣṭa have in themselves the power to produce results. Fruits come from the Lord (Īśvara), although in their particularity they may depend on karma or on apūrva (III.2.41 B, 732). This represents a shift from level 1 to level 2 thinking. At level 1, the affirmation of the effectiveness of action or adṛṣṭa in producing results serves Śaṅkara's argument by defending and reconciling the accounts of transmigration found in the Upaniṣads (at III.1.6 and III.1.8) and by refuting the Vaiśeṣika view of the role of adṛṣṭa (at II.2. 12; cf. Halbfass 1980, 286-7). At level 2, the understanding of causation focuses on the transcendent power of God. From this perspective, the level 1 idea — held by the Mīmāṃsakas among others — of the automatic mechanism of karmic retribution, must be swept aside.

Level One Discrimination: Beyond the Particularity of Personal Continuity

The ideas about action and transmigration examined above involve two aspects of empirical time that are drawn together in the level 1 framework: (1) continuity and permanence; and (2) change and modality. We have seen how, in Śaṅkara's treatment, the "constants" of psychological being — buddhi, vijñāna, and remembrance (pūrvaprajñā) — are similarly of mixed character and, in fact, are themselves implicated in the transmigratory process. The individual self, in association with these factors of continuity, moves through time within saṃsāra because of the experience and agency in particular time and space that these factors depend on and give rise to.

The experience and analysis of change and continuity at the level of empirical time provides a context for the discrimination of different *kinds* of eternal being. If karma, buddhi, vijñāna, and remembrance are tainted by changefulness, is this not simply a result of their relationship to particularity in space and time? Seen as *capacities*, unrelated to agency or objects, can these constants of human experience be considered truly eternal? Śaṅkara's treatment of knowledge, consciousness and memory at level 1 leads to this insight.

The persistence of knowledge, as noted above, is an indicator of the eternality of consciousness (II.3.18). But in that context knowledge has an object. Śaṅkara discusses the character of knowledge in relation to its agency and objects:

> One may say, "It is I who know a thing now, in the present, and I who knew in the past and the distant past, and again I who will know in the future and far future," and although what is known varies according to its being in the past, the future or the present, there is no variation in the knower, because of its character of being ever in the present (II.3.7 B, 575).

We saw in Śaṅkara's treatment of consciousness, that although he linked consciousness to factors such as buddhi and vijñāna, which have modalities, he did not stress the changefulness or relationship to objects of consciousness itself. This potentially "transcendent" character of consciousness is underscored when Śaṅkara contrasts the nature of action with that of perception (upalabdhi). The self is independent (svatantra, ananyapekṣa) with regard to perception because of its consciousness (caitanya). But with regard to action the self must be dependent on a particular space, time, and cause (II.3.7 B, 614).

Memory, although it may have objects, points to something beyond itself, untouched by modality and change:

> When there is no unchanging entity (kūṭastha) linking [all existence] related to the three times nor a seer of all things (sarvārthadarśin), the everyday actions of memory, recollection and so on — whose support is the store of mental impressions dependent on place, time and cause — cannot occur (II.2.31 P, 75).

Śaṅkara's use of the term darśin (seer, witness) emphasizes the lack of agency or true relationship with the objects of memory in the eternal self whose presence is indicated by memory.

Śaṅkara's analysis of time at level 1 not only suggests the possibility of a deeper understanding of the self but also points to the existence of an eternality beyond individual experience. In his analysis of the Upaniṣadic passages that refer to prāṇa (life force), he distinguishes between the prāṇa that is particular to the individual and cosmic prāṇa. The latter is identified, according to the *Kauṣītaki Upaniṣad*, with intelligence (prajñā), life (ayus), immortality (amṛta) and bliss (ānanda) (I.1.28-31 C, 98-107). The personal prāṇa is, as we have seen, instrumental in perpetuating the individual through death and into further lives, but the cosmic prāṇa is utterly ageless and deathless. This prāṇa is, Śaṅkara insists, none other than Brahman (I.1.23-31; I.3.39).

The Level One Goal: Freedom from Death

The sense of continuity of the self in empirical existence and the law of karma provide a sense of assurance about the orderliness of time. The idea that there is ultimate justice in the process of birth, death, and rebirth may mitigate the sense that death is a disaster. Yet we still wish to escape death, and continued rebirth only means continued redeath. Although the self never really dies, the transmigrating self — associated with the functions of mind, the modes of the intellect, the qualifications of awareness, the contingencies in space and time of remembrance and action — is ever subject to the *experience* of death. The arrow of time moves relentlessly forward, but this movement is not necessarily progress.

Śaṅkara affirms the continuity of the self through the three times, but deprecates the immortality that is achieved through saṃsāra, produced by action in time (III.1.1 C, 553). The goal at level 1 is freedom from death, but the only kind of eternality or continuity we can be certain of at this level of understanding is the immortality of transmigration. Especially when the discrimination appropriate to the level 1 perspective has been awakened, this solution to the problem of personal continuity may seem unsatisfactory. Indeed, this view of the unceasing, inescapable workings of the karmic mechanism may seem intolerably restrictive, and a new perspective may emerge — at level 2.

2. Level Two: Transcendental Time

The second category of time is transcendental time. It is the river of time that exists apart from our particularized experiences in time. It includes in itself all of what the Buddhists call saṃtānas, those streams of momentary events that give the impression of continuity. Time at this level is not dependent on change and motion, as it *contains* all events in time and is itself beginningless and endless.

Many Indian philosophical schools distinguish between empirical and transcendental time.[11] A famous passage in the *Maitrī Upaniṣad* (6.14-16) describes the two kinds of time: that having form (mūrti) and the formless. Embodied (vigrahavān) time originates with the creation of the sun. It has the form of the year and is made up of parts, which are various measures of time. Formless time, the "timeless" (akāla), exists prior to the sun and is partless (akala) (Radhakrishnan 1953, 827-9).[12] This idea of transcendental time having priority *in time* to empirical, particulate time shows that transcendental time is not truly "timeless" but is the eternal, absolute time *within* which empirical time is produced.[13]

Level Two World View: Cyclical Time and Iśvara as the Lord of Time

Eternality at level 2 is "more" eternal than at level 1. The idea of eternity at this level is pravāharūpa nityatā, changing but without any alteration in pattern (Murty 1959, 40). It is pariṇāmi nityatā, eternal but subject to transformation, "in which the idea 'that very thing is this one' is not destroyed, although it is changing" (I.1.4 M, 215). When eternity at level 1 was defined in terms of personal continuity, we saw how this continuity was subject to modality and alteration in its pattern and how the permanence of the transmigrating self was, in fact, *dependent* on the particularity and uniqueness of these modes. Drawing back to consider the character of the universe on a less personal, broader scale, however, Śaṅkara points out that change within cosmic time does indeed exhibit a fixed pattern. It is Brahman and no other who, as Īśvara, is the cause of this beginningless and endless pattern of change.[14]

Śaṅkara maintains firmly that the Vedānta conception, borne out in numerous passages of śruti and smṛti, of Brahman as the efficient cause and the author and ruler of the universe does not compromise Brahman's absolute and eternal nature. At the same time he shows that the various conceptions of the absolute or of the source of the universe in other philosophical schools cannot be eternal in the same sense. In his efforts to show the internal contradictions of his opponent's positions, Śaṅkara presents us with a number of descriptions of the non-eternal that can serve to distinguish level 1 from level 2 concepts of eternality. The way in which the Sāṅkhya, Yoga, Vaiśeṣika and Śaiva schools define God as efficient cause is faulted, says Śaṅkara, because of their ideas of the plurality and particularity of forces (God, souls, nature) involved in the production of the world. These forces, including God, cannot be eternal since whatever is limited (paricchinna) with respect to quantity or extent (iyattā) is seen to have an end (II.2. 38 P, 82). As for the Sāṅkhya prakṛti (nature), it cannot be eternal if it is divided into parts (avayava), and it must have parts if it is the cause of composite things such as those constituting the universe (II.1.29 P, 38). Only Brahman, as Īśvara, the singular and partless cause of the universe, is truly eternal, the Lord of time.[15]

According to Śaṅkara's own summary, nearly the whole first half of his commentary is dedicated to showing that Brahman and no other is the cause of the universe. In large part, this demonstration focuses on the role of Brahman in level 2 terms, as Īśvara:

> the omniscient Lord of all ... [who] through his governorship (niyantṛtva) of the world of creation is the cause of its continuance like a magician because of his magic (māyā), but is the cause, too, of the withdrawal of the

> expansive world into himself like the earth's [withdrawal into herself] of the four kinds of creatures (II. 1.1 P, 1).

This passage refers to the three processes — creation (sṛṣṭi), continuance (sthiti) and dissolution (saṃhṛti, pralaya) — that are the basis for the patterning of the level 2 eternity-in-change. These three processes recur over and over in precisely the same way in cosmic cycles (kalpas). Śaṅkara makes it very clear, in numerous contexts, that Īśvara is the ruler of these processes. Commenting on *Kaṭha Upaniṣad* 2.1.1 — "He is the ruler of the past and the future; He exists today and He will exist tomorrow" — Śaṅkara identifies "Him" as Brahman and insists that "none other than the supreme Lord can be the absolute ruler of the past and the future" (I.3.24 C, 202-3).

In terms of the creation of the universe, Śaṅkara must not only refute the theories of other philosophical schools but must reconcile the various Upaniṣadic accounts of the origination of the various elements of the phenomenal world. The painstaking reconstruction of the exact order of creation — the creation of space, air, fire, earth and other physical factors, or of such factors of consciousness as awareness, intellect, mind and the sense organs — must be undertaken in order to show how everything apart from Brahman is produced and therefore non-eternal and how everything is derived from Brahman (e.g. II. 3.5, II.4.2).

The distinction between empirical and transcendental time is clearly brought out in the notion of the creation of time and of time's dependence on space. Time — like the directions, mind and atoms — is a product, an effect (II.3.7 B, 584). It is not considered to be one of the factors (space, air, fire, and earth) that emerge first in creation. Time, in fact, is subsumed by space: "everything that is produced arises in a place and time (deśakāla), which are included in space (ākāśa), and that place and time of space itself are said to be included by Brahman" (II.3.5 B, 581).[16] Indeed, the Upaniṣads say that all things originate from space. Śaṅkara hastens to tell us that here Brahman is meant (I.1.22 C, 83). Space must be understood to be created before empirical time. Space is created and recreated, in each kalpa, in transcendental time.

The continuance of the world is also entirely dependent on the supreme Lord. Śaṅkara cites passages from the Upaniṣads to prove that it is the Lord who acts as a dam, preventing the intermixture of different worlds and different castes, and who holds the sun and moon in their positions (I.3.16 C, 186-7).[17] Within each kalpa, there is diversity and change, but even this change is orderly and patterned. In his commentary on I.3.33, Śaṅkara seems to refer to the idea of the succession of the four yugas (ages) marked by moral and physical deterioration, an idea elaborated in smṛti literature but not, in fact, met with in the Upaniṣads (Sharma 1980, 145-7). Śaṅkara suggests that knowledge of the nature of the gods may have come from direct perception by ancient and holy seers, and that anyone who denies this possibility denies variety in history. Such a person would, for instance, "have to assume that the rules of caste and stages of life were as unstable in other periods as at present" (I.3.33 C, 228). Ordering and governing all is Īśvara. Śaṅkara identifies Īśvara as the akṣara (imperishable) of *Bṛhadāraṇyaka Upaniṣad* 3.8.7-9, at whose command (praśāsana) the sun, the moon, the divisions of time and the directions maintain their positions (I.3.10-11).

The third of the three processes, dissolution (pralaya), is also ruled by Brahman as Īśvara. At the end of the kalpa, the Lord devours the worlds, withdrawing the universe into himself in reverse order from creation (I.2.9 C, 119; II.3.14 B, 596-8). As in the case of the idea of the four yugas, the Upaniṣads themselves seem not to present the concept of pralaya as a periodic cosmic dissolution, despite Śaṅkara's interpretation of śruti on this point (Deussen 1906, 180-1 and 221ff.). Śaṅkara's treatment of pralaya and the cycle of the kalpas was influenced by subsequent intellectual developments reflected in smṛti literature. It was useful for his tasks of describing Brahman and outlining the means to liberation. By associating Īśvara with cosmic dissolution, Śaṅkara establishes him as the ruler of time and of all transformations in time. The world and everything in the world cease to exist; there is nothing apart from Brahman that can serve as the source of future worlds. Transcendental time continues, containing the processes of and the potential for the endless recreation and re-destruction of the universe.

Śaṅkara tells us that these cosmic cycles, the kalpas, extend into the past and the future. The cycle of saṃsāra is beginningless (anādi) (II.1.35-6 B, 42-3). He finds support for this idea in śruti,[18] smṛti and logic. If saṃsāra were not beginningless, were it to spring into being with creation, argues Śaṅkara, those who had already been liberated might be reborn, and the cause and effect process connecting actions with their karmic results would be put at odds. Śaṅkara must establish the eternal nature of saṃsāra in order to escape the logical fallacy of mutual dependence when his opponent charges that karma and diversity (vibhāga) depend on one another, yet diversity cannot exist in the undifferentiated state of Existence that precedes creation. The role of Īśvara is at stake here, with respect both to the charge that diversity is the consequence of his injustice or cruelty, and ultimately to the issue of his establishing rulership over the process of creation (II.1.34-6 P, 42-3). Also at stake is the inescapable character of the mechanism of karmic retribution and the permanent character of liberation from saṃsāra. The concept of cyclical time allows Śaṅkara to reconcile the theory of karma with the idea of Īśvara as Lord of creation, continuance, and dissolution.[19] The succession of cosmic cycles is the basis for the fixed pattern of change found at the level of transcendental time:

> When successive creations take place as the result of virtue and vice, they are brought into existence exactly like the previous creation.... When this universe gets dissolved, it dissolves by keeping its latent power intact, and the next creation emerges from that latent power.... The pattern of behaviour is the same in every cycle of creation (I.3.30 C, 219-20).

Level Two Discrimination: the Nature of Īśvara's Rulership Over Creation and Transmigration

At this level, an understanding is sought of the nature of Īśvara as the Lord of time, and of the relation of the individual to creation and transmigration. What *is* the latent power that causes the universe to appear over and over again?

The lordship of Īśvara with respect to the three processes of creation, continuance and dissolution is associated with his omniscience:

> The eternally perfect Lord possesses eternal knowledge (nitya jñāna) with reference to creation, continuance and dissolution.... Like the light of the sun, this knowledge is eternally possessed by Brahman as Its very nature (svarūpa), without reliance on any means of knowledge (I.1.5 M, 14-5).

We have seen that the individual self has caitanya (consciousness) as its very nature, and that this consciousness on the human level is linked to intelligence (prajñā) (II. 3.27-8). A parallel conception can be found in the idea that the supreme Lord is eternally inseparable from his intelligence (prajñā), which is characterized by omniscience (I.3.42 B, 368). But this divine intelligence, this knowledge of all events in time and of the very patterning of time, is *not* possessed by the embodied selves of human beings (I.2.21 C, 139), although through the grace of Īśvara yogis may obtain knowledge of the past and future (I.1.5 M, 14-5). Even perfected, divine beings do not have the knowledge of creation possessed by the supreme Lord (II.1.6 P, 11).

If Īśvara is sole author of creation, as a result of his omniscience, how does Śaṅkara explain his agency? In the discussion of level 1 time, it was evident that whatever was associated with action or psychological modality could be considered continuous but not truly eternal. Śaṅkara uses a number of different explanations to maintain the absolute temporal character of Īśvara. In some places, he suggests that it is Hiraṇyagarbha, the "eldest born," the divine presence identified with cosmic intelligence, who is the actual agent of creation (II.4.2 C, 524-5). Śaṅkara also argues that when the Upaniṣads say "the universe differentiated," the use of the intransitive verb "differentiate" (vyākṛ) indicates the "easiness of performance" (saukaryam) of the act of differentiation. Although Īśvara is the creator (vyākartṛ), his action is effortless (I.4.15 B, 402). If the Lord's creatorship is to be understood as different from human action in time, it must be distinguished as not only being effortless but also motiveless. At *sūtra* I.4.24, in the midst of further discussion about Brahman as the cause of the universe, the author refers to the teaching in the Upaniṣads of the "wish" (abhidhyā) for creation. Śaṅkara explains that this teaching leads to the idea of the supreme Self as the agent (kartṛ) of creation through his freedom of will (svātantrya), preceded by "wishing" (I.4.24 B, 427). This idea of wishing or willing seems to compromise the eternality of the supreme Lord as creator, but Śaṅkara elsewhere makes it very clear that Īśvara is not subject to the same kinds of mental modes as humankind:

> Although to us the construction of this world seems to be a very great effort, for the supreme Lord it is simply like an amusement (līlā), because of His immeasurable power. And although we may ascribe some motive to worldly amusements, it is impossible to imagine that in this case there could be any kind of motive, since it is known from śruti that all His desires are fulfilled (II.1.33 P, 40).

The appeal to the metaphor of līlā — the creation of the universe as the Lord's sport, which is effortless, aimless, and spontaneous — serves to define the agency of Īśvara so that it is free from all contingencies and utterly independent. But is the Lord wholly responsible for the diversity of creation and the fact of continuous recreation? If Īśvara himself has no motive in the creation of the world, what then impels this endless unfolding of the pattern of time?

> It can be inferred that even in dissolution, there is a power of differentiation which is entirely dependent on false ignorance (mithyājñāna) and, thus, since false ignorance is totally eliminated by right knowledge (samyagjñāna), the notion that those who are liberated are subject to rebirth is refuted (II.1.9 P, 14).

It seems, then, that individual human ignorance is implicated as the cause of the creation of the world. How can this idea be reconciled with the concept of Īśvara's supremacy? And how is the relationship between Īśvara's creatorship and human action to be understood?

We have already seen that in dealing with the mechanism by which human actions produce their karmic consequences, Śaṅkara insists that Īśvara is the ultimate source of these consequences. As in the case of his creatorship generally, here again, it is because of his omniscience, his knowledge of the nature of creation in all its particularity of time and place, that the Lord can ordain the fruits of actions according to their merit (III.2.38 C, 640-1). Śaṅkara insists on the absolute rulership of Īśvara with respect to all beings and all occurrences. Even bondage to saṃsāra is ordained by him:

> When the individual self is in a condition of ignorance (avidyā) ... the transmigratory state, characterized by agency and experiencership, occurs because of the supreme Self, who oversees all actions and dwells within all creatures ... and liberation is obtained through awareness (vijñāna) which comes about only by virtue of His favour (anugraha) (II.3.41 B, 620).

Yet, as in the case of Īśvara's creatorship, Śaṅkara must again struggle with the problem of the Lord's knowledge and action being bound by the particularity of time and place. In the context of ordaining the fruits of action there can be no question of the Lord's līlā; He must consider human actions. Were He to disregard these actions, neither behaviour based on Vedic injunctions nor ordinary human efforts would have their desired effects. In that case, the authority of śruti would be nullified and space, time, and causation would be meaningless (II.3.42 B, 621). In fact, says Śaṅkara, Īśvara has no creatorship independent of the merit and demerit of human actions (II.1.34 P, 41). In addition, although the agency of the individual is dependent on the Lord, it is still the individual who really acts (II.3.42 B, 620). Once more, there appears to be a tension between the supremacy of Īśvara and the contingency that is inescapable in his creatorship and ordaining of the fruits of actions.

Our level 2 understanding thus involves us with the problems of analysing and identifying the cause of the universe of diversity, change and transmigration. What force is ultimately responsible for maintaining the eternity of saṃsāra through endless cycles of creation, continuance and dissolution?

Level Two Goal: Freedom from Saṃsāra

Despite the popular notion that cyclical time in Indian philosophy denies the reality of time, the sense of bondage to time at level 2 is clearly even more absolute than at level 1. Transcendental time is confining, repetitive, beginningless and endless. "This eternal (saṃtata) series of worthlessness, of endless sorts, is manifest to all of us" (I. 3.1 M, 258).

The level 2 world view focuses on Īśvara's power and supremacy. Śaṅkara makes every effort to demonstrate that the Lord, who is none other than Brahman, exercises rulership over everything in all time and is superior to those gods or powers postulated by other systems. This perspective is suitable as the foundation for a religious practice based on devotion, and for a mythology centred on the supreme God. Indeed, Śaṅkara reflects this theistic orientation in some of his references to smṛti texts and in his mention of the Lord's grace.[20] But Śaṅkara, of course, does not stop here. He is not, in his *Brahmasūtra-bhāṣya*, addressing himself to those who would worshipfully accept the lordship of the ruler of time, entrusting themselves to the grace of the Lord. Nor does

Śaṅkara suggest that we may become like Īśvara, becoming ourselves masters of time. Īśvara's omniscience, as noted above, cannot be an attribute of the individual self. Even if we could possess this omniscience, we would discover that mastery over time does not lead to freedom from time, since the knowledge and agency of the supreme Lord is, in some sense, contingent on human ignorance and action bound in time. How is the relation between Īśvara's creatorship and these contingencies to be understood? How can Īśvara's omniscience and rulership in transcendental time be truly independent of human dealings in empirical time?

> Omniscience depends on the distinctions of the seeds of the world, which are name and form, consisting of ignorance (avidyā).... Name and form, invented (kalpita) by ignorance, are as if part of the being of the omniscient Lord and are indescribable as real or unreal; they are the seeds of the manifestation of saṃsāra and are spoken of in śruti and smṛti as the māyā of the omniscient Lord, as power (śakti), and as prakṛti. But the omniscient Lord is other than these (II.1.14 P, 23-4).

Having established the character of transcendental time, Śaṅkara is now ready to lead us away from attachment to this level 2 time with its mythic and devotional religious orientation and its philosophical substantialization of absolute time. We may now be ready to try to resolve the tensions created by the new understandings emerging at this level, to discover who the omniscient Lord "really" is, and to gain the realization that may dispel ignorance, allowing passage outside the eternity of saṃsāra and freedom from the rulership of the Lord of time.

3. Level Three: Time Dissolved

The third category of time is "time dissolved." If level 1 time is imagined as drops of water joined in a stream and level 2 time is the river of time, the image of time at level 3 may be the river-bed, stable and immutable. Eternity at level 3 is still more absolute than at the preceding levels. At level 2, the level of transcendental time, eternity is time-bound; while at level 3, eternity is timeless. At level 3, there is a shift from the language of creation to the language of cause. The subject is less often Īśvara and more often Brahman. Īśvara is the Lord of all the three times, ordaining the results of past actions in future time. He rules the three processes of creation, continuation and dissolution, which occur and recur in a fixed order: the pattern of time at level 2 is directional. But when Śaṅkara speaks, at level 3, of Brahman as the material cause of the universe, he speaks of causation outside of time, since the cause is forever present in the effect. Brahman as cause is timeless, "not," as Mahadevan says, "in the sense of endless duration, but in the sense of eternity and completeness, requiring neither a 'before' nor an 'after'" (1953, 70).

Very often, especially in refuting the cosmogonical and causal theories of other schools, Śaṅkara combines level 2 and 3 approaches. There are some important continuities in the perspectives of these two levels. The level 2 characterization of Īśvara as omniscient and omnipotent applies to Brahman as well as to Īśvara, and Śaṅkara's analysis at level 2 has introduced us to the idea that the "seeds of the world" and the power of creation, māyā, rest in Brahman. Elsewhere, however, Śaṅkara clearly indicates the difference between level 2 and level 3 conceptions of time and eternity, with respect to the nature of Brahman, the individual self (ātman), and liberation (mokṣa). Because of the timeless reality of the self, it is in essence untouched by the modalities that produce bondage to saṃsāra. It is already liberated, eternally free (nityamukta). By being in everything, Brahman is eternally possessed by everyone. The self is not really the locus of any action (kriyā) and liberation cannot be dependent on any activity (kārya, vyāpāra). Thus liberation is not something that is produced (utpādya) nor obtained (āpya) nor perfected (saṃskārya) nor the result of modification (vikārya) (I.1.4 M, 223-4). To borrow Alan Watts' phrase — 'This is It'. The perspective of level 3 is that of the eternal present, a vision of the world, individual being, and cosmic Being entirely dissociated from all processes in time.

Level Three World View: Brahman as Cause, and the Timeless Reality of the Self

At level 3, we find a resolution to the problem raised at level 2 concerning contingency in Īśvara's role as efficient cause of the universe, that is the tension between Īśvara's supremacy and his seeming dependence on various factors in his creatorship and ordaining of karmic fruits. The theory of causation that Śaṅkara defends at length in his commentary destroys the meaning of time and agency in causation.[21] This theory, satkāryavāda, maintains that the effect is pre-existent in its material cause, and that the cause endures in the effect. Brahman, as Being Itself, is the material cause of the universe. This concept of causation releases Brahman from any association with the contingencies of time and change: "it cannot be imagined that the supreme Self has any connection with particularities of place, time, and so forth" (IV.3. 14 B, 998). This causal theory further assists Śaṅkara in his efforts to refute the views of other schools. It also helps him to interpret the teaching of the Upaniṣads that "all this is but the Self" (*Chāndogya Upaniṣad* 7.25.2) and "all this is certainly Brahman" (*Chāndogya Upaniṣad* 3.14.1) (quoted at II.1.9, II.3.6, etc.).

Śaṅkara, in his refutation of the Buddhist position, argues that we know through common experience, by recognition or inference, that there is something that persists in things (II.2.22 P, 66). It is also known that the cause continues in the effect, even in cases where it appears to be destroyed. Logic and observation show us that an effect that is existent cannot have its cause in non-existence (II.2.26 P, 70). To avoid the logical fault of infinite regress, a primary material cause must be admitted, says Śaṅkara. And, as we know from śruti that Brahman's very nature is pure existence, it is therefore Brahman which is that cause (II.3.9 C, 460-1). Not only does the cause persist in the effect as the substrate of its very being, but in just the same way the effect exists in dependence on its cause even before it is produced (II.1.7 P, 12). Śaṅkara interprets the statements of the Upaniṣads to support a view of causation in which the three times — past, present and future — have no meaning:

> Just as the cause, Brahman, does not part from existence (sattva) in all the three times, so also the effect, the world, does not part from existence in all the three times. And yet existence is one; thus, again, it is shown that the effect is not other than the cause (II.1.16 P, 26; also II.1.9 P, 14).

If the effect exists always, either potentially or manifestly, resting in Brahman as existence, then the world is as eternal as is Brahman. "The power [to produce an effect] is the very nature of the cause; and the effect is the very nature of this power" (II. 1.18 P, 27). The relationship of non-difference between Brahman and the world is that of the dependence of the effect on the cause. "Effects do not exist apart from Brahman" (II.1.14 P, 19). Brahman is absolute, all-inclusive, limitless in space and time (I.3.9 C, 173-4). The world is equally eternal, but this temporal status is only a derivative one.

The individual self, however, has the same absolute and independent character as Brahman. "Although the body becomes ashes, the self is not destroyed, and since it has the nature of being always present, one cannot suppose that its nature is otherwise" (II.3.7 B, 575). In contrast with those things that are eternal but subject to transformation (pariṇāmi nitya), the unembodied or liberated self is truly unchangingly eternal (paramārthika kūṭastha nitya). It is all-pervading, like space, free from any modification, eternally satisfied, partless, and by its nature self-illuminating (I.1.4 M, 215-6). The individual self thus has exactly the same *kind* of eternal nature (kūṭastha nitya) as that attributed to Puruṣa or Brahman, the imperishable and unchanging, which is eternally pure, enlightened, and free (I.1.4 M, 242). This level 3 eternity is that of Puruṣa, described in *Muṇḍaka Upaniṣad* as "higher than the highest imperishable (akṣara)." As Śaṅkara explains, the imperishable itself is the unchanging power belonging to the Lord, the latency that is the source of the world (at our level 2) and is, in turn, higher than its own modifications (at level 1) (I.2.22 C, 143).

Level Three Discrimination: Understanding Ignorance

At level 3, Śaṅkara tries to show us how to discriminate between kinds of non-difference and Brahman in order to lead us to the realization that the world does not exist apart from Brahman and that the individual self is none other than Brahman. This is the knowledge of Brahman that constitutes liberation. This is the knowledge that destroys ignorance (avidyā) This is the knowledge that the Upaniṣads seek to convey. Śaṅkara uses his skill to remove any doubts or misconceptions that may obscure this knowledge, refuting the views of other philosophical schools and revising the conceptions he himself has presented from the point of view of levels 1 and 2. Knowledge of Brahman can only be achieved through understanding the nature of ignorance, and its power to produce the idea of difference where there is really non-difference. The analysis of the nature of the individual self must come to terms with the problem of ignorance in order to establish, at level 3, the absolutely timeless character of the self. This means going beyond the previous understandings of the continuity and permanence of the self, so as to evoke the realization of the self's identity with Brahman.

Śaṅkara identifies ignorance as the ultimate source of the individual soul's bondage. He defines ignorance as "the understanding of the self as being what is not the self, the body and so on" (I.3.2 M, 258). "It is only because of possessing ignorance that the worldly dealings of the individual continue incessantly" (I.4.3 B, 380):

> Saṃsāra, characterized by the not doing of good and so on, is an error (bhrānti) caused by nondiscrimination [between the self and] its qualifications (upādhis), the collection of causes and effects made up of name and form called into being by ignorance (II.1.22 P, 32; also II.3.50 C, 516).

Knowledge of Brahman is said to produce a dissociation from those elements originating in ignorance that produce particularized knowledge (I.4.22 C, 288-9). Knowledge of Brahman burns away the "seed-power" (bījaśakti), constituted by ignorance, that has its abode in the supreme Lord, and is like a great sleep in which the transmigrating souls rest without awareness of their own nature (I.4.3 B, 377-8).

Over and over again in his *Brahmasūtra-bhāṣya*, Śaṅkara stresses that knowledge of Brahman means understanding the nature of Brahman as the material cause of the universe. Unlike other, especially later, Advaitins who are careful to describe Brahman as cause only in the sense of vivarta (manifestation),

Śaṅkara does not avoid talking about Brahman as the cause of the universe in terms of pariṇāma (transformation) (Potter 1965, 165-7; cf. Balslev 1983, 70-1). In some cases, Śaṅkara is simply following the lead of the author of the *Brahmasūtras*, who refers directly to the transformation of Brahman (I.4.26) or, by mentioning the analogy of the transformation of milk into curds (II.1.24), indirectly indicates this idea. But Śaṅkara is skilled enough as a commentator that he could certainly have interpreted these sūtras so as to deny that Brahman, in fact, is subject to transformation. While Śaṅkara accepts the validity of the analogy of milk and curds, his commentary makes it clear that Brahman is not truly transformed:

> Brahman becomes involved in all activities such as transformation because of the differences of forms, differentiated or uncreated, characterized by name and form and imagined by ignorance, which cannot be described as real or unreal; in Its true (paramārthika) form, It remains beyond all activities and untransformed (II.1.27 P, 37).

At level 2, as we have seen, Śaṅkara indicates that it is ignorance that is the basis for the re-creation of the world following pralaya. It is also the basis for the diversity known to the omniscient Īśvara, making possible his role as creator and ordainer of karmic fruits. At level 3, ignorance is identified as the source of bondage of the individual soul. Here, considered in the context of Brahman as material cause, ignorance accounts for the appearance of change, for the very emergence of the effect from the eternal and changeless Brahman. The concept of ignorance is relevant to the problem of the relation between cause and effect: "The cause is not commingled with the effect, [although] ignorance mistakenly identifies the cause with the effect and its properties" (II.1.9 P, 14). By understanding the role of ignorance, we see how Brahman can be the cause of the whole universe and at the same time remain untouched by its diversity and mutability.

It is clear that Śaṅkara considers human ignorance the fundamental problem, the source of misapprehension about the true nature of Brahman and the cause of bondage to saṃsāra. While ignorance is linked to changefulness and particularity in time, the knowledge that destroys this ignorance is absolutely eternal. Such knowledge cannot be a product of our experience in empirical time, nor of logical argumentation. Our only means of attaining to the knowledge of the true nature of the self and of Brahman, says Śaṅkara, is through the Vedic texts:

> Being eternal and a cause of the awakening of knowledge, and by virtue of being concerned with an unchanging subject, the Vedas can produce correct knowledge, which is impossible for any logician of past, present or future to deny (II.1.11 P, 16-7).

Statements about Brahman in the Vedas relate only to the awakening of understanding, in fact, and have no other purpose (III.2.21 B, 715). Śaṅkara reiterates many times that the whole point of the Upaniṣads is the presentation of the nature of Brahman. In some cases, he shows how the Vedic texts deal with this task from different points of view or, as we might say, on different levels — and how the level 2 perspective is to be superseded by the level 3 perspective. The śruti texts concerned with the origin and so forth of the world, says Śaṅkara, are meant to bring about the understanding of the unity of Brahman as the source of the universe. But these texts should be considered subordinate to those texts that reject all distinctions in describing Brahman (IV.4.13 B, 998-9). It is not only the nature of Brahman, but the identity of the self with Brahman, that is the object of the Upaniṣads (II.3.29 B, 610):

> And when non-difference is taught, through such instructions of non-difference as tat tvam asi (that thou art), then the transmigratoriness of the individual self and the creatorship of Brahman vanish, since the aggregate of activities having to do with distinctions appearing because of false ignorance is removed (II.1.22 P, 32).

Level Three Goal: Knowledge of Brahman

The Upaniṣadic texts present the object of knowledge, Brahman, and through their teachings allow the individual to dispel ignorance and attain liberation. Śaṅkara draws a sharp distinction between those Vedic texts that are concerned with injunction and prohibition, directing the individual toward particular kinds of actions, and those that are concerned with revealing the nature of Brahman, which have no connection with action:

> When "Brahman is one only, without second" and "that is the truth, that is the self, that thou art" are made known, knowledge arises by itself. By that knowledge ignorance is removed so that this whole world consisting of name and form superimposed by ignorance is dissolved like a dream-image. But when Brahman is not made known thus, even if one is told a hundred times [by way of injunction], "Know Brahman, sublate the world," he will not achieve knowledge of Brahman or the sublation of the world-appearance (III.2.21 B, 713).

Knowledge is not a kind of action. Action depends on someone who acts, while knowledge is dependent only on its object (I.1.4 M,227; III.2.21 B, 715). Knowledge of Brahman simply *is*. It is not something to be done, or not done, or done in another way. Its object, Brahman, is not in any way subject to human agency and is not something that can be rejected or accepted (I.1.4 M, 227-8). Knowledge of Brahman is liberation, not something that can be produced. It is eternally present (III.4.52 C, 811). Liberation and those who are liberated exist without connection to action or change in time.

Although knowledge is not action and liberation is not produced, Śaṅkara makes an effort to show how Vedic ritual and actions, especially those of meditation, are conducive to the attainment of knowledge and liberation. He says that once knowledge has emerged, it does not depend on other factors or actions in order to produce its result, liberation. But the emergence of knowledge is dependent on other factors, which are mentioned in the Upaniṣads, such as sacrifice, charity, austerities and duties appropriate to the different stages of life (III.4.26 C, 783-4; IV.1.16 C, 841-2). Śaṅkara supports the idea found in smṛti texts that the repetition of mantras, fasting, worship of gods and virtuous deeds performed in earlier lives may assist in the attainment of knowledge (III.4.38 C, 794). He even goes so far as to say that obligatory sacrificial rites like agnihotra, whether or not they are associated with meditation, may destroy accumulated sins that stand in the way of realizing Brahman. They thus become indirect causes of this realization "so that in collaboration with such proximate causes of enlightenment as hearing, reflection, faith, meditation, devotedness, etc., they come to have the same result as the knowledge of Brahman has" (IV. 1.19 C, 845).

Śaṅkara's efforts to accommodate orthodox, popular, and ascetic ways of action into a system propounding the nonassociation of liberating knowledge with action spring from two motives. On one hand, he faces the problem of reconciling authoritative texts and traditional practices with one another. On the other, he needs to make clear that liberation is truly possible. This second point is a very serious one, related to the whole didactic effort of the *Brahmasūtra-bhāṣya* and to the conception of sādhana Śaṅkara propounds. Śaṅkara has to link the finite empirical world to the infinite, timeless realm of release from that empirical world in order to show that what we *do* makes a difference to our spiritual fate, even if ultimately there is no doer, no doing, and nothing to be done.

These same two motives — reconciliation of śruti and presentation of sādhana — also shape Śaṅkara's level 3 treatment of the nature of liberation and the path that leads to it. They involve him in the same kind of tension, moreover, between timelessness and action in time. We have seen how the Upaniṣads outline the various courses taken by the transmigrating souls after death. Śaṅkara in several places discusses the path of the gods leading to Brahmaloka. This path is travelled by those who have meditated with the help of the sacred syllable OM on the supreme Brahman. This path is attained because of *knowledge*, not through faith or the practice of austerities (I.3.13 C, 178-80; III.3.31 C, 700). Śaṅkara quotes *Bṛhadāraṇyaka Upaniṣad* 6.2.15 on the destiny of those who depart by this path: "in those worlds of Brahma they live for long periods" (Radhakrishnan 1953, 314). Śaṅkara then goes on to argue that the mention of a plurality of brahmalokas and of the realm of Brahman as *containing* the individual selves show that the travellers on this path attain to the conditioned Brahman (kāryabrahman), rather than the supreme Brahman (IV.3.8 B, 996).

In this discussion, Śaṅkara has to contend with the problem of interpreting various Upaniṣadic passages in the light of his own position that liberation or realization of Brahman cannot depend on any activity such as departing, travelling, approaching or acquiring, which are based on ideas of action, change, and difference (I.1.4 M, 223-4; IV.2. 13 B, 979). It is not possible, says Śaṅkara, to consider that the person who engages in such activity in time could be liberated in eternity. "He desires relative immortality (āpekṣika amṛtatva) in accordance with the inferior knowledge which has not completely burned ignorance and afflictions and, in that case, setting out on a path is a possibility .... In the case of absolute immortality (antika amṛtatva), there is no departure and no course to follow" (IV.2.7 B, 973; IV.2.12 B, 977).

Śaṅkara must also deal with the several opinions presented by the *Brahmasūtras* on the issue of whether those who follow the path of the gods reach the conditioned or the supreme Brahman including the opinion of the author of the sūtras, Bādarāyaṇa, who, in fact, seems to accept that these travellers are truly liberated (IV.3.15; Potter 1980, 253). The Upaniṣads themselves say that those who follow this path do not return (*Bṛhadāraṇyaka Upaniṣad* 6.2.15: teṣām na punar āvṛttiḥ). Bādarāyaṇa's last sūtra echoes this statement: "there is no return, on the authority of scripture" (anāvṛttiḥ śabdāt) (IV.4.22).

Again, Śaṅkara needs not only to make sense of the texts and traditions of Vedānta but also to assure those who meditate on Brahman that their efforts are finally conducive to the supreme goal of liberation. With some difficulty, Śaṅkara manages to bring together the idea of realization of the conditioned Brahman and the idea of final liberation in the concept of progressive or gradual liberation (kramamukti):

> When the dissolution of the world of the conditioned Brahman (kāryabrahmaloka) is imminent, those in whom right understanding has arisen while there, together with Hiraṇyagarbha who is the overseer of that place, attain the transcendentally pure, supreme state of Viṣṇu. Because of the mention of non-return in śruti, this kind of progressive liberation must be admitted (IV.3.10 B, 997).

Those liberated ones (muktas) who attain to the world of the conditioned Brahman are endowed with lordly powers (aiśvarya). They acquire all the powers of Īśvara, in fact, except those of creation (IV.4.17 B, 1017). But they possess these powers only temporarily (IV.4.22 B, 1020). "Later, they become indifferent, through seeing the decay of these lordly powers; fixed entirely on the knowledge of the supreme Self they enter completely into liberation (kaivalya)" (III.3.32 B, 818). These great sages (maharṣis) are not, at the time of their departure from this life, possessed of complete knowledge of Brahman. But their knowledge of the conditioned Brahman evidently produces for them the possibility of a *kind* of liberation, freedom from rebirth, since the supreme Brahman is ultimately the basis of the conditioned Brahman:

> Non-return is entirely valid for those for whom the darkness [of ignorance] is destroyed by right vision, because their final aim is eternally established liberation (nirvāṇa); non-return is valid for those who take refuge in the qualified (saguṇa) [Brahman], since they also certainly resort to that [unqualified Brahman or eternal liberation] (IV.4.22 B, 1020).

In the two passages in the *Brahmasūtra-bhāṣya* (III.3.32 and IV.3.10) where Śaṅkara discusses the final liberation of these perfected beings, they, along with Hiraṇyagarbha or Brahmā, attain this liberation *in time*, evidently at the time of pralaya, cosmic dissolution. It is not clear whether their liberation, once achieved, is truly permanent, or whether they may be subject to rebirth in succeeding kalpas, as Hiraṇyagarbha and Brahmā will be.[22]

This intermediate realm of liberation, of non-absolute knowledge and relative immortality, is problematic. Its very existence in Śaṅkara's system serves to underscore the contention that there are several levels in Śaṅkara's treatment of time. Although Śaṅkara insists that knowledge is one only, and liberation as the result of knowledge is one only, there are clearly several ways of seeing that one. Śaṅkara at level 3 does not deny the existence of the world, since the world's existence rests in Brahman as Existence. But at level 3, time no longer functions in terms of defining the three times of past, present, and future. We understand, therefore, that time does not truly shape our existence and that liberation is now. Yet time is still an issue, at least from an epistemological point of view, from the perspective of the human being in the world. Level 3 understanding provides a way of knowledge in which eternal truth is revealed, but we (and Śaṅkara) must still struggle with the problem of how we may *become* one with this timeless truth without being involved in *becoming*.

4. Level Four: Time Destroyed

At level 3, we found time dissolved through the denial of the reality of change. What endures is singular Existence, the cause of all manifold and changeful effects, Brahman. The knowledge that the phenomenal world has but a derivative reality and eternality produces the apprehension that changeful time is a false qualification of Brahman, which as the cause is unrelated to particular time (at level 1) or to the three times (at level 2). Knowledge of the nature of Brahman at level 3 and recognition of the individual self as non-different from Brahman produce release from the changeful character of time. Whoever has attained this understanding does not return, but is liberated from rebirth in this world. What further level of time can there be? If level 3 represents timeless eternity, does Śaṅkara posit a still greater infinity? What other sort of relationship can Brahman or the individual self have with time?

The answer, I would argue, is that there is a fourth level of understanding time in Śaṅkara's *Brahmasūtra-bhāṣya*, which is that of *non*-relationship with time. At this level, Śaṅkara deals with the problem of time in more radical terms than those of the preceding three levels. He offers no explanation whatsoever for finite being. At this level, time is destroyed. At level 3, our knowledge is of Brahman as unchangingly permanent (kūṭastha), the source of the world in the eternal present, the ground of all existence. At level 4 we, so to speak, drop through the ground. The distinction between level 3 and level 4 is not ontological or metaphysical. Instead, it is a matter of epistemology or axiology, a difference in how one looks at things or how one values them (Deutsch 1969, 15-7; Potter 1965, 166-7). The distinction is one of perspective, and the level 4 perspective is that of the person who has become completely liberated. From that point of view, the problem of going anywhere, obtaining anything, becoming anything — the problem of action in time — is not an issue, and, perhaps, never was an issue:

> The knower of Brahman recognizes "I am Brahman, whose essence is non-agency and non-experiencing in all the three times; from this point on, I realize that even formerly I was neither agent nor experiencer, nor am I now, nor will I be in the future." And just so is liberation produced. Were it otherwise, if actions accomplished in former times were not destroyed, there could be no liberation. What is experienced, associated with place, time and cause, must be produced in accordance with the fruits of actions; but the fruit of knowledge is not similarly produced because of its association with immortality (IV.1. 13 B, 954).

It is from this point of view that Śaṅkara espouses what Potter calls "leap philosophy," the view of freedom and causation in which it is believed that self-knowledge can be attained only by a sudden leap of insight. This stands opposed to "progress philosophy," in which action, devotion, or understanding are seen as leading to the goal (Potter 1965, 93-4). As Potter points out, Śaṅkara "seems to teeter between leap and progress philosophy," and this mixed legacy has produced Advaitins who stand on either side of the issue (Potter 1965, 100). We have seen Śaṅkara struggling at level 3 with the problems of progress philosophy. At level 4, "in the last analysis he will perhaps have no causal theory at all" (Potter 1965, 165).

It is rather difficult to fit our consideration of the level 4 perspective into the categories of world view, discrimination, and goals, as we have done at the preceding levels. For the person who is liberated, the world has vanished. There are no differences between which to discriminate, and the goal has been realized. Looking at the problem another way, world view (Brahman), discrimination (knowledge), and goal (liberation) are identical at level 4. The point of view presented at level 4 is of utter Unity, of nothing apart from the attributeless (nirguṇa) Brahman. From the level 4 perspective, too, the very idea of levels of reality or levels of understanding would be invalid.[23]

The tasks that Śaṅkara has set himself in his *Brahmasūtra-bhāṣya* — teaching a means (sādhana) to liberation, reconciling śruti, and refuting other philosophical systems — relate almost entirely to levels 1, 2, and 3. Therefore, it is not surprising that we find Śaṅkara engaged much more frequently at these levels than at level 4.[24] But Śaṅkara does indeed point to the existence of the level 4 perspective. It is of ultimate significance to his system as the absolute knowledge that is absolute liberation.

Level Four World View: Brahman as Wholly Other

In his commentary on *Brahmasūtra* II.1.9, Śaṅkara quotes "the teacher learned in the meaning and tradition of Vedānta," Gauḍapāda, on the "awakening" of the individual into the state of birthless, dreamless, sleepless non-duality (II.1.9 P, 14). In the Upaniṣads, this state is called turīya, "the fourth," the other three states being waking (viśva), dreaming (taijasa), and deep sleep (suṣupti). The four states are said to be analogous to the four "quarters" of the sacred syllable OM, which are the letters A, U, M and the partless whole (Deussen 1906, 309-12 and 390-5). In the *Brahmasūtra-bhāṣya*, Śaṅkara frequently refers to the three states, but for a more systematic treatment of the three and for his conception of the nature of the fourth, we turn briefly to his commentary on Gauḍapāda's *Kārikās* on the *Māṇḍukya Upaniṣad*. Śaṅkara says that it is only from the point of view of the waking state that one is aware of the three states of experience. An analysis of the three leads to the realization that the self (ātman) is the one element, characterized by consciousness, that unifies the experience of the three (Nikhilānanda 1968, 27; 22, 49-50, 74-5; cf. Śaṅkara's discussions of consciousness and of the continuity of the self through sleep in *Brahmasūtra-bhāṣya* II.3.18 and 27-9 and III.2.9). In the third experiential state, deep sleep, one experiences this consciousness in its purest form; it is blissful, objectless, nondual consciousness (Nikhilānanda 1968, 1-2; cf. *Brahmasūtra-bhāṣya* III.2.7, IV.4.16). Yet it is not infinite bliss, because it contains the causal element, the seeds of the phenomenal world (Nikhilānanda 1968, 59-60; cf. *Brahmasūtra-bhāṣya* II.3.31). The fourth state, turīya, is absolute and infinite. From the point of view of this state, the sounds and quarters of OM, identified with Brahman, disappear, and the realization of turīya arrived at through the negation of the three is attained in this very life and remains forever (Nikhilānanda 1968, 74-7, 80-1, 295). Although deep sleep and turīya share the quality of non-dualism, the third state lacks the knowledge that destroys the causal condition (Nikhilānanda 1968, 30, 59). The knowledge that distinguishes turīya is the understanding that the self is different from the consciousness of the other three states and the realization of unrelated, attributeless, absolute Brahman (cf. IV.4.2 C, 896).

This notion of the self and of Brahman as wholly *other* than phenomenal experience and reality seems to mark an epistemological "flip" at the level of turīya, and at our level 4.[25] Śaṅkara in his *Brahmasūtra-bhāṣya* has, at level 3, taught us that Brahman pervades the world, that the world is ontologically dependent on Brahman, and that consciousness — reflection on the nature of the self and Brahman — is conducive to the awakening of the knowledge that is liberation. The level 3 teaching of the nature of Brahman is central in Śaṅkara's bhāṣya as a means of refuting rival philosophies, interpreting śruti, and guiding students. In fact, Śaṅkara most frequently mentions the attributeless or supreme Brahman *not* in the context of a level 4 discussion but to establish the level 3 position, in contradistinction to the level 2 perspective or to an opponent's view, by referring to Brahman as pure Existence. But we have seen how Śaṅkara, at level 3, points to something that transcends level 3. He points to Brahman entirely unrelated to the world, to liberation that is not produced, to absolute immortality, to the knower of Brahman as one who experiences nothing, not even relationship with Brahman — to something utterly beyond (para).

The notion of otherness and of complete non-relation to time at level 4 is expressed by Śaṅkara when he talks of liberating knowledge as the destruction (upamarda) of the world, of the "entire appearance" (III.4.16 M, 673; III.2.4 B, 693). Of course, says Śaṅkara, it is beyond the powers of a single person actually to destroy the world, and even were this possible, we observe that, in fact, the world continues, although people have attained liberation. The pravilaya (dissolution, melting, vanishing, sublation) of the world is not analogous to the melting of butter. It is instead like the curing of the condition of partial blindness (timira) (III. 2.21 B, 712-3). Here we see clearly that the difference between level 4 and the preceding levels is a matter of perspective. And although the "entire appearance" may persist, it has nothing to do with the one who has attained final liberation. For the one who has attained "relative immortality" in Brahmaloka, "for him it is day for ever" (*Chāndogya Upaniṣad* 3.11.3 Radhakrishnan 1953, 386). But of the supreme state of identity with absolute Brahman, the Upaniṣads say: "there the sun does not shine, neither do the moon and the stars..." (quoted at IV.4.29 C, 910).

Level Four Discrimination: Absolute Non-Dualism

At level 3, our discussion of the means of knowledge focused on the problem of action with respect to a goal unattainable through action. At level 4, the focus is on the problem of the relationship of knowing. The absolute nondualism of level 4 seems to make knowledge *of* Brahman impossible. Knowledge, in the end, is non-different from Brahman, and the self, as the knower, has no existence apart from Brahman. Śaṅkara, on a number of occasions, affirms that indeed Brahman cannot be an object (avastu, aviṣaya) (I.1.4 M, 222-3; II.3.46 C, 511). The authority of the Vedas as the source of knowledge of Brahman is therefore meaningless at this level, although Śaṅkara, of course, does not say so. He does, however, maintain that the practice of meditation, involving as it does subject/ object dualism, cannot be considered as having reference to the supreme Brahman (I.1.12 C, 62-3). In this, he apparently abrogates the level 3 statement that the supreme Brahman *is* the object of meditation undertaken with the help of the syllable OM (I.3.13 C, 178-80).[26]

Commenting on the meaning of the Upaniṣadic passage "not this, not this" (neti neti), Śaṅkara says: "it does not mean that Brahman Itself does not exist. And that very fact is shown by asserting that Brahman does exist which is beyond all else and which is not denied." What neti neti indicates is simply that Brahman cannot be classed with objects of knowledge, since it is beyond speech and mind (III.2.22 C, 625-6).[27] The denial of access to knowledge of Brahman through any process or any relationship puts Śaṅkara firmly on the side of "leap philosophy." Any "progress" toward liberation derived from the study of the Upaniṣads, meditation on Brahman, or the mastery of "lower level" discrimination (not to mention moral or ritual behaviours) can only be seen as preliminary or even incidental from the level 4 perspective. Śaṅkara never denies the validity of the level 3 understanding of Brahman as cause, which he has laboured to establish throughout his commentary. However, his indication at level 4 of the nature of Brahman's existence as being of a wholly other character than the existence of things in the world leads us to believe that, after all, there is a further and final knowledge to be realized.

Level Four Goal: Jīvanmukti

The level 4 perspective is that of the person who has been completely liberated. True knowledge of Brahman results in immediate liberation (I.1.4 M, 217; I.1.12 C, 63; III.3.32 B, 818). "When there is no [karmic] obstruction to what has been undertaken [in pursuit of knowledge] knowledge may come into being here in this world" (III.4.51 B, 924). In contrast to the path of those destined for Brahmaloka, liberation in life (jīvanmukti) is absolute emancipation involving no departure, no journeying, no acquisition, no attainment — no action and no object. This liberation is in reality already present. It is something that is eternally established (nityasiddha), since it is the acknowledgment of one's own nature (IV.3.14 B, 1001). This is the leap of understanding, which is not knowledge *of* anything, because there is no difference between the knower and what is known.

At level 4, the problems of the *means* to knowledge and the *attainment* of liberation are resolved. The only lingering tension has to do with the issue of arabdhabhogakarma, that is, karma that has already begun to produce results in the present lifetime, which must be completely experienced before the person who has realized liberation is entirely released from the world. Until this karma has been gradually destroyed or as long as there is an "office" (adhikāra) to be fulfilled in the world, the liberated person is still propelled through timeful, phenomenal existence by the momentum of karmic cause and effect like an arrow shot from a bow (III.3.32 B, 818). The world is destroyed for the jīvanmukta but the jīvanmukta continues to exist in the world until the falling off of the body (śarīrapāta) (III.3.30 B, 812; IV.1.15 B, 958).

> Once false ignorance has been burnt away by right knowledge, then it is fit that, when the karma that has already begun to bear fruit has been worn away, the man of knowledge will inevitably realize liberation (kaivalya) (IV.1.19 B, 964).

We may sense an internal contradiction in the idea that while liberation totally transcends the world, the jīvanmukta is present in the world. But this conundrum, embodied in the person of the jīvanmukta whose very embodiment is problematic, is, in fact, the best proof of the efficacy of the sādhana that Śaṅkara presents. The person of the jīvanmukta stands as a legitimization and vindication of the path of Vedānta whose authority surpasses even that of the Veda. At other levels we have seen how the tensions and limitations inherent in a level's outlook may incite a shift in perspective, leading to the next level. At level 4, the problem of jīvanmukti prompts us not to look ahead for further insights at succeeding levels, but to look back to understand the significance of the level 4 perspective for the preceding levels. Although there is a radical disjuncture between level 4 and the preceding three levels, the idea of jīvanmukti maintains the connection between level 4 and the other levels. The concept of jīvanmukti is the thread that runs all the way from the empirical sense of existence in time at level 1, the idea of personal continuity associated with karma, through the other levels, and straight to level 4, where the very idea of time is destroyed.

Conclusion

The four-tiered system of levels has been useful as a model for analysing the various approaches to the concept of time in Śaṅkara's *Brahmasūtra bhāṣya*. The analysis on four levels has helped us to appreciate the completeness and sophistication of Śaṅkara's presentation and has shown us how Śaṅkara's method of teaching works as a progressive sādhana in which *every* level of his students' understanding is taken seriously. Apart from the question of time itself, there are a number of related issues and ideas, important to the system of Advaita Vedānta and formulated by Śaṅkara in various ways — such as the nature of Brahman, the self, the world, and liberation — that we have also been able to analyse, at least in terms of their links to the problem of time, within the framework of the four-level system. But before suggesting that this system indeed has wider applicability and potential for enhancing our understanding of Śaṅkara's philosophy in general, we must consider whether this four-level model really reflects Śaṅkara's own approach or merely our interpretation of Śaṅkara.

Certainly Śaṅkara does not explicitly present a system of four levels, nor is the structure of his bhāṣya tied to a progressive explication of the four levels. In terms of the order of presentation of his ideas, Śaṅkara is bound to follow the structure of the sūtras on which he is providing a commentary. Apart from this limitation, his own style is one in which ideas are introduced and referred to in a kind of kaleidoscopic display. He does not start with basic and obvious principles and present his system in an orderly sequential unfolding. Śaṅkara, instead, from the very first page and in every section of his bhāṣya, discloses the whole multi-layered truth from various points of view, with diverse emphases, and with reference to several levels of discrimination. The burden of this essay has been to show how Śaṅkara thus brings forward a number of different perspectives, how these various approaches can be differentiated from one another, and how they fit, not into a two-level, but into a four-level typology. Yet if these perspectives are distinguishable from one another, why doesn't Śaṅkara highlight their existence, making explicit his progressive sādhana? Why doesn't he *tell* his students that they must master each kind of discrimination before passing on to the next level of understanding and ultimately attaining complete liberation? Why does he seem instead to gloss over the differences in levels, to obscure the boundaries between levels?

First of all, we must recognize that there *are* important continuities and linkages amomg the various levels, that the boundaries *are* somewhat indefinite. Representing Śaṅkara's various approaches schematically within the four-level framework elucidates the internal coherence of each of the several planes of understanding. But it should not mislead us into thinking that each level is a watertight category or that every person, perception or statement can be definitively classified as belonging to a single level. A certain topic of discussion (e.g. Īśvara as creator) or citation of a given Upaniṣadic text (e.g. "neti neti"),[28] does not necessarily signal discourse at a particular level. In many places we find that Śaṅkara may combine perspectives in his treatment, and this is only possible because of the fact that there is continuity between levels.

His motives for combining levels bring us to our second observation. Śaṅkara evidently has good reasons for *not* wanting to make the boundaries between levels very prominent. The main reason has to do with the fundamental principle of Advaita Vedānta: that unity alone is the highest truth, and that truth is one only. There can be, in reality, no gradations of right knowledge and there is but one result of knowledge — liberation. Śaṅkara is for this reason understandably reluctant to point up differences among the several perspectives he presents, to make obvious the revocation of one position in favour of a "higher" truth. Where two positions are brought forward that seem to be in conflict with each other, Śaṅkara at times distinguishes between what is taught "for the sake of meditation" — that is, the inferior Brahman associated with attributes — and what is taught concerning the supreme Brahman (IV.3.9 B, 997; IV.3.14 B, 1001). This distinction between teachings relating to the conditioned Brahman and those relating to the supreme Brahman is not met with very frequently in Śaṅkara's commentary. The distinction is an issue at level 3, but there we found that Śaṅkara tried to maintain the validity of *both* kinds of teachings rather than indicating that one should supersede the other. Where contradictory positions are said to belong to various Advaitins in the sūtras themselves, Śaṅkara resorts to the explanation that such views may be presented in order to stimulate the development of wisdom (prajñāvikāsana) IV.3.14 B, 1002). Śaṅkara successfully avoids having to repudiate any of the ideas he has himself established, although many of these ideas are, in fact, irreconcilable.[29] Thus he creates the impression of a homogeneous, coherent and singular view of the truth of Brahman.

In addition to the central philosophical principle of unity, Śaṅkara is also concerned with the exegetical principle of unity, with reference to his task of interpreting and reconciling śruti. He adopts the Mīmāṃsā concept of the purport (tātparya) of a text and labours to establish that there is a single purport of the Upaniṣads: the making known of Brahman (I.1.4 M, 181; II.3.6 C, 451) (Murty 1959, 76-81). Here again, there is a strong motivation for Śaṅkara to minimize the importance of the existence of different levels, if the Upaniṣads are to be presented as having a unity of purport. Meanwhile he capitalizes on the existence of these levels in his interpretation of apparently contradictory texts.

Śaṅkara, when presenting his own philosophical conceptions, or when treating the authoritative texts and traditions of Advaita Vedānta, is non-confrontational. He avoids the juxtaposition of conflicting views and in this way enhances the effect of the unity of his message. When he deals with the views of rival philosophical schools, he looks specifically for the internal inconsistencies of his opponents' positions and actually contrasts the logical defects of these positions with what he presents as the internal coherence of the Advaitin position. Some of his most clever argumentation occurs when, having pointed out a defect in a rival's position, he has the opponent counter that the same defect clings to the Advaitin view. Very often it is only by shifting levels that Śaṅkara can successfully argue that this is not the case. He allows himself the possibility of changing perspective, changing the grounds on which debate proceeds, but he denies that possibility to his opponents. To maintain this advantage in the important task of refuting rival philosophical schools or dispelling doubts that arise with respect to the Advaitin position, it is clearly in Śaṅkara's interest *not* to call attention to the variety of levels his argument proceeds from.[30]

Finally, Śaṅkara has good reasons for wanting to minimize the different levels from the point of view of his didactic purpose. Rather than focusing on how the discrimination attained at "higher" levels transforms or invalidates previously acquired understanding, Śaṅkara stresses the usefulness of the insights of *each* level. If, in the final analysis, his is a "leap philosophy," he nonetheless does not deprecate the world view, the tasks of understanding and the goals that shape the conceptions and practices of all of those who have not yet made the leap. Śaṅkara is very serious about providing a sādhana, a practical means of realizing spiritual ends. By de-emphasizing the differences between levels, he can attract people of all degrees of attainment, making meaningful their experiences, neither disparaging "lower" levels of understanding nor encouraging pride in those who might wish to identify themselves with the spiritual accomplishments of a "higher" level.

However else Śaṅkara's sādhana may be institutionalized, the issue of the attainment of knowledge and the question of who has been liberated are not meant to be resolved with reference to an explicitly drawn-up set of criteria. The series of levels cannot serve as a kind of curriculum that advances one toward graduation into emancipation, because knowledge of Brahman cannot be acquired in this way. Insight into the true nature of Brahman is not, ultimately, dependent on anything else. Therefore, Śaṅkara does not codify the levels as steps in a ladder. Instead, he seeks to enlighten his students by again and again presenting the different perspectives together, as if they were one, by using the points of view of the different levels in continual alternation with one another so that eventually one of them, and then perhaps, later, another of them will provide a context for the awakening of knowledge.

The multiple truths that Śaṅkara presents are not really reducible to one truth or even to two truths. By looking at Śaṅkara's teachings in the *Brahmasūtra- bhāṣya* within the framework of a four-level model, we have been able to recognize the fullness and subtlety of his vision of the truth of Advaita

Vedānta and to appreciate the sophistication of his method of imparting that truth.

NOTES

1. At all the various stages of the writing of this essay, from its inception, I have benefitted from discussion with and suggestions from Katherine Young. I am indebted to her for providing the idea of the four-level system, as a framework for my analysis of Śaṅkara's concept of time.

References to the *Brahmasūtra-bhāṣya* are made by first citing chapter, pāda, and sūtra of the *Brahmasūtras* where Śaṅkara's commentary appears and secondly citing page numbers in one of the several editions used, with the following abbreviations:

B: The *Brahmasūtra Śaṅkara Bhāṣya* with commentaries, ed. Anantkṛiṣṇa Śāstrī (Bombay: Pāṇḍuraṅg Jāwajī, 1938).

C: *Brahma-Sūtra-Bhāṣya of Śrī Śaṅkarācārya*, trans. Swami Gambhirananda (Calcutta: Advaita Ashrama, 1977).

M: *Brahmasūtra-Śaṅkara-Bhāṣya with the commentary Brahmavidyābharaṇa of Śrīmad-Advaitānanda-Swāmipāda*, ed. S.R. Krishnamurthi Sastri (Madras: Samskrit Education Society, 1976).

P: *The Brahma-Sūtras of Bādarāyaṇa with the commentary of Śaṅkarāchārya: Chapter II, Quarters I and II*, ed. S.K. Belvalkar (Poona: Belvakunja Publishing House, 1938) — page numbers cited refer to the second part of the book, the Sanskrit text.

All translations and paraphrases from the *Brahmasūtra-bhāṣya* are my own, except where "C" is cited as the source.

In references to other primary sources, translations are my own, except where the translator's name is given in parentheses.

2. I have been influenced in my understanding of the manifold constitution of each level by Frederick Streng's analysis of the "existential character" of ontological formulations (1982, 371). Eliot Deutsch, whose scheme of ontological levels in Advaita Vedānta is somewhat different from the typology presented here, also insists on the idea of a *cluster* of concepts at each level: "A level of being ... has special and distinguishing epistemological, logical, and axiological characteristics" (1969, 25-6).

3. For example, see the various papers in *The Problem of Two Truths in Buddhism and Vedānta*, ed. Mervyn Sprung (Dordrecht: P. Reidel, 1973).

4. At II.3.32, Śaṅkara gives manas, buddhi, vijñāna, and citta as the predominant aspects of mind — in this list ahaṃkāra is replaced by vijñāna (awareness).

5. Elsewhere, Śaṅkara suggests that the organs in general survive death and influence future births (III.1.4 C, 558; IV.2.8 C, 857).

6. In his commentary on *Bṛhadāraṇyaka Upaniṣad* 4.4.2, Śaṅkara explains that the "awareness" of the soul is like consciousness in a dream and is in consequence of past actions; pūrvaprajñā is the sum of impressions (vāsanās) of past experiences,

which take part in initiating new actions as well as bringing past actions to fruition (Madhavananda 1965a, 705-7). Cf. also *Brahmasūtra-bhāṣya* 3.1. 1 (C, 555-6).

7. Śaṅkara explicitly equates vijñāna and buddhi also at II.3.40 (B, 618), with reference to *Taittirīya Upaniṣad* 2.5.1, insisting that is not the Self, constituted by vijñāna, but rather the intellect that has agentship in the performance of sacrificial rites. Elsewhere, vijñāna is identified as one of the mental functions (see note 4 above).

8. The memory of divine beings is even more persistent, more eternal than that of humans; it seems to survive not only death but cosmic dissolution (pralaya) according to Śaṅkara's discussion of the role of memory in the periodic recreation of the world and the persistence of the Vedas (I.3.30) (see Murty 1959, 39-40). To establish the eternality of the Vedas, Śaṅkara must also address the problem of memory in relation to language (I.3.28), again apparently referring ultimately to the memory possessed by sages or divine beings. "The power of the seers who visualize the mantra and brāhmaṇa portions of the Vedas are not to be measured in terms of our power" (I.3.33 C, 228). This power of memory is perhaps best seen in terms of the level 2 or 3 framework of the understanding of time and the eternal. (Cf. "When true memory [of "I am Brahman"] is regained, all the knots become untied" (*Chāndogya Upaniṣad* 7.26.2) (III.3.32 C, 704); (Sjoman 1986, 200; Eliade 1963, 330-2).

9. Śaṅkara, in his *Brahmasūtra-bhāṣya*, steers clear of the discussion of the nature of the moment (kṣaṇa) which is of such importance to other philosophers concerned with the problem of time, particularly those within the Buddhist, Yoga, and Vaiśeṣika schools (Balslev 1983, 48ff, 80ff, 113ff; Bhaduri 1975, 206-13; Hiriyanna 1957, 121-6). In refuting the Buddhist doctrine of momentariness, he does remark that every existent must persist for at least three successive moments — the moment of its arising, of its being, and of its destruction (II.2.20) — confirming the view that action is momentary.

10. Śaṅkara elaborates on the mechanism of the process by which Vedic ritual can produce post-mortem effects: liquid oblations made into the sacrificial fire are transformed into apūrva as a subtle medium which envelops the sacrificer at death and carries him to heaven (III.1.6 C, 562).

11. The Jainas distinguished between formless, eternal time and measurable, changing time (Mandal 1968, 76ff). The Vaiśeṣikas held that time was real, unitary, eternal, all-pervasive, and independent of events, and that empirical time was simply the relationship between infinite time and finite actions or objects (Potter 1977, 91-3; Bhaduri 1975, 183-7 and 193-7; Hiriyanna 1957, 121-6). The Buddhist logicians of Dignāga's school were at pains to refute the Sarvāstivādin and Vaiśeṣika views of the reality of absolute time. Absolute time, according to Dignāga, is merely a thought construction (cf. note 12 below) (Shastri 1964, 187-8 and 204; Stcherbatsky 1930, 84-7 and 111). Western science has based itself on empirical, particulate and measurable time, but in recent years, the theory of relativity and quantum mechanics have raised the question of whether we, too, must consider the conception of continuous time, of time continuous with space, and of time independent of the "arrow of time" (Bohm 1980, 19ff. and 210-2).

12. The point of the Upaniṣadic passage is the identification of Brahman with the "timeless" and of the phenomenal world with partite, empirical time. Śaṅkara drives home the message of the unequal ontological status of these two kinds of time in *Vivekacūḍamaṇi* 497: "... kalpas, years, seasons, and so on are imagined (kalpita) to exist in partless and changeless time." Cf. also Śaṅkara's commentary on *Bṛhadāraṇyaka Upaniṣad* 4. 4.16, glossing "[The Lord] below which the year with its days rotates": "... *the year*, representing time which limits everything that is born, *with its* own parts, the *days* and nights, *rotates*, occupies a lower position without being able to limit It..." (Mādhavānanda 1965a, 742).

13. This concept of transcendental time is clearly expressed in the ideas of śuddha kāla in the Śaiva Siddhānta system (Sivaraman 1973, 237) and of eternal time in the Sāṃkhya system of Vijñānabhikṣu (Sinha 1983, 37-8). In both cases, transcendental time, eternal and all-pervading, is the domain in which cosmogonic processes occur (including the creation or emergence of empirical time), and therefore exists at a level *above* empirical time. But this transcendental time exists at a level *below* the truly timeless domain of Śiva or puruṣa, level 3 time.

14. This shift from the level 1 to the level 2 concept of time is similar to what Ruth Katz describes in her analysis of the *Bhagavadgītā*: Kṛṣṇa's instruction of Arjuna and the vision of himself as the Lord, as devouring Time itself, that Kṛṣṇa grants to Arjuna "functions like a suddenly widening camera angle, a back-stepping from the human to the superhuman viewpoint," from which time is seen as progressing "in an eternal pattern independent of human actions" (1981, 105). Katz seems to suggest that the *Gītā* may include not only these two perspectives on time, but a level 3 point of view as well, when she mentions that, at *Gītā* 8.20ff, the truth of God is said to lie beyond the cosmic cycle (106).

15. As Śaṅkara says in his commentary on *Bhagavadgītā* 10.33, where Kṛṣṇa, showing his divine form to Arjuna, declares himself to be imperishable time, "'time' can be understood as referring to moments (kṣaṇa) and so forth, or as the supreme Lord who is the time even of time."

16. The priority of space over time seems quite deeply entrenched in Hindu philosophy. This philosophical orientation has been compared to the Greek perspective on the nature of the world, and contrasted to the Judaeo-Christian viewpoint, in which time is held to be more important than space (Needham 1965, 47-8; Nakamura 1960, 51-2; Bohm 1980, 211). According to Schayer many of the oldest Indian conceptions of time, such as those of the Upaniṣads, are characterized by "physicalism" or "somatism," describing time as filling space (1938, 7).

But all Indian philosophers do not share the idea that time is subordinate. Bhartṛhari gives time a prominent place in his system: time is not a product, but a power, the efficient cause of creation (Coward 1982, 278-9). Also among Vaiṣṇava and Śaiva theistic schools, we find the idea of time as a power, as the vehicle of creation (Herbert 1978, 118 and 124-6). Gauḍapāda refers in his *Kārikās* on the *Māṇḍukya Upaniṣad* (I.6.8) to such beliefs: "those who look upon time as real declare time to be the manifestor of all beings" (Nikhilānanda 1968, 40). It is interesting that Śaṅkara in his commentary on this kārikā does not even bother to refute this position, as he does the other concepts of creation mentioned by Gauḍapāda. The

Śvetāśvatara Upaniṣad (1. 2-3) also brings up the possibility that time is the cause of the universe, only to reject the idea, identifying the cause as the power of the divine.

17. According to Bhartṛhari, it is time itself that has this function of "damming" and ordering the parts of the world (Coward 1982, 282-3).

18. At both I.3.30 and II.1.36, Śaṅkara cites *Ṛgveda* 10.190.3 as referring to the creation of the sun and moon as in earlier kalpas (yathāpūrvamakalpa). Deussen (1906, 220-1) says that Śaṅkara misinterprets this text in order to support the theory of beginningless saṃsāra held by the Vedāntins who had preceded him, a theory in conflict with the concept of creation presented in the early Upaniṣads, but one which is the logical outcome of the notion of the law of karma. The issue of when the concept of cyclical time emerges in Indian history is also addressed by Sharma, who maintains that "there seems to be no unequivocal reference to the cyclical notion of time in the Śruti ... [h]ence the cyclic notion of time cannot be said to have been prevalent in Vedic times" (1980, 147), and by Barua, who cites various evidence, including that of Jaina and Buddhist texts, as indicating that the conception of kalpas and mahākalpas, as well as yugas, was present before the middle of the first millennium B.C.E. (1970, 211-2).

19. In Śaṅkara's argument for cyclical time, we may assume that his opponents would be the Mīmāṃsakas, who accepted neither the creatorship of Īśvara nor the theory of cosmic cycles (Dasgupta 1975, 402-3). The idea that the cyclical view of time dominates Indian thought and shapes Indian philosophy and attitudes to history is widely held. Sharma (1980) gives a long list of works in which this stereotype is elaborated, to which I will add: Nakamura (1960, 54-5 and 133-5 and 1966, 82-3); Organ (1976, 56-7); Brandon (1965, 1-5); and Eliade (1963, 341-4). Sharma persuasively argues that this notion is, indeed, a stereotype, which does not do justice to the variety of concepts of time expressed in śruti and smṛti literature. Indeed, even for Śaṅkara, as is shown in the present analysis, it is only at *one* of several levels of understanding that the cyclical view is important in his treatment of time.

20. Īśvara is said to show his grace (prasāda, anugraha) to yogis (I.1.5 M, 14-5), to Hiraṇyagarbha (I.3.30 C, 218), and to those who obtain liberation (II. 3.41 B, 620).

21. In contrast to the Vaiśeṣika theory of causation, the Advaita Vedānta position is that time is irrelevant even in terms of defining causes and effects. Śaṅkara, for instance, commenting on Gauḍapāda's *Kārikās* 4.15-20, argues against a theory of causation based on succession in time, supporting Gauḍapāda's statement that the wise hold to the concept of the nonevolution (ajāti) of things (Nikhilānanda 1968, 224-7).

22. Elsewhere Śaṅkara makes it clear that those who travel the path of the gods do *not* enjoy permanent liberation. Discussing the line "they do not return," in his commentary on *Bṛhadāraṇyaka Upaniṣad* 6.2.15, he notes that in the Mādhyandina recension the word "here" is included — hence, "they do not return here." "Therefore we understand that they return after the lapse of the present cycle" (Mādhavānanda 1965a, 909-10).

23. Deutsch makes this point very clearly in concluding the discussion of what he considers as the "levels of being" in Advaita Vedānta. Deutsch's levels are Reality (comparable to our level 4), Appearance (comprising the three types, the "real existent," the "existent," and the "illusory existent"), and Unreality. "... From the standpoint of Reality there is no distinction between Appearance and Unreality, or between Itself and anything else: from the standpoint of Reality there is and can be only Reality. The distinctions ... may be necessary and valid as mental organizations of experience from the standpoint of rational-sense consciousness. The distinctions, in short, may be justified as philosophy; albeit they are rejected in Reality" (Deutsch 1969, 26).

24. It is only when one compares the ideas presented by some modern interpreters of Vedānta to those in the *Brahmasūtra-bhāṣya*, that one is in for a surprise. While Śaṅkara for the most part stays clear of discussion at level 4 and never really forces the point of the ultimate reality of the level 4 position, denying the validity of previous understandings, we frequently find modern authors promoting the level 4 perspective with some vehemence as the central position of Advaita Vedānta (e.g. Raju 1953, 115; Reyna 1971, 233).

25. Although it is rather neat that turīya, the fourth, seems to be equivalent to our level 4, the correspondence between the other states and our levels is far from exact. Level 3, for instance, *is* marked by dualism to some extent, unlike the third state, suṣupti. Nonetheless, there are interesting parallels between the "lower" three states and three levels of time in terms of cosmological conceptions. Śaṅkara identifies viśva as virāṭ, which includes adhyātma (the individual self) and adhidaiva (the appearance of the sun, moon, and stars — which are the apportioners of time, the indicators of change on our level 1). Taijasa is identified with Hiraṇyagarbha, and here we see a parallel in the theme of creation, at level 2. Suṣupti or prājñā is the unmanifest, bearing the seeds that produce effects; the idea of Brahman as cause, on our level 3, is similarly seen as possessing the power, māyā, to produce the world as effect (Nikhilānanda 1968, 1-2 and 14).

Alex Wayman analyses the Indo-Tibetan Buddhist conception of time in terms of the three categories of "Profane Time" (empirical time, the realm of reason), "Great Time" (nirvāṇa with remainder, mythological time, the realm of the bodhisattvas), and "No Time" (nirvāṇa without remainder, "the revelation of reality, everywhere, always") and suggests that there may also be a fourth category, which includes the other three, in the Mahāyāna idea of "nirvāṇa without fixed abode" (apratiṣṭhita nirvāṇa) (Wayman 1969, 47-62). Wayman indicates that these four categories of Buddhist time correspond to the four states of waking, dreaming, deep sleep, and turīya. These four categories of Buddhist time also closely resemble the four levels of time we have uncovered in the present analysis, with the difference, perhaps, that while the Buddhist's fourth category is inclusive of the other three, Śaṅkara's level 4 is wholly *other* than the preceding levels.

26. In the *Yogasūtras* (I.17-18), we find the idea that there are four kinds of concentration (samādhi) that rest on the contemplation of objects, and a *fifth samādhi*, which, as Śaṅkara in his commentary explains, is non-cognitive, objectless, and seedless (nirbīja) (Leggett 1981, 76-8). We may compare this fifth state with the condition of consciousness realized at level 4.

27. This discussion in the *Brahmasūtra-bhāṣya* is elaborated in Śaṅkara's commentary on *Bhagavadgītā* 13.12, where Brahman "is said to be neither existent nor nonexistent" (na sattannāsaducyate). Śaṅkara interprets this passage as meaning that Brahman "is not within the range of understanding acquired through the apprehension 'it is' or 'it is not'." Brahman is not a thing (vastu) in the same way as other things are, it is not within the range of intellect, it is inaccessible to speech, it is imperceptible, beyond the senses.

28. We have just seen how, at level 4, Śaṅkara says that the meaning of "neti neti" is that Brahman cannot be an object, that Brahman's Existence is of another character than the existence of mundane things (III.2.22 C, 625-6). But almost in the same breath, Śaṅkara cites this same text as demonstrating that Brahman, as Existence, is the cause of all of phenomenal existence, in level 3 terms (III.2.22 C, 626; also III.2.30 B, 723).

29. Potter considers that "Śaṃkara failed to see the contradictions in the different portions of his writings" because he tended to see problems in terms of epistemology or "value," rather than as metaphysical issues. "What Śaṃkara is interested in is not the *truth* of alternative accounts of ultimate causation but rather the relative *importance* of the seeker's believing in one of them" (Potter 1965, 167).

30. As one example of how level-shifting works to Śaṅkara's advantage in debate with his opponents, we may consider how Śaṅkara uses a particular argument himself at level 2 (that karma and diversity can be mutually dependent since the transmigratory state is beginningless — II.1.35-6), but when he shifts to a level 3 discussion, refuting the Sāṃkhya, Śaiva, and Vaiśeṣika views that Īśvara is only the efficient and not the material cause, he denies the validity of the same argument when it is used by his opponents (that Īśvara and karma can be mutually dependent because of the beginninglessness of the world — II.2.37).

BIBLIOGRAPHY

Balslev, Anindita Niyogi. 1983. *A Study of Time in Indian Philosophy.* Wiesbaden: Otto Harrassowitz.

Barua, Benimadhab. 1970. *A History of Pre-Buddhistic Indian Philosophy.* Delhi: Motilal Banarsidass.

Bhaduri, Sadananda. 1975. *Studies in Nyāya-Vaiśeṣika Metaphysics.* Poona: Bhandarkar Oriental Research Institute.

Bohm, David. 1980. *Wholeness and the Implicate Order.* London: Routledge and Kegan Paul.

Brandon, S.G.F. 1965. *History, Time and Deity.* Manchester: Manchester University Press.

Coward, Harold. 1982. "Time (*Kāla*) in Bhartṛhari's *Vākyapadīya*." *Journal of Indian Philosophy* 10:277-87.

Dasgupta, Surendranath. 1975. *A History of Indian Philosophy*. Vol. 1. Delhi: Motilal Banarsidass.

Deussen, Paul. [1906] 1966. *The Philosophy of the Upanishads*. Trans. A.S. Geden. Reprint. New York: Dover.

Deutsch, Eliot. 1969. *Advaita Vedānta: A Philosophical Reconstruction*. Honolulu: East-West Center Press.

Eliade, Mircea. 1963. "Mythologies of Memory and Forgetting." *History of Religions* 2:329-44.

Halbfass, Wilhelm. 1980. "Karma, *Apūrva*, and 'Natural' Causes: Observations on the Growth and Limits of the Theory of *Saṃsāra*." In *Karma and Rebirth in Classical Indian Traditions*. Ed. W.D. O'Flaherty. Berkeley: University of California Press.

Herbert, G.S. 1978. *Time: A Metaphysical Study*. Trivandrum: College Book House.

Hiriyanna, M. 1957. "An Indian View of 'Present Time'." In *Indian Philosophical Studies*. Mysore: Kavyalaya Publishers.

Katz, Ruth. 1981. "Human and Divine Time in the *Bhagavad-gītā*." *Journal of Studies in the Bhagavadgītā* 1:100-112.

Mahadevan, T.M.P. 1953. *Time and the Timeless*. Madras: Upanishad Vihar.

Mandal, Kumar Kishore. 1968. *A Comparative Study of the Concepts of Space and Time in Indian Thought*. Varanasi: Chowkhamba Sanskrit Series.

Murty, K. Satchidananda. 1959. *Revelation and Reason in Advaita Vedānta*. Waltair: Andhra University Press.

Nakamura, Hajime. 1960. *The Ways of Thinking of Eastern Peoples*. Tokyo: Government of Japan/UNESCO.

—. 1966. "Time in Indian and Japanese Thought." In *The Voices of Time*. Ed. J.T. Fraser. New York: Braziller.

Needham, Joseph. 1965. *Time and Eastern Man*. Glasgow: Royal Anthropological Institute.

Organ, Troy. 1976. "Causality: Indian and Greek." In *Philosophy East and West: Essays in Honour of Dr. T.M.P. Mahadevan*. Ed. H.D. Lewis. Bombay: Blackie and Son.

Potter, Karl H. 1965. *Presuppositions of India's Philosophies*. New Delhi: Prentice-Hall.

—, ed. 1977. *Encyclopedia of Indian Philosophies: The Tradition of Nyāya-Vaiśeṣika up to Gangeśa*. Princeton: Princeton University Press.

—. 1980. "The Karma Theory and its Interpretation in Some Indian Philosophical Systems." In *Karma and Rebirth in Classical Indian Traditions*. Ed. W.D. O'Flaherty. Berkeley: University of Califonia Press.

Radhakrishnan, S., trans. 1953. *The Principal Upaniṣads*. London: Allen and Unwin.

Raju, P.T. 1953. *Idealistic Thought of India*. London: Allen and Unwin.

Reyna, Ruth. 1971. "Metaphysics of Time in Indian Philosophy and its Relevance to Particle Science." In *Time in Science and Philosophy*. Ed. Jiri Zeman. Amsterdam: Elsevier.

Śankarācarya. n.d. Śrībhagavadgītābhāṣyam. Śrīraṅgam: Śrīvanivilāsa-mudrāyantrālaya.

—. 1938a. *The Brahmasūtra Śaṅkara Bhāṣya with Commentaries*. Ed. Anantkṛṣṇa Śāstrī. Bombay: Pāṇḍuraṅg Jāwajī.

—. 1938b. *The Brahma-Sūtras of Bādarāyana with the comment of Śaṅkarāchārya: Chapter II, Quarters I and II*. Ed. S.K. Belvalkar. Poona: Belvakunja Publishing House.

—. 1965a. *The Bṛhadāraṇyaka Upaniṣad with the Commentary of Śaṅkarācārya*. Trans. Swami Mādhavānanda. Calcutta: Advaita Ashrama.

—. 1965b. *Vivekachudamani of Shri Shankaracharya*. Trans. Swami Madhavananda. Calcutta: Advaita Ashrama.

—. 1968. *The Māṇḍukyopaniṣad with Gauḍapāda's Kārikā and Śaṅkara's Commentary*. Trans. Swami Nikhilānanda. Mysore: Sri Ramakrishna Ashrama.

—. 1976. *Brahmasūtra-Śaṅkara-Bhāṣya with the commentary Brahmavidyābharaṇa of Śrīmad-Advaitānanda-Swāmipāda*. Ed. S.R. Krishnamurthi Sastri. Madras: Samskrit Education Society.

—. 1977. *Brahma-Sūtra-Bhāṣya of Śrī Śaṅkarācārya*. Trans. Swami Gambhirananda. Calcutta: Advaita Ashrama.

—. 1981. *Śaṅkara on the Yoga-sūtras (Vol. I: Samādhi)*. Trans. Trevor Leggett. London: Routledge and Kegan Paul.

Schayer, Stanislaw. 1938. *Contributions to the Problem of Time in Indian Philosophy*. Krakow: Nakladem Polskiej Akademii Umiejetnosci.

Sharma, Arvind. 1980. "The Notion of Cyclical Time in Hinduism." In *Textual Studies in Hinduism*. New Delhi: Manohar.

Shastri, Dharmendra Nath. 1964. *Critique of Indian Realism*. Agra: Agra University.

Sinha, Braj M. 1983. *Time and Temporality in Sāṃkhya-Yoga and Abhidharma Buddhism*. New Delhi: Munshiram Manoharlal.

Sivaraman, K. 1973. *Śaivism in Philosophical Perspective*. Delhi: Motilal Banarsidass.

Sjoman, N.E. 1986. "The Memory Eye: An Examination of Memory in Traditional Knowledge Systems." *Journal of Indian Philosophy* 14:195-213.

Sprung, Mervyn, ed. *The Problem of Two Truths in Buddhism and Vedānta*. 1973. Dordrecht: P. Reidel.

Stcherbatsky, Th. [1930] 1962. *Buddhist Logic*. Vol. 1. Reprint. New York: Dover.

Streng, Frederick J. 1982. "Three Approaches to Authentic Existence: Christian, Confucian, and Buddhist." *Philosophy East and West* 32:371-92.

Wayman, Alex. 1969. "No Time, Great Time, and Profane Time in Buddhism." In *Myths and Symbols: Studies in Honor of Mircea Eliade*. Eds. J.M. Kitagawa and C.H. Long. Chicago: University of Chicago.

THE BASIC TYPES OF RENUNCIATION IN HINDUISM: WITH SPECIAL REFERENCE TO ŚAṄKARA'S GĪTĀ-BHĀṢYA

Roger Marcaurelle

During the last fifteen years, secondary literature on renunciation has put right the over-emphasis of earlier Western scholars on the world-negating aspects of this dimension of Indian religious and cultural life. However, confusion still abounds in today's literature on renunciation. The vagueness of its terminology prevents an understanding of the network of relations that upholds this theme in Indian spirituality. What is required are systematic definitions and a basic typology of renunciation.

This essay, which will be limited to the Hindu context, will begin by outlining instances of confusion in secondary literature on renunciation. Examples will be taken mainly from the works of Karl Potter, Kapil Tiwari, Haripada Chakraborti, M.M. Agrawal, Robert Minor and Surendranath Dasgupta. Of course, statements in primary literature may also seem ambivalent and unconcerned with systematic and univocal definitions. But, this only highlights the need for more careful definitions. Four basic types of renunciation will then be defined, clarifying categories already found in the *Bhagavadgītā* (*BG*). We will formulate them with as little ambiguity as possible, basing them on the *object* being renounced. This object can be: (1) the physical action or material possession as such; (2) the result, or metaphorically, the "fruit" of action (phala); (3) a layer of mental activity; and (4) the authorship (agency) of action (kartṛtva), through direct experience of ātman or Self, which is unconditional by nature (prakṛti). These types of renunciation will be defined in terms of their respective characteristics as well as their relations and possible combinations. This typology will be presented from the perspective of Advaita (non-dualism).[1]

It may be argued that while this essay tries to provide a sound basis for interpreting renunciation, its components are themselves born of what is already one interpretation of renunciation among others possible. This is an unavoidable part of the hermeneutical enterprise, in which one always intuits the whole by the parts and the parts by the whole, back and forth in a continuous refining process.

Is Abandonment of the Results of Action the "Core" of Renunciation?

In his book *Dimensions of Renunciation in Advaita Vedānta*, Tiwari defines renunciation indiscriminately as abandonment of: (1) the results of action (1977, 80); (2) egoism — his translation of the Sanskrit term ahaṃkāra (1977, 17, 40); and (3) ignorance (1977, 73). In his conclusion, he identifies renunciation in Śaṅkara as "spiritual action sustained by jñāna" (1977, 141) — jñāna being direct experience of the Self. Tiwari suggests that all these perspectives merge in the nature of one and the same kind of renunciation. But, as we shall see, Śaṅkara considers renunciation of the results of action as meaningful even in the case of a man still ignorant of the Self. We thus question Tiwari's equating the abandonment of the results of action with the abandonment of ignorance in knowledge of the Self.

In his *Ancient Indian Asceticism,* M.G. Bhagat stresses that true renunciation is not mere physical abandonment of activity and apathic indifference. In his view, the essential Indian teaching on this theme is "renunciation in action, not renunciation from action" (1976, 316). He then defines the right perspective as renunciation of the fruits (karmaphalatyāga). And, in his *Presuppositions of India's Philosophy*, Potter writes that although the positions of various Indian philosophers vary widely as far as the theory of paths is concerned, "one point on which everyone agrees, however, is the importance of non-attachment to the fruits of actions as the core of renunciation" (1965, 38).

No one can deny the importance of non-attachment to the results of action in Hinduism and especially in the *Bhagavadgītā*. But the question whether it constitutes the very heart of renunciation requires a close examination of this important type of abandonment and its relation to other fundamental types of renunciation.

What does the tradition usually mean by renunciation of the results? The definition given by Agrawal represents the thinking of modern scholars: "[It is] not that one should not be concerned with the results of one's actions, but that one should not make the fruits of actions one's *motive* for acting" (1982, 44). This definition assumes that the motive will be conducive to the welfare of the environment. Agrawal explains that while no actor can avoid the primary motive that his good actions will benefit others, renouncing the fruit of action would be to disallow the rise of a second motive that would be centred on the interest of the actor (1982, 45). Other writers such as Franklin Edgerton (1952, 57) and

Sarvepalli Radhakrishnan (1923, 572) apparently refer to the same thing when talking, respectively, of unselfishness or disinterestedness.

The key to understanding the specific value of this type of renunciation appears from time to time in secondary literature, but very few writers acknowledge it or employ it consistently. Potter, for example, says that "renunciation constitutes a route to the removal of bondage" and that "complete freedom is the removal of all karma." He also asserts that "renunciation must be with respect to the fruits of actions" (1965, 23). In the Advaita context, for example, complete freedom is mokṣa, a state of consciousness where one's identity has become the infinite and inactive ātman and where, as a consequence, inner "removal of all karma" has occurred. Does the fact of renouncing the fruits — that is, of not seeking the results of one's actions on oneself (as already defined) — necessarily mean that one is free from all action and free from the sense of being an actor limited by time, space and contingencies? Potter implies that this is so since, for him, on the way to complete freedom, the main object of renunciation has to be the fruit of action. Bhagat (1976, 240) and Dasgupta (1952, 488) adopt the same viewpoint, upholding the commonly held opinion that action is not binding to one who does not expect the fruits of action. Bhagat adds that by abandoning all expectation for results, one will be able to surrender "one's will, desire and action at the feet of the Lord" (1976, 241-242).

If renunciation of the results is to be understood as the absence of a motive of self-interest, which occurs in the *active* field of mental fluctuations (vṛttis), it cannot be likened to the absence of identification with the boundaries of all processes of action. The latter is characteristic of mokṣa and, as recognized by the Advaita tradition, is ensured by the *inactive* nature of the ātman with which one has become identified. In other words, if Agrawal's definition is to be maintained, methodological consistency requires that renunciation of the results be clearly distinguished from renunciation of authorship (the sense of being the doer of one's actions). Otherwise, vagueness, confusion, contradiction and misinterpretation are bound to invade the very subject that one is supposed to clarify. The possibility of avoiding this inconsistency by altering Agrawal's definition will be considered below.

Most authors of secondary literature cite the *Bhagavadgītā* to support their contention that abandonment of the fruits is the heart of renunciation. However, this work does not teach the equivalence between abandonment of authorship and abandonment of the fruits defined by Agrawal. Indeed, it presents renunciation of authorship as distinct and most important.

In *BG* chapter 12, Kṛṣṇa admonishes Arjuna to unite with him (12.8) or, if that is impossible, to reach him through the "yoga of practice" (abhyāsayogena) (12.9). If this, too, is impossible, he is told to do actions for his sake (madartham) (12.10), or, as a last resort, to abandon the results of all actions (12.11) (sarvakarmaphalatyāga). This essay does not permit a full discussion of the subtlety of the different levels of consciousness and practice referred to here. It is quite clear in this context, however, that renunciation of the results of action cannot be equated with renunciation of authorship. First, in the above sequence, renunciation of the results is far removed from that of union with Kṛṣṇa. Unity with Kṛṣṇa implies that one's identity is beyond the activity of the three guṇas, which belong to prakṛti alone, and that one has therefore abandoned the sense of being an actor. Hence, the renunciation of authorship implied in this union and the abandonment of the results are clearly distinct. Second, although abandonment of the fruits seems to be the most accessible type of renunciation, it represents a last resort and so could hardly be described as the most precious or fundamental type. It is, therefore, abandonment of authorship that is the "core" of renunciation.

The apposition of abandonment of results and renunciation of authorship in several verses dealing with liberation, could, admittedly, lead one to think that they amount to the same thing in the *Bhagavadgītā* (see verses 2.51; 4.14; 4.20; 5.12; 9.28; 12.12). In other passages of the same work, however, liberation is said to come from knowledge of the non-dual, inactive dimension of consciousness that is the Self (see verses 2.39; 3.31; 4.16; 4.22; 4.41; 5.3; 9.9; 10.3; 13.34; 18.17; 18.66). Thus, it could be argued that the link between these two types of renunciation is one of cause and effect rather than of identity. Depending also on the sequence of the terms in the apposition, these passages could say that one has to abandon the results to prepare or assist abandonment of authorship. They could also mean that one will no longer be attached to the fruits of actions *because* one has already reached inner detachment from the actions themselves.

Śaṅkara separates these two types of renunciation in his commentary on the *Bhagavadgītā*. First, he writes that in verse 12.12, the option of abandoning the fruits (given at the end of Kṛṣṇa's sequence of means in verse 12.11) is addressed to the person ignorant of the ātman. Hence, it is directed to one who has not yet achieved renunciation of authorship (which he calls here abandonment of all desires [sarvakāmatyāga] through direct experience of the Self). He then states that if renunciation of the fruits of action is praised in verse 12.12, it is due not to its identity with, but to some similarity (sāmāya) with, renunciation of all desires (or authorship) reached by the knower of the Self: "There is similarity between renunciation of the fruits of actions on the part of the ignorant and renunciation of all desires. Through this similarity, renunciation of the fruits of all actions is praised" (sarvakāmatyāgasāmānyamajñakarmaphalatyāgasyāstīti tatsāmānyātsarvakarmaphalatyāgastutiriyam). Moreover, Śaṅkara suggests in his commentary on verse 4.14 that it is the abandonment of authorship which finally ensures full renunciation of the results: "I am not a doer, [thus] I have no longing for the result of action" (nāhaṃ kartā na me karmaphale spṛhā).

Maharishi Mahesh Yogi, a modern commentator in Śaṅkara's tradition, sees the same causal relation in his commentary on the *Bhagavadgītā*. He writes:

> when the doer is attached to the action, the result of the action is naturally attached to the doer. But when the doer is not attached to the action, the results are not attached to him (1969, 218).

For his part, Minor sees renunciation of the results and of authorship not as "two distinct objects but as the same viewed from two angles, [in other words, as] two sides of one coin" (1980, 465). The first side is the "realization of the distinction of the true self from Nature" (1980, 465). It is the experiential knowledge that one is not acting at all but has abandoned all identification with action. The second is "the practice of action without attachment to the results of the action" (1980, 465). Minor's unifying perspective holds true in the case of one who practices both renunciation of the fruits and of authorship at the same time. It does not account for the abandonment of the fruits for one who is ignorant of the ātman and still has the sense of being an actor.

Although rightly insisting on the importance of reaching the inner state of non-involvement with action, Minor over-emphasizes abandonment of the results when he identifies types of renunciation. Commenting on a verse that mentions freedom from action as a condition for knowing Kṛṣṇa, he defines saṃnyāsayoga only as renunciation of the results (1982, 300). Contrary to Śaṅkara, he suggests in at least one instance that renunciation of authorship is a result of renunciation of the fruits: "non-attached to the results of action and, *thus*, 'perfect in actionlessness'" (emphasis added; 1982, 485).

It seems better to separate clearly renunciation of the results of action as defined by Agrawal from that of authorship. For terminological purposes we may give it two main values, one for the state of ignorance and one for the state of liberation, the latter resulting from the complete renunciation of authorship as conditioned by Nature (prakṛti). It is only the second type of renunciation of the fruits that becomes one side of the coin, the other being the renunciation of authorship. We shall come back to this point in the course of enumerating the possible combinations of our main types.

Renunciation is often understood as abandonment of desires on the basis of expressions such as niṣkāmakarma (action without desire). Since we have defined abandonment of the results of action as the absence of a motive of self-interest, and since renunciation of desires also has motives as its objects of abandonment, they appear to be synonyms. Accordingly, renunciation of desires (fruits, results, or motives of self-interest, whatever the synonym) can have a value for both contexts of ignorance and knowledge of the Self.

Secondary literature often talks of renunciation of desires in terms of unselfishness (Edgerton 1952, 57-58), or of "complete eradication of egoism"

(Tiwari 1977, 40). But does someone behaving in a generous and altruistic manner necessarily know the Self? While we cannot endorse such a conclusion, the reverse is true in the context of Hinduism: being unidentified with authorship, one who knows the Self will necessarily behave as a mere instrument of nature or God, and only then will be really free from selfishness. Therefore, even when preceded by the epithet "complete," the term unselfishness cannot clearly describe the full range of renunciation of desire, since it leaves aside the fundamental aspect of its possible coexistence with the experience of the Self. As we have seen in the case of renunciation of the fruits, disinterestedness also has a value for a man still ignorant of the Self. It reaches its climax only when abandonment of desires is the natural result of abandonment of authorship — through identification with the Self that is uninvolved with any activity (which belongs to prakṛti), including that of having a desire. Eliot Deutsch concurs, stating that according to the *Bhagavadgītā*, niṣkāmakarma is possible only through discrimination between the Divine and nature (1986, 164). Using Sanskrit terms, we could say that niṣkāma is conditional to naiṣkarmya, i.e. to actionlessness based on direct experience of the Self as actionless.

Is Renunciation an Attitude?

When defining mental renunciation (as distinct from physical), most secondary literature describes it in terms of an "attitude" of non-attachment or of "indifference" in relation to either the results or authorship. Potter states that discrimination of the Self and the attitude of non-attachment represent for most "path philosophers" the "immediate conditions of freedom" (1965, 40). He does not specify the link between the "conditions" and the "freedom." Rather, he tends to confuse cause and effect by defining both of them as attitudes. Freedom "is not a result at all but an attitude" (1965, 19).

Needless to say, an attitude is a blend of mental and emotional *activity* and, according to Advaita, the absolute freedom of the Self is not. While Potter acknowledges that the state of liberation is not a result of action, he overlooks the fact that neither is it an attitude, at least according to Advaita. It does not pertain to the field of activity but rather to the self-illuminating, inactive and unbounded nature of the Self. Moreover, if freedom in the knowledge of the Self were an attitude, then one would also have to consider discrimination of the Self (Potter's first "condition of freedom") as an attitude. This would obscure even further its distinction from the second "condition," consisting also in an attitude of separation; that is, of non-attachment. Unfortunately, Potter's terminology on renunciation fails to clarify this issue.

Minor defines non-attached action as "acting with an attitude of renunciation" (1982, 206). Elsewhere, he still considers it an attitude, although he clearly defines jñāna as the discrimination between the Self and prakṛti, which takes place beyond prakṛti itself: "The place of the search for jñāna is as the means of attaining the attitude appropriate to the furtherance of non-attached action (karmayoga)" (1980, 347). Along the same lines, he contends that renunciation entails "renouncing of attitudes which cause attachment to action" (1980, 342). This notion of attitude is so pervasive that renunciation has become the attitude of giving up an attitude. Minor has clearly not grasped the full consequences of his definition of jñāna. Since only that which is beyond action can free one from the limitations of action and its fruits, and since jñāna or discrimination of the Self is beyond all activity, the renunciation it establishes is not of the nature of an attitude. It is beyond the *thought* that one does not feel attracted towards the results of action or the *reflection* that one's identity is indeed beyond all activity.

Even when defining renunciation as unity with either saguṇa or nirguṇa brahman (1977, 25), both of which transcend the activity of nature, Tiwari still understands renunciation as a "spiritual attitude" (1977, 17) and as an "attitude of mind" (1977, 102). In his book on yoga, C.T. Kenghe also erroneously presents discrimination between action and inaction as an attitude:

> The Gītā therefore advises that a Yogin should always consider Nature as doer and himself as non-doer. It is such an attitude that leads to complete unattachment and evenness of mind (1976, 100).

This quotation immediately follows a discussion in which he explains that the *Bhagavadgītā* advocates renunciation of the fruits alone rather than actions themselves. To us, the full explanation of the teaching of the *Bhagavadgītā* on the discrimination between nature and the Self demands the introduction of a third object of renunciation apart from physical actions as such and the fruits of action. This third object is that of authorship. Even the notion of a "meditative act," which Tiwari takes from the *Upaniṣads* (1977, 23), does not account for the full range of renunciation, because especially in Advaita the renunciative or introverting activity of meditation is meant to transcend all activity, including its own process of transcending. It follows that the basic state of renunciation to which it leads cannot be an act, even a meditative one, since it consists in the experience of being devoid of all activity and authorship. As Le Saux aptly comments, at this level "il n'est point en vérité 'd'acte' possible de renoncement" (1979, 204).

The Distinction between Mental and Physical Renunciation

We have thus far been discussing types of renunciation that are mental. They occur in consciousness alone; that is, in the mind, in the Self or in both. They do not involve physical abandonment of possessions and reduction of physical activity in one's daily routine, and are of a qualitative nature only. Another major kind of renunciation is quantitative in character. It entails physically leaving one's possessions and eliminating at least some kinds of activities in one's life. The type of activity that is particularly subject to physical abandonment in the Hindu context is the performance of Vedic rituals prescribed in the scriptures. We shall call this type physical renunciation.[2]

The relation of physical renunciation to the other types is likewise confused in secondary literature. Tiwari properly attempts, for example, to restore mental renunciation as the primary type for Śaṅkara, as opposed to the physical kind, the importance of which has been generally over-emphasized in the Indian, as well as in the Western, understanding of this philosopher. But he does so in a way that is blind to the prescription of physical renunciation in Śaṅkara's commentaries. Tiwari concludes at the end of his book on renunciation in *Advaita Vedānta*: "By non-performance of action, or karma-saṃnyāsa, the advaitins only mean that the Brahmavid or Brahmasaṃstha acts but automatically or spontaneously without any strain or struggle, due to the realization of the cosmic consciousness outside of which nothing remains" (1977, 139). Although it is true that the mental value of karmasaṃnyāsa often escapes readers of Śaṅkara, one can find passages where the philosopher clearly uses the same or similar expressions to formulate an injunction concerning physical renunciation.[3]

Another confusing tendency on the part of some authors is to use the word "renunciation" without noticing or specifying changes of type that may occur as one passes from one scriptural statement to another. For example, shifts occur in values of renunciation within the single page by Chakraborti cited below, but the author treats the reference or content of the theme of renunciation exactly the same in all of the passages he quotes. He writes [and I have added in brackets the reference or the question one is led to ask for each passage quoted]:

> The ancient sages who had attained this self (Bṛh. Upa., 4.4.23) cared little for children and renounced their homes [physical renunciation].... The Kaṭha Upa. (6.14) and the Bṛh. Upa. (4.4.7) prescribe the renunciation of all desires and attachment [renunciation of authorship] as the requisite of immortality: "when all desires that lodge in one's heart are liberated, a mortal becomes immortal and he reaches Brahman".... The works of the later period repeat the same thing [physical or mental renunciation, or both?]. The Sāṃkhya and Yoga systems preached renunciation [of

> authorship] as a direct means of attaining self-realization. The Mahābhārata also speaks of renunciation as the culmination of the giving up of all duties [mental and/or physical renunciation?]: "O Brāhmaṇa, what will you do with wealth or friends or a wife, for you shall have to die? Seek the self that has entered the cage of your intellect." The Nārada-Parivrājaka Upa. (77) prescribes again renunciation from the student-life itself [physical renunciation] of that very student who is already disgusted with this world and becomes free from any impulsion of desire [renunciation of the results alone or of authorship also?] (1973, 29).

Chakraborti summarizes the vague blend he has made of renunciation in a single sentence: "As early as the Ṛgveda man withdrew from the outside world to discover his inner being in the depth of his heart" (1973, 30). Does "withdrew from the outside world" mean practicing yogic or other sorts of techniques while still keeping one's possessions as a householder, or engaging in those practices only after complete physical renunciation? Unfortunately, nothing in his comments clarifies what this withdrawal entails in the Hindu scriptures or in subsequent history.

Unlike Chakraborti, Potter is quick to affirm that the meaning of renunciation can differ from one Hindu work to the other. For example, it may differ from Śaṅkara to post-Śaṅkara Advaita. In addition, he recognizes that this meaning is intimately related to the commentator's specific understanding of the state of, as well as the means to, mokṣa. Writes Potter: "Whereas most Hindus view saṃnyāsa as an advanced spiritual state, it is a peculiarity of Śaṁkara's thought that he construes this stage as identical with liberation while living, that is, with jīvanmukti" (1981, 35). It is true, as Potter says, "that Śaṁkara, when speaking of saṃnyāsa, frequently describes it in terms that seem appropriate only to the liberated person" (1981, 35). Thus, according to Potter, renunciation of all actions in Śaṅkara's commentaries is to be understood in the light of the "thesis that Self-knowledge necessarily renders action of any kind impossible" (1981, 35).

Because we are talking here of a qualitative renunciation of authorship through knowledge of the Self, we contend that this impossibility of acting is valid as a living reality only on the level of the identity with the Self. It is not valid on the level of the individual self, which continues to act even after liberation and which represents through its daily actions the jīvan or living and practical aspect of jīvanmukti. Potter erroneously applies this intrinsic absence of activity characteristic of Self-knowledge alone to the physical dimension of renunciation. This is evident when he tries to make a case for the impossibility of Śaṅkara's being the real historical founder of the monastic tradition that has been associated with his name for centuries:

> we may well doubt that the philosopher Śaṃkara had anything at all to do with the founding of the Daśanāmins. It would have been out of character for him to form a social institution around what he considered to be a saṃnyāsin, since he insisted that they were incapable of action and thus entirely outside of society (1982, 121).

In our opinion, it is wrong to conclude that because one is "incapable of action" — in other words, because through renunciation of authorship one has eliminated all identification with the will to pursue activity — one has necessarily left behind social activities on the physical and mental levels. Absence of action on the level of Self-knowledge does not necessarily mean the same on the physical and mental levels. Potter himself prevents such erroneous transfer of value when, in another work, he specifies about the liberated person: "from the 'higher standpoint' (pāramārthika) he is liberated and thus incapable of ordinary knowledge, action, and experiences, but from the 'lower standpoint' (vyāvahārika) he is a saṃnyāsin or renunciate, capable of all such things" (1981, 34).

The Basic Types of Renunciation and their Combinations

Having shown the necessity of clearly distinguishing the basic types of renunciation, it is now time to define them in a more formal way and to consider them in all their possible combinations. They will be defined on the basis of the objects that are abandoned.

The most obvious object of abandonment is a physical action or material property. It could be, for example, the accomplishment of a ritual, the use of fire to prepare one's food, or the repairing of a house. This kind of abandonment involves the physical abandonment of possessions and/or cessation of physical activity, as in the case of a householder physically ceasing to perform Vedic rituals when he has reached a certain age. Or it involves simple avoidance of these possessions and activities in favour of monastic life, as in the case of a student who has not yet acquired possessions and any familial or social responsibility that necessitates the observance of injunctions to perform certain actions. This first type we shall call physical renunciation. Combined with renunciation of the results and meditative renunciation without concomitant knowledge of the Self, it may be said to correspond to the experience of the person living a monastic life but without experiencing the Self. Combined with renunciation of authorship, it automatically includes renunciation of the results and is lived by the monk who maintains the experience of the Self in his daily activities.

The second major object of renunciation is the results of action. Whereas abandonment of action or possessions as visible objects is quantitative, this is qualitative, since it does not involve obvious physical changes. We have used the most common definition for this type, which is the absence of a selfish or self-centred motive to guide one's mental or physical actions. Since it relates to the absence or presence of a motive, that is, of an element of the active psyche, its specific or characteristic sphere, in this definition, is the emotional and mental structure of the individual self. In this sense, it can be called an "attitude," as the absence of a selfish motive will leave room in the active psyche for another affective and cognitive relationship with — or attitude towards — one's mental and physical actions. Being an active modification (vṛtti) of the psyche and a blend of emotional and mental aspects, this renunciation of the results can be understood as an attitude in the same way as we say that, whatever one's level of consciousness, one has had a spontaneous positive attitude towards a particular event.

Now, two questions may be raised here. First, is this attitude only the spontaneous effect of the experience of the Self? If not, is it a general moral guideline worthy of remembrance once in a while? Or is it something to be entertained consciously on a more or less permanent basis as a definite practice of renunciation? Second, is there a criterion in renunciation of the results of action, as defined so far, by which one may establish that one has indeed no selfish motive and is really living what is described by the definition?

Most scholars, we suspect, would answer the first question as Dasgupta has. He asserts that it is not only an effect of the experience of the Self but also a formal practice:

> It is by our attempts at the performance of our duties, trying all the time to keep the mind clear from motives of pleasure and enjoyment, that we gradually succeed in elevating it to a plane at which it would be natural for it to desist from all motives of self-interest, pleasure and enjoyment (1952, 445).

Dasgupta also mentions that this "plane" from which results of action can only be abandoned is nothing other than the experience of the Self: "The person who realizes the true nature of his self, and knows that the self is unchangeable and infinite, cannot feel himself attached to the fruits of his actions and cannot be affected by ordinary mundane desires and cravings" (1952, 457). The question to be asked, then, is whether the practice of "trying all the time to keep the mind clear from motives of pleasure and enjoyment" is even possible or conducive to the experience of the Self. If we recognize the path towards the Self as a process of stopping the excitation of the psyche and opening to the absolute silence of its transcendental level, we may seriously doubt that, if at all possible, this "trying all the time" in the midst of daily activities would ever succeed in transcending its own activity and really open the awareness to the Self.

In light of this, it would seem more realistic and practical to understand renunciation of the fruits of action mainly as an effect of the degree of experience of the Self reached during periods of meditation limited in time. It may be understood also as a general principle to be remembered on occasion, rather than as a constant practice. Therefore, as the *Bhagavadgītā* itself suggests, for the man of action as well as for the monk, meditation (in other words, meditative renunciation) would play the main role, as far as practices are concerned, for developing renunciation of the results of action. These remarks may not end the debate (see also Marcaurelle 1988-1989 for more details). But from the methodological point of view of this essay, it is sufficient to show that, apart from the value of a spontaneous effect issuing from knowledge of the Self, renunciation of the fruits probably means something other than constant striving.

Our second question concerning renunciation of the results of action is whether the definition we have taken from Agrawal contains a criterion to establish that the renouncer really has no selfish motive. It is our contention that it contains no such criterion. How can one be sure that there is no unconscious selfish motive behind a particular action or, for that matter, behind every action a human being performs? And how is one to ascertain that no impression left deep in the unconscious by previous experiences may become surreptitiously the major guiding principle of one's action at the cost of a purely altruistic response to needs of the environment? In other words, what is the criterion for the absence of a selfish motive in one's whole psyche? We find the following answer in Agrawal's analysis: "The disappearance of the motive of self, which is often hidden, is effected naturally when attachment is annihilated. The uncovering of the motives of self and the perception of one's attachment is self-knowledge" (1982, 49).

According to this statement, non-attachment and "self-knowledge" are the criteria for the absence of a motive of self-interest. But what kind of non-attachment is it? If it is with regard to the results, then we would have the following tautology: the criterion of non-attachment to the results (here "motive of self") is non-attachment to the results. If, on the other hand, this non-attachment is based on the unconditioned Self and is therefore primarily in regard to authorship, then Agrawal's definition of knowledge of the Self as uncovering motives and perceiving one's attachment is inadequate and misleading. This description does not refer to the inactive nature of the Self. Instead, it defines aspects of the transformations occurring in the individual self during the process of awakening to the Self. The only passage in which Agrawal clearly suggests self-knowledge as the criterion for unselfish action is the following: "A person with the discriminative knowledge of the self, inwardly unattached, naturally chooses to act from the standpoint of moral respect for persons" (1982, 67-68).

But his preceding definition of knowledge of the "self" makes his position unclear.

According to Advaita, the criterion of complete renunciation of the results of action (or of unselfish action) can only be the most inward type of renunciation, the object of which is authorship. It occurs only when one has realized, deep within one's identity as a non-actor in the silent nature of the Self, that the individual self in its own relative sphere automatically becomes the smooth instrument of the completely beneficial will of nature or God (depending on the viewpoint). Therefore, the criterion to ascertain that one has renounced all selfish motives is abandonment of all sense of authorship in the direct experience of the Self. Renunciation of authorship lets nature automatically work out its cosmic beneficial motives within its own active field (kṣetra), of which the body and the individual self are part. In turn, we may say that the criterion and definition of the renunciation of authorship is the direct experience of the Self as uninvolved with any action and desire/will to act.

A fully valid definition of renunciation of the results of actions cannot be reached without introducing and defining renunciation of authorship. Left to itself, renunciation of results is never integral. It is true that, even without the help of anything else, accomplishment of rituals and of one's duty, without caring for their results, is recognized by the *Bhagavadgītā* and by its Hindu commentators as a purifying process. But for the purposes of a rigorous definition, abandonment of the results of action such as explained by Agrawal and others is an uncertain, unstable and incomplete reality.

Because renunciation of the results can be resorted to by the ignorant and can also be the spontaneous result of the experience of the Self, this type of renunciation allows for the widest range of possible meanings, right or wrong. From one extreme to the other, they include: (1) a constant effort or a controlled attitude to avoid selfish motives; (2) a general understanding recalled once in a while, of the importance of doing the right action without attending to the results; (3) a general or particular, spontaneous, altruistic attitude in the individual self, not concomitant with direct experience of the Self; (4) a general or particular, spontaneous, altruistic attitude in the individual self, concomitant with direct experience of the Self. The last involves the state of being beyond the activity of prakṛti through identification with the Self, and thus a perfect, unselfish instrument of nature on the level of the individual self. From a methodological or non-normative point of view, the most holistic definition of renunciation of the results of action would include all of these meanings.

Whatever the definition favoured by different authors, most would probably agree on the following point: it is the quality of awakening to the Self that determines the degree of unselfishness and the depth of renunciation of the results. More precisely, I would add, especially from the Advaita viewpoint, renunciation of the fruits progressively becomes, on the path to liberation, inseparable from that of authorship. The value of the object of abandonment gradually shifts from the motive of self-interest to *all* motives or desires; that is, to the total absence of identification with even the act of desiring itself, whatever its content. While selfish desire is the characteristic object for renunciation of the results, all desires, inasmuch as they constitute forms of mental activity with which one identifies, represent the specific sphere of renunciation of authorship. Since one continues to identify with the limitations of the individual self when one practises only the renunciation of the results, it follows that it is not specifically the latter that liberates one from the bondage of action but renunciation of authorship.

A fourth major type of renunciation can be equated with the meditative process wherein a layer of mental activity is abandoned in favour of a more subtle one, or of direct self-knowledge. This form of abandonment, which we call meditative renunciation, is expressed well in *Kaṭha Upaniṣad* 2.1.1:

> ... one sees the outer objects and not the inner Self. Desiring immortality, a discriminating man turns his eye within and sees the indwelling Self.

The *Bhagavadgītā* twice associates the expression "renouncing all actions" with the practice of meditation. First in verse 12.6:

> But those who worship me, renouncing all actions in Me, regarding Me as Supreme, meditating on Me with single-minded yoga.

Then in 18.57:

> Mentally renouncing all actions in Me, regarding Me as supreme, resorting to the yoga of the intellect, do thou ever fix your mind in Me.

We can fairly say, therefore, that the meditative process consisting of withdrawing the awareness from gross to finer levels of mental activity towards the Self, is another major form of renunciation in Hinduism.

The Three Modes of Mental Renunciation

Apart from the perspective of the object of renunciation, there is another way to consider similarity (sāmānya) and distinction (viśeṣa) among the four main types of renunciation that we have defined; by taking the angle of the difference between the mental and physical dimensions of life. As its name implies, physical renunciation is of a physical or bodily/material nature. By contrast, abandonment of the fruits of action, meditative renunciation and abondonment of authorship are of the nature of the psyche or consciousness.

Renunciation of the results without concomitant experience of the Self may be called a renunciation in attitude. The mental nature of this renunciation pertains to the individual self. Abandonment of authorship is, on the other hand, renunciation in that Self which is beyond individuality and attitude, as pertaining to prakṛti. The mental nature of this renunciation is beyond the mind itself, in that layer of consciousness which transcends mental activity maintained by prakṛti. While for this reason it does not involve an attitude, it automatically implies a spontaneous and integral attitude of non-attachment to the results of action on the level of the individual self that remains active in daily activities.

The words manasā and cetasā are used in the *Bhagavadgītā* as modifiers of the act of renouncing. Translators have usually rendered these terms as "by the mind" or "by thought." The question then arises: Does the use of manasā and cetasā in the *Bhagavadgītā* correspond to the distinction we made between physical and mental renunciation?

These two words are found twice in the *Bhagavadgītā* (verses 5.13 and 18.57) in reference to abandonment of all actions, the act of renouncing being expressed by the verb sam-ni-ās, rather than tyaj. This confirms that manasā and cetasā are used to distinguish mental from physical abandonment. Indeed, since one of the meanings of sam-ni-ās clearly refers to physical abandonment, it would be expected that its mental character be specified by a qualifier, so as to mean only inner renunciation. According to our three-fold division of mental renunciation, do manasā and cetasā then refer to renunciation in attitude and meditative renunciation only, or also to renunciation in the Self? Since in the contexts in which these two expressions occur, the object is "all actions," and since, as specified by both qualifiers, its abandonment is of a qualitative nature alone, their reference must only be renunciation of authorship. This involves renunciation in the Self and not renunciation of the fruits without concomitant experience of the Self. However, because verse 18.57 also suggests a context of meditation (buddhiyogam), it may also refer to meditative renunciation.

It is significant that in the *Upaniṣads*, the word manasā refers to the mind as an instrument that may be both able and unable to lead to self-knowledge. Various passages state that Brahman or the Self (ātman) can be known only through the mind; that is, manasā or cetasā.[4] Śaṅkara's answer to an objector in his commentary on verse 2.21 of the *Bhagavadgītā* suggests that the mind or manas is given this ability for supreme knowledge because it is impossible to attain the Self by means of the senses (see Potter 1981, 297). Yet in verse 2.3.12 of *Kaṭha Upaniṣad*, the word manasā is used for the assertion that no more than speech or the eye is the mind able to reach the Self (naiva vācā na manasā prāptum śakyo na cakṣuṣā). This statement does not necessarily contradict the previous ones on the power of the mind. Rather, it shows that the mind plays the major role in the opening of awareness to the Self, while keeping a nature different from that of the Self as far as individual life is concerned. This confirms the importance we give, in the study of mental renunciation, to determining whether this double-faceted mind of a renouncer experiences the Self or not.

Seemingly, the double nature of the mind or manas can be subsumed by the concept of mediation. Since the range of the mind extends from absorption within the boundaries of action to the silence of eternal freedom in the Self, one dimension of it is ignorance, and the other is direct knowledge of the Self. Because it also mediates between these two poles of experience, it can be seen as a means, from the perspective of the gradual process of purification and opening of awareness to the Self. Yet it can also be viewed as an irrelevant device, when understood from the perspective of the dissolution of the relation of means and goal when realization of the Self actually occurs in the "depths" of consciousness.

The semantic extension of manasā includes both the states of ignorance and knowledge of the Self. Therefore, we can say that it corresponds to the range encompassed by what we have called mental renunciation. This includes renunciation in attitude (abandonment of the fruits of action without concomitant experience of the Self), meditative renuciation, and renunciation in the Self.

Conclusion

This essay has demonstrated the need to identify clearly the main types of renunciation and their possible combinations in the Hindu context by shedding light on the frequent lack of clarity and consistency encountered in secondary literature dealing with categories of renunciation. Having determined the different types of renunciation on the basis of the main objects that may be abandoned, we established the necessity of distinguishing renunciation of the results of action from that of authorship of action. Renunciation of the results has been defined as unselfishness and seen as the "core" of renunciation by many modern scholars. But we have seen that, at least for Advaita, the central role is played by renunciation of authorship as it strengthens that of the results and gives it full depth and permanence. Without concomitance with abandonment of authorship, renunciation of the results of action remains uncertain. It can even become a source of self-delusion if it is understood as a constant striving in the midst of daily activities. In this context, contrary to what is often suggested, renunciation of the results alone does not lead to freedom from bondage. It needs the renunciation of authorship, which comes with the experience of the unbounded reality of the Self, thereby providing freedom in relation to both action and its results. However, due to the relevance of unselfishness to which it refers, even when it is not accompanied by renunciation of authorship, abandonment of the results of action has a wider semantic extension than the other types.

The other feature commonly attributed to renunciation was its definition as an attitude. We have shown that this term does not account for the full range and reality of renunciation. It is often used in a misleading way when understood as the main means or goal of complete inner renunciation. At least for Advaita, all attitudes can belong only to the individual self, never to the inactive Self. Whether or not it is accompanied by renunciation of authorship, an attitude can describe only the reality of renunciation in the sphere of the individual self. When renunciation has reached its full extent in Self-knowledge, it is beyond attitude. This level of renunciation beyond attitude gives full validity to the sphere of renunciation which can be described in terms of attitude.

When distinguishing between physical and mental renunciation of "all actions," again the key for Advaita is renunciation of authorship. When it is absent, then all actions are abandoned only physically. But when it is present, they are renounced in the Self, whether or not they are also on the physical level. Yet since renunciation of authorship is not at all of the same nature as physical renunciation, it can be combined with an active social life as far as the individual self is concerned.

The following chart summarizes the types we have defined on the basis of the object and nature of renunciation:

MAIN TYPES OF RENUNCIATION

TYPE	OBJECT	NATURE
1. Physical renunciation	action or material possession as such	physical
2. Renunciation of the results of action	results of action (particular selfish desires)	mental (renunciation in attitude)
3. Meditative renunciation	a layer of mental activity	mental
4. Renunciation of authorship	authorship of action (all desires, selfish and unselfish)	based on direct Self-knowledge (renunciation in the Self)

The combinations of these types can be summarized as follows. Type 1 and/or type 2 are not necessary and/or sufficient conditions for type 4. Type 4 is a sufficient condition for type 2 but does not necessarily entail type 1.

This typology can clarify the contextual meanings and measure the semantic extension of different traditional Sanskrit terms related to renunciation such as vividiṣāsaṃnyāsa (renunciation of the seeker), vidvatsaṃnyāsa (renunciation of the knower), vairāgya (non-attachment), viveka (discrimination), sarvakarma-saṃnyāsa and tyāga (renunciation of all actions). It can also help recognize shifts of emphasis from one value of renunciation to another in a single work or author or in the course of the history of Advaita or of other schools.

NOTES

1. It would be interesting to use this typology for other schools of thought. For example, according to both Advaita and Viśiṣṭādvaita (qualified non-dualism), Self-knowledge is beyond the activity of Nature or prakṛti . Therefore, even our definition of renunciation of authorship could partially apply to Viśiṣṭādvaita as well, in spite of its different understanding of the nature of that Self that is beyond prakṛti.

2. In a previous paper (Marcaurelle 1985-1987), I have used the expressions qualitative and quantitative renunciation, respectively, for what I now call mental and physical renunciation. I chose these new terms to facilitate understanding.

3. See, for instance, his commentaries on *Bṛhadāraṇaka Upaniṣad* 3.5.1 and 4.5.15; *Chāndogya Upaniṣad* 2.23.1; *Māṇḍūkya Kārikā* 2.36-37; *Bhagavadgītā* 18.3. Karl H. Potter also overlooks these passages when he writes: "It is evident that Śaṃkara does not teach withdrawal from the world at any point along the path of spiritual progress, even at the saṃnyāsa or jīvanmukta stage" (1981, 35). For a detailed analysis of physical and mental types of renunciation in Śaṅkara's works, see my PhD dissertation (Marcaurelle, 1993).

4. See, for example, *Bṛhadāraṇyaka Upaniṣad* 4.4.19; *Muṇḍaka Upaniṣad* 3.1.9; *Kaṭha Upaniṣad* 2.1.11.

BIBLIOGRAPHY

Agrawal, M.M. 1982. *The Philosophy of Non-Attachment*. New Delhi: Motilal Banarsidass.

Bhagat, M.G. 1976. *Ancient Indian Ascetism*. New Delhi: Munshiram Manoharlal.

Chakraborti, Haripada. 1973. *Asceticism in Ancient India*. Calcutta: Punthi Pustak.

Dasgupta, Surendranath. 1952. *A History of Indian Philosophy*. Vol. 2. Cambridge: University Press.

Deutsch, Eliot. 1968. *The Bhagavad Gītā*. New York: Holt Rinehart and Winston.

Edgerton, Franklin. 1952. *The Bhagavad Gītā, Translated and Interpreted*. Vol. 2. Cambridge: Harvard Oriental Series.

Kenghe, C.T. 1976. *Yoga as Depth-Psychology and Para-Psychology*. Vol. 1. Varanasi: Bharata Manisha.

Le Saux, Henri. 1979. *Initiation à la spiritualité des Upanishads*. Sisteron: Editions Présence.

Maharishi Mahesh Yogi. 1969. *Bhagavad-Gita*. New York: Penguin Books.

Marcaurelle, Roger. 1985-1987. "Śaṅkara's Hermeneutics on Renunciation in the *Gītā*." *Journal of Studies in the Bhagavadgītā* 5-7: 98-126.

—. 1988-1989. "States of Consciousness and Meaning in the *Bhagavadgītā*: The Contribution of Maharishi Mahesh Yogi." *Journal of Studies in the Bhagavadgītā* 8-9: 25-47.

—. 1993. *Śaṅkara and Renunciation: A Re-interpretation*. PhD dissertation, McGill University.

Minor, Robert N. 1980. "The Gītā's Way as the Only Way." *Philosophy East and West* 30:339-354.

—. 1982. *Bhagavad-Gītā: An Exegetical Commentary*. New Delhi: Heritage Publishers.

Potter, Karl H. 1965. *Presuppositions of India's Philosophies*. New Delhi: Prentice-Hall of India (Private) Ltd.

—. 1981. *Encyclopedia of Indian Philosophies*. Vol. 3. Delhi: Motilal Banarsidass.

—. "Śaṃkarācārya: The Myth and the Man." *JAAR Thematic Studies* 18:111-125.

Radhakrishnan, Sarvepalli. 1923. *Indian Philosophy*. London: George Allen and Unwin Ltd.

Śaṅkara. 1978. *Works of Śaṅkarācārya in Original Sanskrit*. Vol 2. *Bhagavadgītā with Śaṅkarabhāṣya*. Delhi: Motilal Banarsidass.

Tiwari, Kapil N. 1977. *Dimensions of Renunciation in Advaita Vedānta*. New Delhi: Motilal Banarsidass.

THE VIŚIṢṬĀDVAITA IDEA OF PERVASION (VIBHU) ACCORDING TO THE YATĪNDRAMATADĪPIKĀ

Zayn Kassam-Hann

Introduction

This essay will examine the statement made in the *Yatīndramatadīpikā* that Īśvara is of the nature of vibhu or all-pervasiveness.[1] The *Yatīndramatadīpikā* is a seventeenth-century tract written by the Viśiṣṭādvaita thinker, Śrīnivāsa. As the title suggests, it aims to shed light upon the teachings of Yatīndra, or Rāmānuja, an important Indian philosopher of the Viśiṣṭādvaita school or Śrīvaiṣṇava tradition. It is a manual of key philosophical concepts for students of Viśiṣṭādvaita and, as such, reflects the doctrines of the Ācāryas of the school in the seventeenth century. Its author traces his lineage back to a nephew of Rāmānuja named Daśarathi, who had been appointed the śrīkāryam (overseer) of the Śrīraṅgam temple by Śrī Rāmānuja. While this function was different from that of chief ācārya or authoritative teacher, it nonetheless required an intimate understanding of the key concepts of the school. The position of śrīkāryam remained in Daśarathi's family until at least 1324 C.E. (Carman 1974, 37). In this lineage was Mahācārya (circa late sixteenth or early seventeenth century), who was the immediate teacher of Śrīnivāsa, the author of the *Yatīndramatadīpikā*.

Rāmānuja had devoted his intellectual efforts towards meeting the challenge posed by the Advaitan view, most forcibly articulated by the renowned Śaṅkara, that Brahman is essentially beyond attributes (nirguṇa). The position held by Śaṅkara was viewed by Rāmānuja as tantamount to denying the very existence of the Supreme Deity. In Rāmānuja's opinion, it promulgated an unbridgeable chasm between the positive, worshipable deity of theistic religion and the unknowable — hence unreachable — Absolute of systematic philosophy. This led Rāmānuja to the conclusion that although the attributes of Brahman cannot be exhausted, the testimony of sacred scripture nonetheless affirms the existence of, and leads the way towards, a God who can be known by his attributes and therefore worshipped. Rāmānuja's resolution of the gap between the God of religion and the Absolute of philosophy, lay, in part, in the observation that substance and attributes do not exist independently. They are eternally and internally connected in what is called the dharma-dharmin relationship.

Another way that Rāmānuja overcame the gap between Brahman, the individuals and the world was by arguing that Brahman, cit (all sentient beings or jīvas) and acit (insentient matter or prakṛti), although three categorically distinct and eternal entities, are inseparably and externally connected in what is called the apṛthaksiddhi relationship. The inseparability of substance and attributes as internal distinctions of Brahman, on the one hand, and the inseparability of the three entities of Brahman, cit, and acit as external distinctions, on the other, allowed Rāmānuja to speak of his system as non-dual (advaita). The internal attributes of God and his external attribution or qualification — through his inseparable connection with cit and acit called his modes (prakāras) or body (śarīra) — meant, however, that the nondualism is qualified or differentiated. Hence the name of the school as Viśiṣṭādvaita, the nondualism (advaita) of that which is (internally and externally) differentiated. This metaphysical organization, which created hermeneutic scope encompassing unity and difference, also provided Rāmānuja a way to deal with the problem of evil. All evil comes about from the asssociation of acit with cit; Brahman as the third eternal entity is kept distinct from any ontic identification with evil or even from an act of will as the creation of evil. Accordingly, Brahman as Supreme Deity is distinguished (viśiṣṭa) by all auspicious attributes and is never tainted with the imperfections of qualities that characterize cit and acit. Brahman is also said to be the controller of cit and acit and the possessor of cit and acit as his body (called the śarīra-śarīrin relationship). This permitted Rāmānuja to talk about the supremacy of Brahman.

Given Rāmānuja's view that substance and attribute do not exist independently, it is not surprising to find that the *Yatīndramatadīpikā*, written almost five centuries later, emphasizes the notion that Īśvara, that is, Brahman, is essentially of the nature of vibhu. The position that the Supreme can be known by his attributes, and thereby worshipped, necessitates his all-pervasiveness, for there can exist no auspicious attribute which does not point to him, whether directly or indirectly. Although this is implicit in Rāmānuja's attempt to establish Brahman's position as the inner controller of cit and acit, it is explicit in the*Yatīndramatadīpikā*. The development of this viewpoint establishes the supreme position of Īśvara with respect to five, not two other substances, as in the time of Rāmānuja. The general definition of substance is given as that which is the substratum of attributes (IV:4).[2] In addition to cit and acit (which in this text are referred to as jīva and prakṛti, respectively), kāla (time), dharmabhūtajñāna (attributive consciousness), and nityavibhūti (eternal realm, identified with śuddhasattva, spiritual matter) are also mentioned. The inclusion of time, attributive consciousness and the eternal realm as eternal substances together with jīva and prakṛti is essential, since each of these eternal substances are instruments for the purposes of divine manifestation (IV:55; V:8; VI:3; VII:15, VIII:7).

The semantic range of the term vibhu includes the meanings night, powerful, eminent, supreme, able to, capable of, self-subdued, firm, and self-controlled. The term also means firm, hard, ether, space, time, the soul, lord, master, sovereign, king, supreme ruler, or servant. In Nyāya philosophy, it indicates that which is eternal, existing everywhere, all-pervading, or pervading all material things. In addition, it is used as a name for Brahmā, Śiva and Viṣṇu. The author of the *Yatīndramatadīpikā* uses it specifically to mean all-pervasiveness (vyāpakatva), pointing out that what is pervaded is not more extensive than the pervader (vyāpaka) in respect of space and time. Moreover, that which is pervaded has an invariable relation with the pervader (II:2). It is in this sense that the term will be used in what follows.

Īśvara, says our text, is essentially of the nature of vibhu (IX:14). This all-pervasiveness is of three kinds:

1. by his essential nature (svarūpa);
2. by his attributive consciousness (dharmabhūtajñāna);
3. by his body (vigraha).

Lest there be any doubt that this classification imposes limitations on the Supreme, the text adds that Īśvara is infinite and thereby free from the three kinds of limitations imposed by being determined in space, time and object. Since such doubts may emerge with respect to Īśvara's attachment to the attributive consciousness and his body, we will examine his relations with them in the latter part of our discussion.

The Divine Svarūpa

Consistent with the Viśiṣṭādvaita view that Īśvara cannot be known save through his attributes, the text lists those attributes that determine his essential nature (svarūpa-nirūpaka-dharmāḥ): truth (satya), consciousness (jñāna), bliss (ānanda), purity (amalatva), etc. Although it purports to be a manual that casts light on Rāmānuja's teachings, we must turn elsewhere for clarification in order to understand what is meant by the statement that Īśvara is vibhu by his svarūpa. As Carman points out, Rāmānuja in his *Vedārthasaṃgraha* accepted the well-known idea that the five qualities of Brahman mentioned in the defining

Upaniṣadic texts are "'defining attributes' distinguished from other less essential qualities in the Divine nature" (Carman 1974, 89). Carman also notes that this list, which includes infinity (anantatva) as one of the five defining attributes, is not necessarily exhaustive, for it is followed by ādi (and so forth). The word ādi indicates that the list cannot be exhaustive because Brahman possesses greatness (bṛhattva) and the power of growth (bṛṃhaṇa) — according to the etymologies of the word brahman — and so cannot be subject to any limitation whatsoever. The defining attributes serve a twofold function: first, they set forth a set of qualities whereby the devotee can meditate upon the essential nature of Brahman (Carman 1974, 88, n.2). Second, they establish his freedom — his stainlessness, as it were — from any kind of limitation. According to Carman, Rāmānuja perceived Brahman's essential nature as being "defined without reference to his relation to any other entity" (Carman 1974, 97).

This highlights one of Rāmānuja's central hermeneutical principles, that of the ubhayaliṅgatva, that is, of Brahman's possessing two kinds of attributes: those that emphasize his positive perfections and those that render him free from any kind of imperfection (Carman 1974, 88). In stressing that Brahman can be defined without reference to any other entity, Rāmānuja sought to distance Brahman from sentient beings (cit) and insentient matter (acit) and their imperfections, while simultaneously denying the Advaitin notion that Brahman is essentially beyond attribution. In specifying the defining attributes of Brahman as those qualities to be included in all meditations upon the essential nature of Brahman, Rāmānuja sought to give weight to his central hermeneutic principle that "Scripture exists to instruct us primarily about the nature of and the way to the ultimate" (Lipner 1986, 28). The question then remains: In what way can Īśvara be considered to be all-pervasive with respect to his svarūpa?

The author of the *Yatīndramatadīpikā* does not provide a direct answer, and so we must examine the attributes he lists (in IX:15) for clues to a possible answer:

(a) attributes that determine the essential nature (svarūpanirūpaka-dharmāḥ): truth, consciousness, bliss, purity, etc.;
(b) attributes of the essential nature so determined (nirūpita-svarūpādharmāḥ): knowledge, power, etc.;
(c) attributes useful for creation (sṛṣṭa-upayuktāḥ dharmāḥ) omniscience, omnipotence, etc.;
(d) attributes useful for providing refuge (āśrayaṇa-upayuktāḥ dharmāḥ): love, excellence of disposition, easiness of attainment; and
(e) attributes for protection (rakṣaṇa upayuktadharmāḥ): compassion and others.

We have already discussed the first item, pointing out that Rāmānuja considers these attributes to be the essential attributes of Brahman, and necessary in all meditations upon his essential nature. These attributes also define, albeit not exhaustively, the attributes attending Brahman as distinct from his relation to any other entity. We may note that each of these attributes, viz. truth, consciousness, bliss, purity, etc., connotes the opposite of characteristics that qualify entities in saṃsāra. That is, Brahman is true being as opposed to saṃsāric, karma-bound or ephemeral beings. He is characterized by knowledge rather than nescience; infinity rather than limitation by time, space or matter; bliss rather than sorrow; and purity rather than evil or imperfection. The term ādi, alluded to earlier, may imply the power of growth inherent in the very term Brahman, thus emphasizing his illimitability. It is quite conceivable that for the author of the *Yatīndramatadīpikā* these defining attributes are sufficient to convey, without need for any explanation, the idea that Īśvara is all-pervasive by virtue of his essential nature thus defined. Certainly both the concept of infinitude and the concept of the limitless capacity of Brahman for growth connote all-pervasiveness, for infinitude suggests that there is no entity into which Brahman's reach may not extend. Similarly, existence (satya) has the connotation that there is no other existing entity which does not derive its reality from him. For example, although jīva is said to be eternal and of the nature of sat, jñāna, amalatva, etc. (VII:7), it is still subsidiary to Brahman and controlled by him (VIII:2). Nonetheless, since the author of our text does not specify what he means, it behooves us to examine the remaining attributes. Do they, in his mind, constitute a sufficiently strong link to the essential nature and thereby explain more clearly how Īśvara can be all-pervasive? The idea of pervasion also calls for an examination of those attributes that enter into a relation with other entities, since the concept of pervader is meaningful in relation to that which it pervades.

The remaining four kinds of attributes — which Carman notes are less essential to the divine svarūpa although not less important from the viewpoint of the creature — are those attributes necessary for the meditations on Brahman in relation to other entities. That is, these qualities "cannot exist apart from the subject to which they belong" (Carman 1974, 88, n.1).

These attributes have generally been termed the kalyāṇaguṇas (auspicious qualities) (Carman 1974, 89). It is difficult to determine in our text the exact distinction between the attributes determining the svarūpa of Īśvara (the five defining qualities) and the attributes listed in the second item above. Śrīnivāsa here has in mind the ṣaḍguṇas (six qualities). Carman lists them as jñāna, bala, aiśvarya, śakti, vīrya and tejas (Carman 1974, 92). The usage of the term nirūpita indicates that these attributes are the effect of, or in some manner rest upon, the five defining attributes. Thus they may be considered secondary qualities in contrast to the primary qualities that determine the svarūpa. While these qualities are in no way less important than those that define the svarūpa, their distinction lies in indicating, as was mentioned earlier, that aspect of Brahman which stands in relation to other entities. This separation between the attributes of the svarūpa and the svarūpa so determined, serves once again to reveal the twofold aspect of Brahman: (1) that which marks his essential supremacy in rendering him separate from all other entities; and (2) that which simultaneously establishes him, with respect to his connection with the universe, as the sovereign over all other entities. The author of the *Yatīndramatadīpikā* seems to have had a similar purpose in mind when he draws a distinction between the five defining qualities and the auspicious qualities. In this respect he is simply following Rāmānuja's own distinction between the essential qualities and the auspicious qualities. However, the manual draws distinctions in a more explicit manner than Rāmānuja did.

The statement in our text that describes the forms of Īśvara can explain this observation. Following a list of Īśvara's attributes is a description of the divine being as the creator, protector, and destroyer of the universe. Then we are told that the "Īśvara of such description abides in a fivefold form as para, vyūha, vibhava, antaryāmin and arcāvatāra" (IX:15-17).

The importance of describing Brahman in such a manner lies in establishing his stainlessness with respect to all other entities. At the same time, rather than treading the ideological path of the Advaitin, and thereby concluding that Brahman is beyond attributes (nirguṇa), the Viśiṣṭādvaitin seeks to give reality to the creator of the world. This is accomplished by insisting that although Brahman, in his essential nature, is free from the attributes attending the universe, He is in reality its sovereign, and is so not by virtue of any nescience but of his own divine will. (We remind the reader here of the connotation of bṛhattva and bṛṃhaṇa). Thus, both Rāmānuja and Śrīnivāsa draw upon the kalyāṇaguṇas, the auspicious qualities. These are qualities of Brahman brought into emphasis when viewed in relation to something else to establish the creatorship and thereby the sovereignty of Īśvara. The Viśiṣṭādvaitin seeks to maintain the ontological unity of Brahman, whether it be the Brahman of svarūpa description or of kalyāṇaguṇa description. Regarding the all-pervasiveness of Īśvara with respect to his svarūpa, Śrīnivāsa implicitly connects sovereignty to all-pervasiveness. This sovereignty is specifically displayed in the discussion on causality immediately preceding the discussion of all-pervasiveness in our text. In that discussion, Īśvara is identified as the material, efficient and co-operant cause of the universe; moreover, it is specified that causality rests finally with the one (Īśvara) who is also known as Nārāyaṇa (IX:5). An analysis of the mechanics of such causality reveals that in each case, it is Brahman as qualified by various entities, for example cit and acit, and modes such as immanence in time, etc., which acts as the relevant material, or other, cause. However, that is not the main point of our author, who is careful to remind us that the imperfections latent in these entities and modes do not attach to Brahman. Rather, his point is to disengage the student from the Advaitin notion that the cause of the universe is illusory. That is, the Advaitin position that "Brahman itself owing to nescience is involved in empirical existence" (IX:10). The author of *Yatīndramatadīpikā* argues, as did Rāmānuja, that the denotative power of scriptural texts ascribes causality to Brahman, who is real. For instance, prakṛti cannot be considered to be the cause of the universe, since it is not conscious. Neither may the deities Indra, nor Varuṇa, nor Agni be considered the cause because they are subject to karma. Instead, all these terms point the way to causality resting finally in Nārāyaṇa, who is understood here as being synonymous with Brahman or Īśvara.

In his discussion of the five defining attributes of God's essential nature, Carman draws attention to Rāmānuja's definition of the Supreme Self. Rāmānuja indicates the most important names by which Bhagavān-Nārāyaṇa is known in the Upaniṣads. Carman surmises that these names draw attention to three essential points, viz. that Nārāyaṇa is "the ultimate Reality (sat, tattva); He is the Self (ātmā); and He is Supreme (para, parama, uttama)" (Carman 1974, 99). Carman continues:

> It is this last quality, in particular, which defines His distinctiveness from all other entities. Para here means "higher than," not "other than," but it is being immeasurably higher than all other beings, utterly surpassing them in excellence, that constitutes His "otherness" from finite beings. At the same time He is also "under" and "encompassing" all other entities (Carman 1974, 99-100).

From the preceding it is clear that Rāmānuja considered Brahman, whom he also terms Bhagavān-Nārāyaṇa, to be para or supreme. Paratva is considered to be equivalent to īśitṛtva (lordship). In Carman's view, the five defining qualities imply supremacy (paratva) for Rāmānuja, "since they all are defined in such a way as to contrast distinctively with finite selves" (Carman 1974, 98). However, Carman adds, the five defining qualities "would not seem logically to imply īśitṛtva (lordship), which concerns a *relation* to other existing entities" (Carman 1974, 98). In pointing out that Rāmānuja "deals at the same time with both the essential nature of Brahman and His relation to other entities," Carman builds a case for para as an attribute that establishes Nārāyaṇa's relation to and distinctiveness from other entities. This distinction of being "higher than" other entities implies his "otherness" from finite beings. Because Rāmānuja is not clear on the issue, Carman suggests that he may have viewed the essential nature as implying paratva — which is connotative of īśitṛtva.

Śrīnivāsa is a little more explicit than Rāmānuja with respect to Īśvara as Lord. In his explanation of the para form of Īśvara, he states:

> What is called Para is Nārāyaṇa ... who is qualified by the infinite, auspicious attributes such as knowledge, power, etc. (IX:18).

In an earlier statement (IX:5), causality rests finally with Nārāyaṇa. The sovereignty of Īśvara with respect to the universe is indicated to the devotees by virtue of the para form in which Īśvara abides. However, IX:18 indicates that it is Īśvara of the description of the ṣaḍguṇas who is referred to as para. That is, the qualities of the para form of Īśvara are not strictly the qualities that define Brahman's essential nature. They are those qualities that have been termed auspicious and that are brought to the fore when Brahman is considered in relation to other entities. Our text thus draws a stricter distinction between the description of the svarūpa of Brahman, which retains his purity from the imperfections of relational entities, and that which establishes him in sovereign relation to the universe (the Brahman of ṣaḍguṇa description). Of course, one must bear in mind that the latter is not ontologically different from the former. The distinction posed here is that the Brahman of ṣaḍguṇa description is no less important than the Brahman of svarūpa description. It is to be viewed in relation to the specific "meditation" of him, for example, creation, providing refuge, etc.

Rāmānuja is not clear on whether lordship (īśitṛtva) belongs with the five defining attributes or with the ṣaḍguṇas. It is instructive to note that Śrīnivāsa places the lordship of Īśvara clearly with the auspicious attributes, that is, with the ṣaḍguṇas. This is logically consistent with Rāmānuja's definition of the qualities of the essential nature as those qualities that must be mentioned in all meditations because they indicate Brahman in his essential nature without reference to any other entity. Lordship implies entities over which it is exercised, and therefore it logically must be included in those descriptions of Brahman that contain references to other entities. Śrīnivāsa does not specify exactly what he means when he says that Īśvara is all-pervasive by virtue of his essential nature. He may mean either or both of two things: (1) that He is so in a general manner, by the connotations of the attributes of the essential nature such as infinitude, by the implications of the usage of the term ādi, and by the etymologies of the word Brahman as possessing greatness and the power of growth; or (2) that He is so in a specific sense, by his lordship which implies his supremacy, which is itself included in the secondary description of his auspicious qualities. In his essential qualities and his auspicious qualities, it is the very same being that is referred to. The distinction is made, however, so as to render him both free from the limitations of other entities and, concurrently, the same real being who enters into a relationship with other entities, thus vilifying the Advaitin positions mentioned earlier.

We now turn to the statement that Īśvara is all-pervasive with respect to his attributive consciousness (dharmabhūtajñāna) and his body (vigraha). In these discussions our focus will be on Īśvara as He stands in relation to the world.

The Attributive Consciousness

In its chapter on the attributive consciousness (dharmabhūtajñāna), our text states that it is always eternal (nitya) and all-pervasive (vibhu) with respect to Īśvara (VII:2). The definition of vibhu includes as one of its meanings that it is eternal (nitya). While dharmabhūtajñāna is all-pervasive, it is of the nature of dravya-guṇa (substance-attribute). Substance is defined as "that which is the abode of states." There is no contradiction in dharmabhūtajñāna being simultaneously substance and attribute. Like light, says our text, it is possible for attributive consciousness to extend beyond its substrate. It is substance in that, like light, it is the possessor of attributes such as diffusion (VII:9). It is attribute because, as with light, it not only reveals itself but also manifests other objects for a knower or percipient other than itself. It is clearly identified as an immaterial substance that exists not for itself but for another (VI.1). Immateriality is identified as self-luminosity. It is itself a non-conscious (acetana) substance (VII:1) and hence, although self-illumined, it cannot know either itself or the other entities that it reveals. It can only show these to a knower.

To whom does it show itself and other entities? One of the attributes listed both in the description of Īśvara's essential nature and in the list of auspicious qualities is jñāna. It is evident therefore that Īśvara is the knower of that which dharmabhūtajñāna shows. Thus, the relationship between Īśvara and dharmabhūtajñāna is one of perceiver and means of perception, respectively. Dharmabhūtajñāna is the means of perception in that it casts light over itself and other entities. The objects of perception are itself, the world and the selves, as dharmabhūtajñāna casts light over them and shows them to the percipient, who is Īśvara. The knowledge of Īśvara is "of the nature of universal realization" (sarvasākṣātkārarūpam) (VII:13). That is, with respect to Īśvara, the attributive consciousness reveals all things in their entirety, without any fragmentation. The knowledge of Īśvara is for this reason all-pervasive, since those things that are pervaded, that is, the objects of his perception, do not extend beyond his reach. In this respect dharmabhūtajñāna functions as the means through which Īśvara perceives. Is He dependent on his means of knowledge, thereby introducing a limitation upon his self-sufficiency? Our text replies that He is not, for knowledge is one of the attributes of the essential nature of Brahman, and so the being (satya) of Brahman cannot be found without its jñāna, amalatva, anantatva, ānanda, etc. (ādi).

While dharmabhūtajñāna is classified as an eternal substance along with jīva and prakṛti, can it be said to be in a śarīra-śarīrin (body-possessor of body) relationship with him? It is said that He "has everything except Himself and his consciousness as His body" (IX:1). The term used for "his consciousness" is svajñāna. Jñāna, in turn, is identified as one of the synonyms of dharmabhūtajñāna (VII:11). We would argue that since the jñāna of Brahman is an internal distinction, both with respect to his svarūpa and his auspicious qualities (ṣaḍguṇas), it is conceivable that none of these may be considered to be in a śarīra-śarīrin relationship with him. Certainly the question may be posed why the remaining ṣaḍguṇas are not also given eternal attribute status as in the case of dharmabhūtajñāna. One possibility is that in addition to Brahman's innate capacity for growth, knowledge is essential to provide direction to that growth. It is considered sufficiently important to be given the status of an eternal self-luminous substance, existing solely for the purpose of a knower, be that Īśvara primarily, or the jīva secondarily.

In summary, the relationship of Īśvara with the attributive consciousness is an internal relationship by means of which Īśvara controls or otherwise expresses his supremacy over the universe. It would not be fitting for this relationship to be subsumed under the śarīra-śarīrin relationship, which, as we will see below, is characterized as an external rather than an internal relationship. Śrīnivāsa terms it more precisely a dharma-dharmin relationship, that is, a substance-attribute relationship in which Īśvara is the dharmin with respect to dharmabhūtajñāna.

A similar case arises in the relationship between the individual self (jīva) and dharmabhūtajñāna. The individual self is part of the body of Īśvara and the dharmabhūtajñāna is its invariable accompanier. The individual self knows of changes only through it, as manas (mind) and its synonyms. All the various states of perception (pratyakṣa) — inference (anumāna), verbal testimony (śabda), etc. — which are the basis for epistemology, are termed "particular modes of the dharmabhūtajñāna." Yet at the same time they are the innumerable attributes (guṇa) of the individual self (VII:13). In this case, we again see that although dharmabhūtajñāna is an insentient substance that is the substratum of various modes and states, it functions as the various attributes of the individual self, which is the sentient cognizer of the states and changes presented to it through the mind and its knowledge. The essential nature of the jīva is described as jñānatva, aṇūtva, amalatva, etc., knowledge being considered to be an attribute of the essential nature of the jīva. The jīva is regarded as being distinct from: (1) manas, also identified as buddhi, etc. (IV:10), which is listed as one of the synonyms for dharmabhūtajñāna (VII:11) as the instrument of consciousness; and (2) knowledge itself, by virtue of the consciousness, "I know by mind" and "I know" respectively (VIII:3). For both Īśvara and the jīva, jñāna is classified as one of the attributes of their essential natures. Simultaneously, they are both held to be distinct from their consciousness, for jñāna has no significance except in so far as it is the means of perception for them. The dharmabhūtajñāna is all-pervasive with respect to Īśvara, but not so with respect to the individual self. The jñāna of the individual self is only a mode or dharma of the dharmabhūtajñāna of Brahman. Although the relationship between the jīva and the dharmabhūtajñāna is an inseparable relationship similar to the relationship between Īśvara and dharmabhūtajñāna, in the case of the jīva, dharmabhūtajñāna is not merely a dharma, but is both dharma and dharmin. It is the dharmin of which the jīva's jñāna is a dharma, while in the case of Īśvara, its dharmin-ness is co-extensive with its dharma-ness and hence cannot be differentiated.

We have seen that dharmabhūtajñāna is a key concept in the relationship of Īśvara with the world and the selves. This indicates that the statement that Īśvara is all-pervasive with respect to the attributive consciousness must indicate the Īśvara of ṣaḍguṇa qualification, since this admits of relations with the universe. The auspicious attribute "knowledge" becomes operative through dharmabhūtajñāna as his instrument without causing any loss of stature for Īśvara, because He is the substrate of which his knowledge is the attribute. The knowledge of Īśvara in this instance is universal, and it is in this regard that it is all-pervasive.

The Divine Body

We turn now to the third manner in which Īśvara is considered to be all-pervasive, that is, by his body (vigraha) (IX:4). As has been said, our text identifies six eternal substances (IV:5). Of these, all except Īśvara himself and the dharmabhūtajñāna form the body of Īśvara. The relationship between Īśvara and his body is said to be that of śarīra-śarīrin (body-possessor of body). We have already drawn attention to one of the definitions given of body (śarīra), viz. that it is "that substance which is different from Īśvara and His knowledge." Another definition characterizes it as that substance "which has an inseparable relation (apṛthaksiddhi) with the sentient invariably as ādheya (supported), vidheya (controlled) and śeṣa (subsidiary)" (IV:53).

Bearing this latter definition in mind, let us look at Īśvara's relationship with the universe. The universe is held to be the effect of which Brahman is the cause. The analogy given for this relationship is that the universe is the manifestation of something that is yet in an unmanifest state, just as a pot is the manifestation of a pre-existent state, namely a lump of clay. The clay is prakṛti, and the universe is Īśvara modified by prakṛti, or acit, and jīva, or cit. This process of change from one mode to another is known as satkāryavāda, that is, the universe is already existent, sat, although not in the form that it is now. Brahman is the material, efficient and co-operant cause of the universe. It is the material cause in that the "object which is competent to undergo modification in the form of effect" (prakṛti) cannot exist apart from it. The other two causes are instrumental in modifying and producing the effect. Therefore, to use the example of a potter, the potter is the efficient cause of which the clay is the material cause, and the potter's wheel is the co-operant cause. Although Brahman is not identical with the effect, He is nonetheless non-different from it in the sense that the substance of the universe cannot exist apart from Brahman, who is the antaryāmin (indweller) and śeṣin (controller) of the universe. Hence, it is in this sense that we understand the statement that Īśvara is vibhu by virtue of his body.

The body of Īśvara, says our text, is twofold — eternal and non-eternal:

> ... the eternal is the body of Īśvara, which is of the nature of prakṛti made up of the three guṇas, time, the jīvas, and the divine, auspicious figure in Vaikuṇṭha. And the natural forms of Garuḍa, Śeṣa and others who belong to the class of nityasūris (are also eternal) (IV:55).
>
> The non-eternal is twofold: non-karma-made and karma-made. The first consists of the forms of Īśvara, such as mahat etc. Likewise are forms of Ananta, Garuḍa etc. assumed at their wish. The karma-made is also twofold: karma-made assisted by one's own will and purely karma-made. The former is that of Saubhari, etc., and the latter that of others (IV:56).

Īśvara is said to be all-pervasive and infinite. In being infinite, He is free of the three-fold limitation of determination by space, time and object (deśa, kāla, vastu) (IX.14). Nonetheless, our text declares Īśvara as abiding in five forms listed as para, vyūha, vibhava, antaryāmin and arcā (I:5; IX:17). The verb avasthita (to abide in) is used in the case of arcāvatāra, antaryāmin and vyūha; āvirbhāva (to descend into) in the case of vibhava; and the verb "to be" is understood in the case of para. The tension underlying Īśvara's "manifestation," so to speak, as his body, whether eternal or non-eternal, and in these five forms, lies in whether He is thereby limited in any way. Is his all-pervasiveness compromised? Moreover, is this the chasm that impels the Advaitin therefore to speak of Īśvara as bound by nescience when in connection with the universe?

We have already noted how the distinction between the para form and the divine svarūpa enables the conception of a real being who is empowered with lordship over all other entities without being tainted by the qualities attached to them (e.g., evil). The vyūha form, which is for the purposes of creation and of meditation upon by the devotees (IX:19), is said to be the para form of Brahman abiding (avasthita) as the fourfold vyūha form. It is interesting to observe that the qualities describing this fourfold form are the ṣaḍguṇas listed above as the auspicious attributes attending Nārāyaṇa, who is the form of Brahman-in-relation as distinct from Brahman-in-himself. Īśvara's "creation up to the four-faced (Brahmā)" (IV:71) is said to be immediate, and it is mediate after that. The significance of this statement, in my view, lies in the attempt made by Śrīnivāsa to maintain the distance between the divine svarūpa and the direct mechanics of creation, thereby re-emphasizing the importance of the two-fold aspect of Brahman outlined above. Of the vibhava form — the descent of Īśvara in the form of avatāras (principally ten) — our text points out that "the cause for the descent is (Īśvara's) will only, and not karma" (IX:25). The modes of each of the ten avatāras are potentially infinite, although not all are necessarily full or to be worshipped. The antaryāmin form, whereby Īśvara abides (avasthita) with the heart as the friend of the individual self in its states of experiencing heaven, hell, etc., is perceptible to the yogis alone (IX:26). There are, we may surmise, potentially as many antaryāmin as there are jīva. However, although Īśvara "co-exists with the individual self, He is untouched by the taints inherent in it" (IX:26). Arcāvatāra is that form of Īśvara which accepts (svīkṛtya) for its body the substance chosen by the devotees, and abides (avasthita) with it in a non-material (aprākṛta) body. Arcāvatāra is said to be pūrṇa (full, replete) in this form (IX:27).

Our author has, in his descriptions of each of these forms, intimated two significant points. First, Īśvara is all-pervasive with respect to these forms because in the para and vyūha forms it is the Īśvara of ṣaḍguṇa description that is made manifest. In the vibhava, antaryāmin and arcāvatāra forms, his modes are potentially infinite, and his connection to these forms is through śuddhasattva, self-luminous, immaterial substance. As such, He is untainted by its connection with cit and acit. These forms are assumed at his will even if at the devotee's request, and He may choose to withdraw from them. The purpose of his manifestation in these forms is for the well-being of the universe, for meditation by the devotees, and for the granting of refuge to the devotees. In them, He is not subject to karma and so nescience, thus nullifying the Advaitin argument.

Second, his connection with cit and acit by virtue of the immaterial substance, śuddhasattva — which exists primarily for his sake, and which is controlled by him — places a mediatory substance between himself and the limiting adjuncts of cit and acit. This secures for him a purity that could not be possible were He to be directly attached to them. At the same time, He is pūrṇa in all these forms. Although the forms themselves are disparate, they are the means by which the devotee may perceive that vision of him which the devotee is capable of, or which He chooses to reveal to the devotee. It may be argued that the devotee can still see the full form of Īśvara through the grace of Bhagavān by way of physical perception, since the indriyas (sense-perception organs) are controlled by the manas and hence related to dharmabhūtajñāna, to which perception of the immaterial is possible. Or the devotee may resort to perception independent of sense (apekṣa), or to prior or ancient perception (I:16). In the final analysis, the vision of Brahman rests upon his grace.

NOTES

1. The author wishes to gratefully acknowledge the many suggestions made by Professor Katherine K. Young, McGill University, in the development of this essay.

2. All references to the *Yatīndramatadīpikā* are made in parentheses indicating chapter and verse numbers. Swāmī Ādidevānanda's translation appears in all quotations.

BIBLIOGRAPHY

Carman, John Braisted. 1974. *The Theology of Rāmānuja: An Essay in Interreligious Understanding*. New Haven and London: Yale University Press.

Lipner, Julius. 1986. *The Face of Truth: A Study of Meaning and Metaphysics in the Vedāntic Theology of Rāmānuja.* Albany: State University of New York Press.

Ādidevānanda, Swāmī, trans. 1967. *Yatīndramatadīpikā. Sanskrit text, English translation and notes.* 2d ed. Mylapore, Madras: Sri Ramakrishna Math.

Vidyarthi, P.B. 1967. *Knowledge, Self and God in Ramanuja: A Study in the Theoretical Foundations of the Theism of Ramanuja.* New Delhi: Oriental Publishers and Distributors.

PART II

STRATEGIES FOR INTERPRETING INDIAN TEXTS

THE MĪMĀṂSĀ THEORY OF TEXT INTERPRETATION

Shrinivas Tilak

Introduction

Traditional religious discourse has been the subject of increasingly radical analysis in the post-modern West.[1] What happens when a religious discourse is textualized? What is the semantic status of a sacred text with reference to its potential reader? Is it possible to determine and organize the meanings of a sacred text without appealing to an author who establishes and validates its meaning (Clooney 1987)? Similar questions arose in the Indian tradition.

Since the meaning of the Saṃhitā portion of the Vedas (the earliest sacred texts, composed sometime between 1900 and 1200 B.C.E.)[2] was initially deemed indisputable, a general theory of interpretation was not found necessary. Even the early Brāhmaṇa texts (c. 1200-1000 B.C.E.) were less concerned about a text's meaning than about its transmission and survival. Vedic texts were compiled, put into private circulation, and valorized without much concern regarding the identity of their authors. The anonymity of texts caused no difficulties since their antiquity, whether real or imaginary, was regarded as a sufficient guarantee of their status. The authority of the Saṃhitās was a matter of faith, and the religious meaningfulness of the Vedic sacrifices and rituals was not subject to disputes or controversies.

But with the continuing expansion of Vedic culture and the elaboration of rituals and sacrifices in the later Brāhmaṇas (c. 1000-800 B.C.E.), conflicts arose over competing commands and the priorities of sacrificial detail. Concern about the proper interpretation of the Vedic Saṃhitās also appeared in the later Brāhmaṇas. In the subsequent stratum of literature, the Āraṇyakas (c. 800-600 B.C.E.), an emphasis on the oneness of truth created the agenda of a unified meaning of the Saṃhitās and Brāhmaṇas. And in the next stratum, the Upaniṣads (from c. 600 B.C.E.), promotion of asceticism (involving withdrawal from sacrificial action, if not all action) challenged the very basis of Vedic ritual. The rise of heterodox schools such as Jainism and Buddhism (c. 600-400 B.C.E.) threatened to undermine further the Vedas and their commands to perform ritual action by changing the locus of authority from revelation to personal experience rooted in spiritual knowledge and meditation. Sacrificial action was denounced as a barrier to enlightenment, and the Vedas were deemed superfluous.

The Mīmāṃsā Theory of Text Interpretation

The principal concern of Mīmāṃsā, which is one of the six major systems of philosophy (darśana) in India, is the interpretation of the actions enjoined in Vedic texts. Derived from the Sanskrit verbal root "man" meaning to think or investigate, Mīmāṃsā means systematic reflection. The Mīmāṃsakas believed that the proper performance of Vedic sacrifices depends upon the correct interpretation of Vedic injunctions. Aphorisms attributed to Jaimini (*Jaimini Sūtra*, henceforth abbreviated as *JS*), form the first systematic work composed with that task in mind.[3]

This school of thought emerged to preserve the "authority" of the Vedas (and their commands to perform sacrifices) in the face of various challenges such as promotion of the concepts of: (1) a single truth embodied in the teachings recorded in sacred texts attributed to a historical person; (2) renunciation instead of action; and (3) experience instead of revelation. Central to these issues was the nature of the text, its meaning and its interpretation. Accordingly, the notion of hermeneutics first emerged in Indian tradition with the discussion of different ways of interpreting injunctions (vidhis) in the Vedas. The Vedic injunctions prescribe different sacrificial actions to suit various goals, and yet all Vedic injunctions were recognized to be free from errors and contradictory meanings. Consequently, a particular problem for the Mīmāṃsakas was how to correlate meaningful sacrificial action with objective textual interpretation. This problem provided the impetus for the development of rival theories of meaning that located objective textual interpretation in words (śabdārtha, śābdabodha), in sentences (vākyārtha), or in both words and sentences. These developments, in turn, gave rise to theories of text interpretation as well as to an incipient hermeneutics in ancient India.[4]

The Mīmāṃsā theory of interpretation is based upon an analysis of the *imperative* (liṅg) mode, because the core of the Vedas is defined by commands to perform sacrificial acts accompanied by recitation of sacred mantras. These commands also guide everyday acts. What transpires in the imperative mode between the injunctions to act and live is the emergence of apūrva, the verbal realization of a signifying consequence. This signifying consequence, however, is synonymous not with a psychological intention, but exclusively with an action that takes place in the world.

To command or to signify is to use language, and to use language is to do so according to certain lexical and syntactic rules that are related to actual use in the world. The Mīmāṃsakas thought that Sanskrit is regulated by real usage as codified by Pāṇini, and not by abstract prescription or speculative freedom.[5] In their opinion, a word has a strict and inborn (nitya) meaning, a specific purpose. In a text, meaning is generated by the inborn meaning of words in association with a strictly ordained series of syntactical bridges to other words and meanings. Even figurative language in the Vedas is part of the actual, not virtual, structure of language (although it is otherwise elusive and at the mercy of the virtuosic interpreter). It is, therefore, a resource of the collectivity of language users.

According to Jaimini, the Vedas are apauruṣeya, that is, they are not the work of human or even divine authors (*JS* 1:1.5). This basic claim of Mīmāṃsākas such as Jaimini may be restated as the "semantic autonomy" of the Vedic texts. The concept of apauruṣeya is the chief hermeneutical strategy to explain the logic of human action. It provides a framework that permits actions to express both a diversity of interests and an underlying authority. The Mīmāṃsakas also invoked this claim in the context of their definition of dharma as that which motivates people to do right actions (codanālakṣaṇo'rtho dharmaḥ, *JS* 1:1.2).[6] Action, they contended, is the very essence of human existence. Without action knowledge is fruitless, and without action happiness is impossible. The Mīmāṃsakas undertook the scrutiny of all actions enjoined in the Vedas on this basic premise. For this purpose, they divided the Vedic corpus into two broad divisions — sacred formulae (mantras) and injunctions (vidhis). A key hermeneutical concern for the Mīmāṃsakas was the interpretation of Vedic injunctions that motivate people to act.

The Mīmāṃsākas devised a method of explaining the formal structure of the Vedic texts to clarify the meaning and significance of sacrifices and ceremonies. Although it was applied principally to injunctions dealing with sacrifices, this method was soon extended to the interpretation of legal texts in order to settle doubtful points. It also generated a lively controversy over the nature of the inerrancy and eternity of the Vedas as a text. In fact, an important stage of Indian hermeneutics may be traced to the attempts by Mīmāṃsakas such as Jaimini, Śabara, Kumārila, and Prabhākara to defend their position against attacks by thinkers belonging to both orthodox schools — the Naiyāyikas and the Vaiyākaraṇas — and heterodox schools — the Buddhists, particularly those advocating the doctrines of emptiness (śūnyavāda) or consciousness only (vijñānavāda).

The Mīmāṃsā Theory of Meaning in the Context of the Larger Indian Debate

Indian theories of meaning started by acknowledging that both words and sentences are used meaningfully. But they differed regarding just how meanings understood from sentences are related to meanings of individual words (padas) in sentences. Indeed, the principal bone of contention was whether or not sentences and their meanings are to be recognized as independent of words and their meanings. Traditionally, the compound śābdabodha, the central concept around which the notion of meaning revolves, is defined as comprehension or import that pertains to words (śabdānāmayam, śābdaścāsau bodhaśca). Śābdabodha, thus, is the cognition of the meaning of words in a sentence. When comprehending the meaning of any sentence, a person first understands its denotation and then its denotative potentiality (abhidhāśakti). Recollection and determination of meaning is effected by considering these two together. This process, in turn, engenders the import or the meaning of the sentence (Rao 1969, 1).

The general theory of linguistic meaning was further developed by various schools. The Vaiyākaraṇas (grammarians), led by Bhartṛhari, held that the sentence has a peculiar capacity through which it is capable of expressing meaning (vākyasya vākyārthe śaktiḥ). A mystic entity (called sphoṭa) — which is one, indivisible, eternal, and manifested by the letters of the sentence — is responsible for its meaning; it is called the akhaṇḍavākyasphoṭa. This is the primary sphoṭa. All other varieties of sphoṭa are subsidiary to it. There is no meaning of words apart from the meaning of the sentence. It is only by way of exclusion (apoddhara) that words acquire meanings. Superimposition (adhyāsa), moreover, relates words to their meanings. The division of the sentence into words, therefore, is false (*Vākyapadīyam* II:10, Hattori 1980, Rao 1969, 30).

An opposing theory holding that the meaning of a sentence is the relation of the individual meanings expressed by component words (abhihitānvayavāda) was championed by Mīmāṃsakas, led by Kumārila (see his gloss *Ślokavārttika* on *Jaimini Sūtras* 1:1.25). In his view, the sentential meaning is simply the meanings of individual words brought into relation with each other by dint of expectancy (ākāṅkṣā), semantic fit (yogyatā), and propinquity (sannidhi).[7] Words cease to play a direct role as signifiers once they have signified their own meanings; they now convey a sentential meaning.[8] Sentential meanings are also indirectly linked with other constitutive words, through the intermediary of word meanings, by the relation called implication (lakṣaṇā), which also serves to connect words with secondary meanings.

A lively controversy is recorded in the commentaries of Śabara (*Śābarabhāṣya*, henceforth abbreviated as *ŚB*) and Kumārila (*Ślokavārttika*, or *ŚV*) on the *Jaimini Sūtra*. The contribution to hermeneutics that Śabara and Kumārila made is easily discernible in their glosses on *JS* 1:1.5, which discusses at length the problem of the meaning of words according to different schools of philosophy. Jaimini opens his defence of the inerrancy of the Vedic injunctions by boldly proclaiming that Vedic injunctions are the only means to know dharma (*JS* 1:1.2). In the next two dozen aphorisms (*JS* 1:1.6-30), he quickly builds his case for the self-sufficiency and autonomy of the Vedas. In the process, he presents the rudiments of semantics. The relationship between words and their meanings, Jaimini asserts, is invariable (nitya) (*JS* 1.1.5). Communication through language is made possible by two universally intertwined and manifesting factors: (1) the sounded word (śabda); and (2) the object denoted by the word (artha). Together they constitute the self-existent universe of linguistic reality, which is not subject to change, decay or destruction. As they become manifest, a dual world of creation — words and objects — emerges.[9]

According to Śabara, Jaimini thought that language is both an ordained institution (which is unchanging, immutable, logical, rational, and intelligible), and also an instrument (which is contingent and signifies meaning anchored in specific Vedic injunctions). Each injunction is its own unique occasion and, as such, is firmly anchored in the worldly context in which it is applied. And because the Vedas, which are the epitome of divine-human language, are texts that order and textualize sacrificial acts, Mīmāṃsā interpretation accepts as inevitable the interplay between a text and its context (prakaraṇa). It is this interplay that generates meaning, indeed, that makes meaning possible at all.

Because Jaimini contended that words are autonomous with respect to meaning (*JS* 1:1.5, 16 and 18), he did not accept the arguments that: (1) the sentence is the basic unit of meaning; and (2) a word acquires meaning only in the context of a sentence. Truth is an attribute of sentences, not of independent words (*JS* 1:1.24-26). Both Śabara and Kumārila raised questions about the doctrine of śabdapramāṇa (verbal testimony) accepted by Jaimini. What is involved in hearing words? Does the peculiarly linguistic understanding (śābdabodha) amount to knowledge (pramā), or does it depend on certain other conditions?[10] Śabara and Kumārila also provided a detailed account of the Naiyāyika and Buddhist positions (*ŚB* and *ŚV* on *JS* 1: 1.6-11).

The Mīmāṃsakas asserted that there is no possibility of error in the Vedas because truth and meaning, with which Vedic injunctions are concerned, existed before the seers (ṛṣis) who apprehended them. The truth and meaning of the Vedas continue to exist, moreover, even when the seers are long gone. Vedic truths, being eternal, impersonal, and autonomous, have nothing to do with their seers.[11]

The main opposition to this claim was led by the Buddhists (although Jaimini did not identify them as such). They argued that the recurrence of the same word uttered simultaneously by different persons at different places would not be possible if the word were an eternal entity, as claimed by the

Mīmāṃsakas (*JS* 1:1.11). Jaimini rebutted this, arguing that just as many people at different places simultaneously perceive the sun, so they are able to utter the same word with the same meaning (*JS* 1:1.15). To the objection that words undergo modifications, which would not be possible if they were eternal (*JS* 1:1.10), Jaimini replied that no such modifications are possible. What appears to be modified is, in fact, the manifestation of other words (*JS* 1:1.16). Words merely exist unperceived. The fact that verbal utterances are brought about by human agency does not mean that words have a beginning in time and space and so cannot be eternal.

The Mīmāṃsakas also argued that a new word cannot be coined by randomly putting together disparate sounds. The image of a human or divine agent "creating or ordering a language for the purpose of using it as a tool," as advanced by the Naiyāyikas (logicians), was dismissed by the Mīmāṃsakas as a naive fiction (Jha 1978, 56). Languages cannot be invented nor can the meanings associated with words. Mere subjective willing cannot make words say something other than what they do say. This is the objectivity of the language. The Mīmāṃsakas' claim that understanding is essentially linguistic (śābdabodha) differs radically from the view of language favoured by the non-Mīmāṃsakas, who saw language as a tool for manipulating or transforming consciousness (*Ślokavārttika* on *JS* 1:1.20-22).

The Naiyāyikas endorsed Kumārila's line of argument but added that the knowledge of purport (tātparya) is a necessary condition of verbal import (śābdabodha). Purport is the ancillary cause (sahakārīkāraṇa) of the word in generating verbal import. It is crucial in sentences with double meanings. In their opinion, it is either the context (prakaraṇa) or the intention of the writer (vaktṛtātparya) that settles the meaning of the sentence. The *Muktāvalī*, an important Nyāya text, said that since the context varies, it cannot be the comprehensive cause (anugatakāraṇa) of determining meaning. Udayana, the great Nyāya thinker, argued that purport is a necessary concept in addition to word-meaning (padārtha) and sentence-meaning (vākyārtha). He defined it as "the nature of that word which is used with a particular intention by the speaker (yaduddeśena śabdaḥ pravṛttaḥ sa tatparaḥ) (*Nyāyakusumāñjali* II:13-14, cited in Rao 1969, 235). Purport, therefore, according to the Naiyāyikas, is a separate potentiality (vṛtti) by which meaning is understood. There is, then, no case at all for the Mīmāṃsakas' concept of implication (Rao 1969, 235).

The Naiyāyika view of purport was contested by Prabhākara, the Mīmāṃsā thinker, in his gloss (*Bṛhatī* on *Jaimini Sūtras* 1:1.25). A word that means something, he argued, is always a related word, and the intended meaning is always a related meaning. This theory of meaning-in-relation is known as anvitābhidhānavāda (the expression of things as they are syntactically related). According to Prabhākara, each word bears not only its own meaning but also its syntactical relation to other words in the sentence. By their recalling capacity (smārikā śaktiḥ), words merely recall substances. But it is their comprehensional capacity (anubhāvikā śaktiḥ) that expresses the sentential meaning (Rao 1969, 92-93). A word such as "pot," for instance, means "pot" as related to enjoined activity.[12] An accomplished act or a ready-made object does not generate any useful meaning. Meaning is located in something to be achieved. Thus, the import of all Vedic injunctions aims at establishing kārya, or what is to be done or achieved.

Prabhākara found Kumārila's views on sentential meaning too cumbersome, since three capacities are attributed to words: (1) for their meanings; (2) to effect relation among them; and (3) to effect the first two capacities. In his own theory only one capacity of words, in the form of syntactical connection, is required. Thus, there is brevity in his theory (*Nyāyaratnāvali*) (Rao 1969, 94).

Dignāga, the Buddhist thinker, proposed a controversial theory based on the concept of apoha in his *Pramāṇasamuccaya.* He thought that a word expresses the object qualified by the exclusion of other things (arthāntaranivṛtti, anyāpoha). Following Bhartṛhari, he claimed that a single word in a sentence has no meaning. The individual meanings of words are conjoined (upaśliṣṭa) giving rise to a "flash" of unified meaning immediately after the speaker's utterance of the sentence. This flash is not brought forth through the process of relating the different concepts formed one by one in accordance with the gradual utterances of individual words. It is immediate and intuitional (note the similarity to the psychological approach of Schleiermacher). Bhartṛhari regarded this immediate flash of meaning as the real meaning of the sentence and expressed it by the term pratibhā, that which appears to the mind, that which becomes clear or manifest. Śabdabrahman, the ultimate reality of the nature of the word (or language), takes the form of pratibhā before it is manifested as phenomenal words. As the primary evolute of the śabdabrahman, pratibhā transcends the temporal sequence of sounds and the diversity of forms that characterize phenomenal words. It is recognized as the prior form of phenomenal words (vāgvikārāṇām prakṛtiḥ). It resides in the mind of the speaker before the sounds are uttered. Through the sounds that constitute the phenomenal words, the listener is awakened to pratibhā.

According to Dignāga, pratibhā is the internal awareness of the idea produced by a sentence. Different individuals may have a different internal awareness, which may not be communicated to others. However, different pratibhās are generalized and regarded as the object denoted by the sentence, since they have a common feature in that they are distinguished from those produced by another sentence. The sentence denotes its meaning through its "differentiation from others" (anyāpoha) (Hattori 1980). Such is the Buddhist theory of the meaning of a sentence (and by extension of a text) on the basis of these important statements of Dignāga.

The Authority of Text or the Authority of Author: The Ancient Indian Debate in the Light of Contemporary Approaches to Hermeneutics

In what follows, an attempt is made to reconstruct the beginnings of hermeneutics in the Indian tradition in the light of current theories of text interpretation provided by David Klemm, E.D. Hirsch, H. Gadamer, Michel Foucault and Paul Ricoeur.

One task of modern hermeneutics is to determine the meaning of an obscure text, which once clearly disclosed the spirit of a community's self-image or self-understanding, and thereby save it from meaninglessness or misinterpretation. According to Klemm, meaning must be objective in the sense that it resides in a text as an ideal object to be recovered by the interpreter. For this type of project, meaning is not the subjective construction of the interpreter; it is objective (Klemm 1986, 1:35).

If Klemm sees the text itself as providing objective meaning, Hirsch sees the author's intention as providing this. Hirsch argues that the author's intention constitutes a text's sole meaning. Validity in interpretation, moreover, demands an unchanging and definite meaning; if meaning changes in different contexts or is indefinite, then interpretation is a free-for-all (Hirsch 1967, 1976). Hirsch's theory of interpretation continues the tradition of Schleiermacher, who also postulated objective meaning and identified it with an author's meaning. Schleiermacher argued that the tools of the philologist succeeded in illuminating only the surface or "vocabulary" levels of the text. By themselves they failed to reveal the deeper, spiritual aspects of the discourse, which Schleiermacher called the "divinatory" or "psychological" level. Understanding an author, then, means more than understanding his or her words. It means understanding the spirit that initiated and controlled authorship. An author's vocabulary is a possession shared with fellow beings. What is noteworthy about an author's work — and the basis of its survival — is what can be done with this common possession (Howard 1982, 9-10). Schleiermacher thought that the unifying insight of the author must be present in each portion of the work's composition. It is an inner dynamic, like that in a bead of mercury which, even when shattered, continues in its fragments to manifest the same shape as the original. The interpreter begins with a part, but looks for the whole which is represented by the author's intention. The actual practice of hermeneutics becomes a part-whole-part movement, a continual dialectical process, which constitutes the famous "hermeneutical circle" (Hoy 1978, 2ff.).

For scholars such as Klemm who argue that texts have an objective sense located in the formal structure of the text itself, interpreting a text is not a matter of empathy with the lived experience of an author. In the words of one modern hermeneuticist:

> Literary interpretation in England and America operates, philosophically speaking, largely in the framework of realism. It tends to presuppose, for instance, that the literary work is simply "out there" in the world, essentially independent of its perceivers. One's perception of the work is considered to be separate from the "work itself". The author's intentions too, are held rigidly separate from the work; the work is a "being" in itself, a being with its own powers and dynamics. A typical modern interpreter generally defends the "autonomy of being" of the literary work, and sees his work as that of penetrating this being through textual analysis (Palmer 1969, 5).

Thus, a major debate in modern hermeneutics concerns whether the text itself or the author's intention provides the objectivity or authority for interpretation.

I shall now reformulate the ancient debate between the Mīmāṃsakas and their opponents by using the arguments of contemporary hermeneutics.[13] This involves constructing two competing arguments, each representing a particular ideal type of hermeneutical inquiry. Using the insights provided by Rogers (1969) and Hekman (1983) on Weber's social theory (1949), each ideal type will be created by emphasizing a point of view. Since the ideal types are a heuristic device and a logical expedient, they need not be found in their entirety in any particular text. Furthermore, the prefix "ideal" has only a logical connotation and does not imply a philosophical point of view. As a methodological tool, the ideal types oscillate between particular historical examples and a general conceptualization.

The purpose of using ideal types is two-fold. First, it enables one to demarcate a point of reference to identify and interpret hermeneutic trends in the extant philosophical literature of the Hindus and the Buddhists. Second, the difference between the actual course of the Indian philosophical tradition and the constructs of ideal-types along the lines suggested here facilitates identification of the motivations of the interpreters (both traditional and modern) of Indian philosophy. The term "Vedic" will be used to refer to the ideal type based principally on the Mīmāṃsā theories of the interpretation of Vedic injunctions. The term "non-Vedic" will refer to the opposing ideal type abstracted from the arguments put forth by the non-Mīmāṃsakas, especially the Buddhists. The terms "Vedist" and "non-Vedist" refer to respective proponents of the two.

Foucault (1979) has persuasively argued that the coming into being of the notion of "author" constitutes a privileged moment of *individualization* in the history of ideas, literature, philosophy, and science. A similar development took place in ancient India with the rise of Buddhism and Jainism. In the Buddhist tradition, for instance, sacred texts began to be accepted as "true" only when clearly identified with the historical Buddha. By extension, determination of actual authorship became a functional principle by which to include or exclude discourse attributed to the Buddha. This development introduced a hermeneutics of control that adversely affected the free circulation, composition, and recomposition of the text. The concept of "author" became an hermeneutical tool to control the proliferation of meaning.[14] By extension, commentaries on other Buddhist texts dealing with spiritual liberation such as the *Theragāthā* by monks and the *Therīgāthā* by nuns provided socio-historical and psychological details about their authors. The authors[15] of such texts were concerned with the historical authenticity of the information provided in them. Descriptions of the experiences of actual, individual authors rather than myths of inspired sages or poets acquired decisive importance for attaining ultimate truth. These developments paved the way for the emergence of the "authors-and-their work criticism" in the sacred literature of the Buddhists and the Jains. Questions such as "should everything individuals wrote, said, or left behind become part of their work and mission?" were raised by those who were compiling the Canon.

Mīmāṃsakas were the first thinkers from the orthodox Vedic tradition to develop the concept of the "authorlessness" of texts in response to the Buddhist and Jain preoccupation with an author. Authority, they contended, lay in the Vedas, and not in any author, as was argued by their rivals. There might be individuals or groups who were authorities *within* the Vedic tradition, but no authorities who stood *over* the tradition of the Vedas (Gachter 1983, 80). The Vedas collectively refer to historical events, it was claimed, yet they are not themselves historical. They refer to past events, which they condense and particularize, yet they do not constitute a record of actually lived experience. Instead, they evoke a memory of actions that are repeated eternally as orders, imperatives, and rewards. The Mīmāṃsā position adopted a view of the Vedas that is this-worldly, though not allowing this worldliness to *dominate* the actual sense of the text.

Insofar as Vedic hermeneutics focused on text-oriented interpretation, the Vedic theory of interpretation had to analyze the phenomena of speech[16] and textual preservation first by oral tradition and then by writing.[17] To the Vedist, transmitted texts such as the Vedas cannot be the recorded speech-event which the Buddhists presumed the dialogues of the Buddha found in the Pali Canon to be. Accordingly, the Vedas constitute, to paraphrase Gadamer, an autonomous piece of work in language. Furthermore, the condition of textualization is central to the hermeneutical phenomenon because, as Ricoeur says, the detachment of a text from its writer/composer/editor gives that particular text an existence and world of its own. Because the text is not merely the fixation of a previous oral discourse, its development escapes the finite horizon experienced by its originator even if that originator was the omniscient Buddha.

For this reason, the Vedist would argue, what the Vedas really mean both at a given period in time and eternally is the issue, not the intention of a human author. For the Vedist, writing is not a faithful reflection of an author's thought.

The objective meaning of a text is, moreover, something other than the subjective intention of its creator and must be so construed. This implies that understanding takes place in a non-psychological, non-subjective and properly semantic space, which the text carves out by severing itself from the mental intention of its creator. As Ricoeur would say, the author has no control over the written word once it has been let loose upon the world and as such cannot be granted a privileged status as an interpreter of the work (Ricoeur 1976, 29).

To Śabara and Kumārila, the encounter with transmitted texts such as the Vedas did not have the nature of simple knowledge, personal experience, or authentication. They rejected the idea that one "understands" a text because of some knowledge of its author. One may, they argued, successfully interpret a particular sacred formula (mantra) or an injunction (vidhi) from the Vedic corpus and yet theoretically disagree with the seer who happened to be its original recipient. A text is understood, they explained, because of its subject-matter. The ground of this shared meaning is not strictly human and psychological. Rather, it is language itself. Hence there exists the possibility of meaningful interpretation of enjoined actions even in "anonymous" texts such as the Vedas (see Kumārila's spirited defence of *JS* 1:1.27 in the *Ślokavārttika*).

The non-Vedic approach, on the other hand, is based on the following two counter-claims that can be traced back to the *Pramāṇasamuccaya* of Dignāga: (1) a text's meaning is the author's intended meaning; and (2) an author's meaning provides a criterion by means of which the validity of the interpretation/s of the work may be judged. The meaning of the text (that is, the one correct meaning which the interpreter should grasp) is the author's intended meaning. This amounts to a claim of identity between the text's purported meaning and its author's meaning. This meaning is authoritative for textual interpretation as well as being identical to it. It constitutes the object of interpretation. It is what the interpreter should search for as a "valid" interpretation of a text (this argument is based on Dignāga's understanding of mānasapratyakṣa as the valid means of knowledge [see Nagatomi 1980]).[18] If the text and only the text is the object of textual interpretation — as the Vedist would claim — then there would be no way of validating different interpretations of the text. The same text could say different things to different readers or listeners.[19] But, presumably, the author (for the sake of argument, the Buddha) meant *something* by his discourse/text. To expect interpreters to speculate on what the Buddha meant is clearly unwarranted.[20]

Accordingly, the author's intention, the non-Vedist would maintain, must be the norm by which the validity of any interpretation is to be measured. Furthermore, this intention is a determinate entity about which objective evidence can be gathered by the interpreter and, when the relevant evidence is in hand, a firm determination of meaning can be made that will be universally recognized as valid. The Vedist's claim that the language of the text is not a speech act or dialogue but rather language evolving its own meaning (consider, for instance, *Ślokavārttika* #37,38 on *JS* 1:1.12) would be countered by the non-Vedists by pointing out that in this event whatever the language of a text says to its readers is its meaning, which amounts to nothing in particular. Alternatively, it may mean whatever we take it to mean.

To the non-Vedist, the Vedist's doctrine of the semantic autonomy of the text turns out to be the doctrine of the indeterminacy of textual meaning. As such, it is an invitation to subjectivism and relativism, because various linguistic norms may be invoked by different people to support a given meaning. The non-Vedist maintains that there are no meanings outside of people who understand something. In textual interpretation, meaning can be either the interpreter's or the author's. Since meaning cannot be just the interpreter's meaning, textual meaning must be the author's intended meaning, which, in turn, is an affair of consciousness, not of words.[21]

A word sequence such as the Vedas, the non-Vedist would argue, means nothing in particular until someone understands something from it. There is no realm of meanings outside human consciousness. Whatever meanings are connected to words, it is a person who is making the connection (samvṛ). The meanings that are actualized by the reader are either shared with the author or belong to the reader alone. Within the Mīmāṃsā system itself, the non-Vedist would point out, two major schools (Abhihitānvayavāda and Anvitābhidhānavāda, led respectively by Kumārila and Prabhākara) emerged that diverged widely over the basic unit of meaning. When such disagreements occur, how are they to be resolved? In view of the semantic autonomy claimed by the Vedist for the Vedas, these differences cannot be resolved, since the meaning is not, as the Vedists have always insisted, what the author meant. If the Vedic claim that the Vedas are without an author is accepted, then the Vedist usurps the legitimate author's place. To banish the original author as the one who determines meaning (by claiming, for instance, that the Vedas are apauruṣeya) is therefore to reject the only compelling normative authority that could lend validity to an interpretation.

At this stage the Vedist would legitimately ask the non-Vedist: What does the author's intended meaning denote? It cannot mean what the author intended to mean but did not succeed in meaning, for then the author's meaning would not be normative for textual interpretation in the way the non-Vedist wishes it to be and what the author intended to accomplish by having written the work — for instance, to inform, illumine or mesmerize the potential reader.[22] It also cannot mean that the author intends a personal range of meanings derived from experience, for the Buddha initially hesitated to share his experience with others. Moreover, the author's intended meaning cannot denote all the meanings the author may have privately entertained before a particular work was produced. For the meanings an author can convey textually are more limited than the meanings the author can entertain in mind. It is impossible to divine the author's non-verbalized intention. It is also false to equate the author's inner reflection with the verbalized achievement in the public work. Consequently, a genuine theory of text interpretation must distinguish between the author's intention (which is neither relevant nor available for scrutiny) and the actual accomplishment, namely, the text itself. The text alone must be the object of interpretation.[23]

The Mīmāṃsakas would base their exegesis of Vedic injunctions on the concept of the semantic autonomy of the text. The self-validation of a text, for the Mīmāṃsakas, originates in its presumed semantic autonomy from the author.[24] The non-Vedist, however, would not likely be convinced by such arguments. He would claim that a text is not a mere locus of objective verbal possibilities. A text is also a record of verbalized subjective actuality. If a text represented merely a set of possibilities, interpretation would be impossible, for no actual reading could conceivably correspond to a mere set of possibilities. Furthermore, if a text represents all possibilities of meaning permissible within the public norms of language, then no single interpretation would be "correct" or "valid." Any interpretation would be correct. Anarchy would follow.

The non-Vedist would also argue that even though it is possible to interpret meaningfully an anonymous text, not all texts need to be viewed as anonymous works. Or, the non-Vedist would argue that no text can speak for itself and every construed text is necessarily attributed to its author. The author's intended meaning is the meaning the author has given the text. Hermeneutics must stress a reconstruction of the author's aims in order to construe the meaning of the text.[25]

Such a non-Vedic theory makes possible a definitive interpretation. It is generally acknowledged that a major religious founder such as the Buddha intended something specific. Consequently, all subsequent interpretations claim to recover and represent that original intention. They are trusted by the followers of that religious founder. All competing interpretations must be considered as incorrect. But, the Vedist would counter (today, at least) that such a hermeneutics is essentially "Romantic" since its primary concern is to establish the intention of the Buddha.[26]

A problem for the Vedist remains. Can a person have truly objective knowledge of a text? Are not a people's interpretations affected by their own experience and historical moment? The traditional Vedist accepting the apauruṣeya nature of text would have to answer "No!" The meaning of the text is eternal. It cannot be affected by personal experience or historical moment. On this point, the Vedist would have to part company with modern thinkers like Gadamer, who argue that readers have a dialogue with a text: interpretation arises out of a process of "conversation" between readers in their own cultural milieu and a text that speaks in an alternative cultural mode. The meaning of a text is in the relation between the text and the reader. It is not found behind the text in the mind or life of the author. Gadamer's concept of the interpretive process is dynamic and interactive. He suggests that a good model for the process that takes place between the interpreter and the text is provided by the dynamics of play (1975, 91ff). In a game, the players willingly relinquish some of their control. As a result, they are taken over by the game in such a way that they experience its challenges, its ups and downs, its to-and-fro movements. When people read a text attentively, they are similarly overtaken by it. The subject-matter is neither defined by the author nor the reader, but by the content of the text that engages, challenges and informs the reader.[27] By involvement with the subject-matter of the text, the reader engages in a dialogue with it. The reader confronts the text as an alternative world with an alternative horizon of meaning. For Gadamer, such an encounter results in a fusion of horizons that will lead to a fundamental change in the interpreter's existential self and world view and application of the meaning of the text to the interpreter's own life (1975, 273-4).

To conclude, Clooney (1987) observes that, according to the Mīmāṃsakas, religion includes meanings and values appropriate to human beings, but the sum of its meaning necessarily exceeds the human perspective. Still, there is no meaning beyond the religious acts themselves; one cannot appeal to a pre-verbal intention to get beyond the words and acts. Both of these points are directly relevant to the modern study of religion.

The Vedic theory of text interpretation provided an important alternative to the hermeneutics of authoritative interpretation proposed by their principal rivals, the Buddhists. The arguments that the Vedists marshalled to refute the author's supreme authority in the understanding of the text may also have provided significant checks on the formation of cults in the brahmanical tradition, for there could be no author with absolute authority.[28] Non-Vedists, such as the Buddhists, favoured a hermeneutics of control whereby interpretation of a text was forced to fit a doctrinal position established by the founder. The concept of canonicity gave further authority to doctrine. The Buddha's once radical rejection of sacrificial actions, for instance, became, over the centuries, simply a received and unquestioned sermon.

The Vedists, on the other hand, continued to maintain that a text discloses a particular albeit eternal view rather than simply expressing a doctrine. The text itself must provide independent criteria (svataḥ pramāṇa) for its interpretation without appeal to an author.[29] In the Vedic view, what is to be understood and appropriated by the followers of a particular text-oriented tradition is the significance of the text itself, which opens its own world of meaning. Textual understanding is dynamic. The direction of thought is opened by study and analysis of the text itself, unfettered by the historical circumstance, personality or the reputation of its author.[30] Referring to Foucault's suggestion that a focus on the author overly restricts the text, Clooney (1987) observes that a text possesses a scope of significance wider than that belonging to any author or reader. Anyone seeking to develop the implications of Foucault's position, Clooney (1987) points out, has a very promising resource available in Mīmāṃsā views of hermeneutics.

Thus, the Vedic theory of text interpretation can provide an important corrective to the cult of the author or the religious founder as the sole and omniscient interpreter of the created text. Often the charisma of the original founder of a religion is routinized through discourses attributed to him, which, when transformed into a closed canon, become the object of veneration and worship. In the process, the intrinsic worth of the text itself is lost. The text becomes the prisoner of its author, who stands firmly behind it (see Ricoeur 1976). By contrast, the Vedic theory puts the focus directly on the text itself. Although in theory there is only one eternal meaning, validation of that is impossible beyond the text itself. With a variety of recognized hermeneutical principles in hand, the Mīmāṃsākas had confidence that the eternal meaning of the text could be recovered. But because it was the scholar's responsibility to recover it, the act of interpretation *de facto* remained open to a degree of creativity, though this could not be acknowledged as such (given their presupposition of the eternality of the Vedas). Gadamer's concept of the dialogic interaction of reader and text would take account of this problem. But it would also undermine the authority of the Vedas. It seems, then, that the Mīmāṃsākas' overt presupposition of the authority of the Vedas and their covert creativity within certain rules of the exegetical game made for a position that is worthy of consideration when the topic is hermeneutics in a cross-cultural perspective.

NOTES

1. I wish to thank Professors Francis Clooney SJ, Boston College, Anand Paranjape, Simon Fraser University, and Katherine Young, McGill University for critically reading the draft and for making perceptive comments. Translations are by the author unless otherwise noted.

2. It is extremely difficult to date early Indian texts. The relative chronology has been suggested by the date of the Buddha, but even the Buddha's death has been re-evaluated in recent years (as has the earliest date for the Saṃhitās). Eventually, linguistic analysis may provide a more precise dating on the basis of internal evidence or show that there is considerable overlap in the various categories of Vedic literature. With these caveats in mind, the Saṃhitās have been tentatively dated 1900-1200 B.C.E.; the Brāhmaṇas 1200-800 B.C.E.; the Āraṇyakas 800-600 B.C.E.; the early Upaniṣads from 600 B.C.E; the late Upaniṣads 400-300 B.C.E.; and the rise of Jainism and Buddhism between 600-400 B.C.E.

3. The date of this work is not known; however, the style of Jaimini's writings has led scholars to suggest that he flourished during the Sūtra period, which extended from 600-200 B.C.E. Keith (1978, 7), however, places him in c. 200 C.E.

4. The closest equivalent term in Sanskrit for text interpretation is vṛtti, which is defined by the Naiyāyikas as the relation between a word and its meaning which is favourable to the recollection of the meaning-producing verbal import (śābdabodhahetupadārthopasthityanukūlaḥ padapadārthayoḥ saṃbandhaḥ (see Rao 1969, 242).

5. Compare the Zahirite interpretation of the Qu'rān as discussed by Said (1979).

6. Borrowing from Ricoeur (1976) a broader sense of "text," the Vedic theory of text interpretation can become a useful tool for analysing socio-religious precepts and practices in a tradition such as India's. Hermeneutics proper begins with the problem of the text conceived as a work. Texts actualize the distinctions that determine discourse, whereas in spoken language or other direct modes of communication, the distinctions remain as mere possibilities. Texts provide distance from speech. Readers have time and opportunity to consider both semiotic and semantic approaches. Ricoeur's version of hermeneutics, therefore, reveals itself as practical philosophy. The text urges the interpreter to act. In Ricoeur's view (Reagan and Stewart 1978), social action can also be interpreted as a text. In one sense, the notion of the text is a good *paradigm* for human action; in another sense, the action is a good *referent* for a whole category of texts. Ricoeur argues that human action is in many ways a quasi-text. It is exteriorized in a manner comparable to the fixation that is characteristic of writing. In becoming detached from its agent, action attains an autonomy similar to the semantic autonomy of a text. It is inscribed in the course of things. Action, like a text, is an open work, addressed to an indefinite series of possible "readers." The judges are not the action's contemporaries, but subsequent people. More recently, Tony Hak (1989), following Peter Zima, has proposed the concept of "text sociology" wherein the object of sociology ["society"] is conceived as "text."

Ricoeur's formulation of the similarity of textual meaning and action has important implications for the social sciences. An action has a certain determinate meaning in any society. It encompasses a range of meanings in the same way that words have a range of meanings. Thus, the meaning of an action, like the meaning of a word, need not be seen as something hidden, inner, or inaccessible to scrutiny. Action, like language, can be explained through reference to shared rules of meaning. Like speech, action can be placed under typologies such as Max Weber's ideal types, which specify the criteria of their proper application (1977, 323; quoting Weber (ideal types) and John Searle (ideal models), Ricoeur (1981), too, acknowledges that such an interpretive typology of action is possible. To grasp why human beings act as they do, we must understand the meaning of their activity. To understand the meaning of conduct, according to Peter Winch (1958), is to grasp the rules that actors follow in doing what they do. Meaningful action is activity oriented to rules, where knowledge of those rules provides the actors "reasons" for the acts they engage in. Understanding meaning and reasons, for Winch, involves relating observed behaviour to rules. Social science is thus an integrative, or hermeneutic, endeavour.

The Mīmāṃsakas have sought to correlate meaningful action with objective textual interpretation. They, too, with their notion of command (vidhi) thought that the text urges the reader to act. But if the concern of the Mīmāṃsakas was with sacrificial action, that of the authors of the Dharmaśāstras, who borrowed a great deal from the Mīmāṃsakas, was with social action, norm and law. Because in the Indian context, social action becomes expressed in text; and text, in turn, prescribes social action, there is a particularly close relationship between the two, especially since, as Ricoeur argues, human action is, in any case, a quasi-text.

7. padāni svam svamartham pratipādayanti vākyam. padārthā eva tvākāṅkṣāyogyatāsannidhivaśāt-parasparasamsṛṣṭā vākyārtha ityarthah. na tu vākyam vākyārtho va pṛthagastiti bhāvaḥ (cited in Cardona 1983, 146-48).

8. padāni hi svam svam padārthamabhidhāya nivṛttavyāpārāni. athedanīm padārthā avagatāḥ santo vākyārtham gamayanti *ŚB* I:116.

9. Jaimini's thesis may be understood in terms of the following imagery used by Gadamer. The word is like a mirror in which the object is seen. The curious thing about this mirror, however, is that it nowhere extends beyond the image of the object (1975, 384). This particular mirror exhausts itself in its act of representing. Whatever imperfections inhere in it distort the object or reality coming to view, but we don't know it from the mirroring itself. The mirroring function — not this or that particular reflection — is what Gadamer understands by the "linguisticality" of man (Howard 1982, 157).

10. In his gloss on *JS* 1:1.5 Śabara argues that śabda is the sign/reason (nimittam) of the thing to be known. For Śabara, the authority of śabda as a valid source of knowledge in meaningful speech is the key issue. He considers the relevance of śabda as a means of right knowledge. Śabda is affirmed in its primordial aspect as a pramāṇa because śabda is reliable and valid apart from any human influence. It is independent of human agency (apauruṣeya) (Gachter 1983, 74).

11. Consider in this context Gadamer's discussion of the analogy of truth and light. Light itself is not seen but only as reflected from the surface on which it plays. The act of understanding, too, is an event that involves a passivity of this sort (1975, 422, 439). Interpretation is the illumination of the act of understanding (see also Hoy 1982, 157).

12. kāryānvito ghaṭo ghaṭapadaśakyaḥ. kāryānvite padānām śaktiḥ (*Bṛhatī,* I:3) (Cited in Rao 1969, 84, n. 4).

13. This reformulation is particularly indebted to Wilson 1978.

14. Foucault (1979) has convincingly demonstrated how the author-function is often used as a societal tool to restrain language, assign responsibility, and confine the meaning of texts (see also Clooney 1987).

15. Early texts of both the Vedic and heterodox traditions were consigned to writing sometime after their original composition. Thus, it is important to acknowledge both the oral and written stages of these texts. Because the oral texts were generally fixed by precise memorization — especially in the case of the Vedas — continuity from the oral to written stage is acepted by scholars.

16. As Professor Paranjpe has pointed out in a personal communication, this claim need not preclude a Vedic contribution to a "person-oriented" hermeneutics (as reflected, for instance, in Śaṅkara's *Vivekacūḍāmaṇi* or *Daśaślokī*).

17. The Vedas were transmitted orally and precisely for centuries even when writing was available. Because of their exact oral transmission they had the nature of a text.

18. The form of this argument is based on Hirsch (1976, 17ff.) who defends the determinacy of authorial meaning and its privileged status.

19. See Hirsch 1967, 10 and Wilson 1978.

20. Dignāga's *Pramāṇasamuccaya* praises the Buddha as the "embodiment of pramāṇa" or "pramāṇa incarnate" (pramāṇabhūta). The final authority by which both Dignāga and Dharmakīrti claimed the validity of their pramāṇa system was none other than the Buddha's words which they accepted as authentic by faith. Thus, the Buddhist pramāṇa system, and, by implication, the Buddhist theory of text interpretation and the authenticity of the Buddha's words stand in a circular relation: the structuring of the former was done within the limits of the latter, and the latter was meant by the former. (This line of argument was suggested by Nagatomi 1980.)

21. See Hirsch 1976, 91.

22. This argument is based on Hirsch 1967, 16, 31-40. See also Wilson 1978.

23. The following remarks of Kumārila (*Tantravārttika* on *JS* 1:3.1.2) are relevant here: "As authors of the past texts are not available for a dialogue now, it must be assumed that what they assert is based upon their personal observation and experience. But the impossibility of such an extraordinary facility in the author has already been set aside in our discussion of the omniscience of the Buddha in the *Ślokavārttika*" (on *JS* 1:1.2, #134 et seq.). Failure to heed Kumārila's admonition would amount to endorsing the intuitionism and psychologism also evident in the theory of Schleiermacher.

24. This argument is based on Śabara's contention that the purpose of any sentence is to have someone understand a particular qualified meaning. If an utterance did not have independent status as a distinct meaningful unit directly related to a sentential meaning separate from word meanings, it would follow that people would not understand any sentential meaning (*ŚB* on *JS* 1:1.16).

25. The current advocate of such a view is, of course, Hirsch (1976, 49).

26. A similar view is also expressed in Lopez 1987 with reference to what he calls Yogācārin and Svatāntrika Buddhism.

27. Ricoeur calls this phenomenon "*la chose du texte*" —a settling of meaning of an ontological kind that no longer belongs either to the intentionality of its "sender" or of its "receiver" but to the being of the utterance itself (Reagan and Stewart 1978, 160). "*La chose du texte*" is, then, at the same time a mode of reality (and so satisfies the "ascending pathway" toward ontology) and a reality whose possibilities we can best describe if we pay attention to the objective social sciences ... (and so satisfies the critical need for a "descending pathway") (see Howard 1982, 170).

28. Clooney (1987) has eloquently pointed out that the Mīmāṃsā theory of *authorlessness*, with its underlying concern to "liberate" the sacred texts from their author, approaches Michel Foucault's influential argument that author-function — despite its appeal to the "infinite creative resources" that are culturally supposed to lie within the speaker — actually restricts texts by ordering them to a designated author, whose intentions determine what the texts are allowed to mean.

29. yaḥ śabdasya śravaṇādeva viniyogaḥ pratīyate sa śrautaḥ ityucyate (*ŚB* on *JS* 3:3.14).

30. See Bilimoria 1989 for further discussion.

BIBLIOGRAPHY

Bilimoria, Purusottama. 1988. *Śabdapramāṇa: Word and Knowledge (A Doctrine in Mīmāṃsā-Nyāya Philosophy).* Dordrecht: Kluwer Academic Publishers.

—. 1989. "Hindu-Mīmāṃsā Against Scriptural Evidence of God." *Sophia* 8: 20-31.

Clooney, Francis X. 1985. "Jaimini's Contribution to the Theory of Sacrifice as the Experience of Transcendence." *History of Religions* 25: 199-212.

—. 1987. "Why the Vedas have no Author: Language as Ritual in early Mīmāṃsā and Post-Modern Theology." *Journal of the American Academy of Religion* 55: 659-686.

Cardona, George. 1983. *Linguistic Analysis and Some Indian Traditions*. Post-graduate and Research Department Series, no. 20. Poona: Bhandarkar Oriental Research Institute.

Foucault, Michel. 1979. "What is an Author?" In *Textual Strategies: Perspectives in Post-Structuralist Criticism*. Ed. Josue Harari. Ithaca, N.Y.: Cornell University Press.

Gachter, Othmar. 1983. *Hermeneutics and Language in Pūrva Mīmāṃsā: A Study in Śabara Bhāṣya.* Delhi: Motilal Banarsidass.

Gadamer, Hans-Georg. 1975. *Truth and Method.* New York: Seabury Press.

Garge, Damodar V. 1952. *Citations in Śabara-Bhāṣya: A Study.* Deccan College Dissertation Series, no. 8. Poona: Deccan College.

Giddens, Anthony. 1979. *Central Problems in Social Theory: Action, Structure, and Contradiction in Social Analysis.* London: Macmillan.

Hak, Tony. 1989. "Developing a Text-Sociological Analysis." *Semiotica* 75: 25-42.

Harari, Josue V. 1979. ed. *Textual Strategies: Perspectives in Post-Structuralist Criticism.* Ithaca, N.Y.: Cornell University Press.

Hattori, Masaaki. 1980. "Apoha and Pratibhā." In *Sanskrit and Indian Studies: Essays in Honour of Daniel H.H. Ingalls.* Eds. M. Nagatomi et al. Dordrecht: Holland: D. Reidel Publishing Co.

Hekman, Susan J. 1983. *Weber, the Ideal Type, and Contemporary Social Theory.* Notre Dame, Indiana: University of Notre Dame Press.

Hirsch, E.D. , Jr. 1967. *Validity in Interpretation.* New Haven, Conn.: Yale University Press.

—. 1976. *The Aims of Interpretation.* Chicago: University of Chicago Press.

Howard, Roy J. 1982. *Three Faces of Hermeneutics: An Introduction to Current Theories of Understanding.* Berkeley: University of California Press.

Hoy, David Couzens. 1978. *The Critical Circle: Literature, History, and Philosophical Hermeneutics.* Berkeley: University of California Press.

Jaimini Sūtra [with the bhāṣya of Śabarasvāmin]. 1976. Vol. 1, pt. 1. 4th ed. Anandasrama Sanskrit Texts, no.96. Eds. K. V. Abhyankar and Ganesh A. Joshi. Pune: Anandasrama.

Jha, Ganganath. [1911] 1978. *The Prabhākara School of Mīmāṃsā.* Reprint. Delhi: Motilal Banarsidass.

—. [1900] 1983. *Ślokavārttika* [Translated from the Original Sanskrit with Extracts from the Commentaries "Kāśikā" of Sucarita Miśra and "Nyāyaratnākara" of Pārthasārathi Miśra]. Reprint. Delhi: Sri Sadguru Publications.

—. [1916] 1974. *Pūrva Mīmāṃsā Sūtras of Jaimini: Chapters 1-3. Translated with an Original Commentary.* Reprint. New York: AMS Press.

Keith, A. Berriedale. [1921] 1978. *The Karma-Mīmāṃsā.* 1978. Reprint. Delhi: Oriental Books Reprint Corporation.

Klemm, David E. 1986. *Hermeneutical Inquiry*. Vol. 1, *The Interpretation of Texts*. American Academy of Religion Studies in Religion, no.43. Eds. Charley Hardwick, James O. Duke. Atlanta, Georgia: Scholars Press.

Lopez, Donald S. Jr. 1987. "Buddhist Hermeneutics: A Conference Report." *Philosophy East and West* 1 : 71-83.

Mazumdar, P.K. 1977. *The Philosophy of Language: In the Light of Pāṇinian and the Mīmāṃsaka Schools of Indian Philosophy*. Calcutta: Sanskrit Pustak Bhandar.

Nagatomi Masatoshi. 1980. "Mānasa-Pratyakṣa: A Conundrum in a Buddhist Pramāṇa System." In *Sanskrit and Indian Studies: Essays in Honour of Daniel H.H. Ingalls*. Eds. M. Nagatomi et al. Dordrecht: Holland: D. Reidel Publishing Co.

Palmer, Richard. 1969. *Hermeneutics: Interpretation Theory in Schleiermacher, Dilthey, Heidegger, Gadamer*. Evanston, Ill.: Northwestern University Press.

Pandeya, R.C. 1963. *The Problem of Meaning in Indian Philosophy*. Delhi: Motilal Banarsidass.

Raju, P.T. 1985. *Structural Depths of Indian Thought*. New Delhi: South Asia Publishers.

Rani, Vijaya. 1982. *The Buddhist Philosophy as Presented in Mīmāṃsā-Śloka-Vārttika*. Delhi: Parimal Publications.

Rao, Veluri Subba. 1969. *The Philosophy of a Sentence and Its Parts*. New Delhi: Munshiram Manoharlal.

Reagan, Charles E. and David Stewart, eds. 1978. *The Philosophy of Paul Ricoeur: An Anthology of His Work*. Boston: Beacon Press.

Ricoeur, Paul. 1976. *Interpretation Theory: Discourse and the Surplus of Meaning*. Fort Worth, Texas: Texas Christian University Press.

—. 1981. *Hermeneutics and the Human Sciences: Essays on Language, Action and Interpretation*. Cambridge: Cambridge University Press.

Rogers, Rolf E. 1969. *Max Weber's Ideal Type Theory*. New York: Philosophical Library.

Said, Edward W. 1979. "The Text, the World, the Critic." In *Textual Strategies: Perspectives in Post-Structuralist Criticism*. Ed. Josue Harari. Ithaca, N.Y.: Cornell University Press.

Ślokavārttika of Śrī Kumārila Bhaṭṭa 1978. [With the Commentary Nyāyaratnākara of Śrī Pārthasarathī Miṣra]. Ed. and rev. Swami Dvarikadasa Sastri. Varanasi: Tara Publications.

Weber, Max. 1949. *The Methodology of the Social Sciences*. Trans. and eds. Edward Shils and Henry Finch. New York: The Free Press.

—. 1977. *Critique of Stammler*. Trans. Guy Oakes. New York: The Free Press.

Wilson, Barrie A. 1978. "Hirsch's Hermeneutics: A Critical Examination," *Philosophy Today* 22 (Spring): 20-33.

Winch, Peter. 1958. *The Idea of a Social Science*. London: Routledge and Kegan Paul.

HINDUISM AND THE STRUCTURAL APPROACH OF MADELEINE BIARDEAU

Julian Woods

The structural analysis of Hindu mythology undertaken by Madeleine Biardeau in her *Études de mythologie hindou* (hereafter *Études*) and in *L'Hindouisme: anthropologie d'une civilisation* (hereafter *L'Hindouisme*) explicates literary structures while demonstrating "unity at a deeper analytical level, based on the explicit or implicit norms carried by all Hindus in their minds" (*L'Hindouisme* 10).[1] This essay examines the strengths and weaknesses of Biardeau's structural method.

Basic Assumptions

Biardeau's presuppositions are based largely on the theories of Georges Dumézil and Claude Lévi-Strauss. She has strong reservations about a Western Indology that portrays Indian culture as a "mosaic without the possibility of a unifying design" (*L'Hindouisme* 10), or that remains satisfied with a linear ordering of the data based on philological, historical, archaeological or anthropological lines of enquiry. She asks:

> And what if this historical model existed only in our minds? Or even if it only implicitly borrowed from the model of our own most recent past? It is a big step and one that cannot be taken without further examination, between the statement that different ethnic and cultural groups had to learn to live together over the centuries, and the assertion that their doing so is enough to explain the socio-religious structure of Hindu India today (*L'Hindouisme* 12-13).

Biardeau is also critical of recent challenges to the integrity of Epic and Purāṇic texts. These include the search for an Ur-text such as that found in the *Rāmāyaṇa* version of H.D. Sankalia, as well as endeavours to produce a critical edition along the lines of the Bhandarkar Oriental Research Institute's version of the *Mahābhārata* (*MBh*). Rather than explaining them as the product of historical accretion, or of some hypothetical interaction of Aryan and Dravidian cultures, she views these texts as a conscious and brilliantly executed attempt by orthodox brahmanical circles to extend the possibility of salvation to the ruling caste of warrior kings (kṣatriyas) without the need for them to abandon their secular duties. She explains:

> For an individual brahmin there is no real problem: a simple change from the status of householder to that of renunciate is all that is required. But what becomes of the kingdom if the king abandons the sacrifice to seek his personal salvation? In short, the choice between life in the world and renunciation cannot be left free of all constraint. What is needed is to reconcile the eternity of the world — that no one wishes to see end — with the discovery of the possibility of a definitive personal salvation (Le *Mahābhārata* I 29).

While this orthodox agenda was no doubt prompted by historical circumstances — alarm over growing administrative chaos perhaps — these circumstances were never revealed explicitly in historical records. They can only be inferred from what can be known of the strategy by which the brahmins were able to transform a traditional sacrificial and ascetic system of values into what amounted to a new religion, the religion of devotion to a supreme divinity known as Bhakti. In Biardeau's view, their strategy transformed the old Vedic and Upanishadic ideals into a mythological panorama of space and time in the form of poetic narratives purporting to report things that "were thus" (itihāsa). For the scholar seeking the symbolic keys to this process:

> it is necessary to reverse perspective. When dealing with a sal or palm-tree, the reason is not because it is a part of the environment familiar to the poet .... On the contrary, it may be because it belongs to his mental environment as a result of its symbolic meaning(s). More generally, different landscapes are not portrayed for their actual location on the map (sic), but because of the positive or negative values they carry (*L'Hindouisme* 15-16).

In analyzing and explaining the radical contradictions that arise in passing from the Vedic/Brahmanic to the classical Bhaktic and Tantric perspectives, a structuralist rather than an historical approach is required. In her approach to the religious data, drawn mainly from text and ritual/cultic practice, she is particularly indebted to Lévi-Strauss. For example, her choice of material is governed largely by structures she considers significant, such as the basic cosmogonic structure of prakṛtasarga and pratisarga (the original and secondary cycles of creation) common to the Purāṇas and the Epics:

> This clearly requires a preliminary breakdown of the myths into their elements and the acceptance of the general principle that different elements of different tales can carry the same symbolic meaning and an equivalent function in the myth; or, inversely, that an identical symbolic element may have different meanings and roles according to the myths and its place in them. All we are doing in this respect is to express the b.a.b.a of the structural method applied here very modestly to a given group of myths (*Études* 54, 20).

Biardeau makes use of historical documents, but without their history:

> stripped of their date, of their origin, but organized and hierarchized according to a system of values drawn from inside the atemporal vision that the Hindu has of his universe.... We therefore propose to look at the Vedic revelation through the eyes of Hindus, albeit without assuming that they all have an equal view of it (*L'Hindouisme* 21).

Her rationale for this ahistorical approach is that myth is a privileged medium which illustrates fundamental questions and expresses governing values of Hindu culture. She has chosen Epic and Purāṇic literatures because they embody the essence of Hinduism and contain the key to a global understanding of Hindu religion:

> ... the origin stories of the Purāṇas, in contrast to those to be found in the Vedic hymns or the Upaniṣads, offer us a speculative effort that no longer expresses this or that aspect of Hinduism but rather the totality of the religious attitudes and beliefs that constitute what is known as Hinduism (*Études* 54, 20).

These assumptions buttress the central thesis that runs through all her work, namely, that Hinduism is not a disparate mosaic but a manifold expression of a single core of values. Her analysis is designed to reveal this:

> Yet it is around this Vedic core that a Hindu structure will emerge, drawing from it a variety of readings which, within certain limits, shift and change over the course of the centuries. The term 'Hinduism' is appropriate to describe this aggregate of readings, together with their structural organization. Closer to the Vedic revelation, orthodox Brahmanism is not the precursor of modern Hinduism; it is the permanent heart, the implicit model for and against which are constituted the Bhakti and the Tantric traditions with all their sects (*L'Hindouisme* 21).

Études de mythologie hindou

The *Études* bear witness to Biardeau's quest to understand the Bhaktic transformation through structural analysis of Hindu myth, with the *Mahābhārata* as a major focus. The term 'quest' is deliberately chosen, since her exploratory approach raises a large number of questions, some of which are consciously left in abeyance. Her work is not presented as the final word. As she herself admits, it is a series of probes, sometimes without issue but always provoking further study. Her intent is always to uncover patterns of symbolic connections that can reveal key structures. For example, she examines the justification of violence (hiṃsā) by the divine incarnation (avatāra) and the sacrificial nature of the war. Like scattered pieces of a jigsaw puzzle, her key ideas are then put together one by one to yield a comprehensive view of Hinduism.

Biardeau does not begin with the *Mahābhārata* directly. She starts instead with a study of its cosmological and eschatological setting drawn from Purāṇas such as the *Brahmāṇḍa*, the *Kūrma*, the *Mārkaṇḍeya*, the *Vāyu* and the *Viṣṇu*. She sees these works as the logical, not temporal, starting point for understanding the remarkable transformation of brahmanical values, beliefs and practices from the traditional Vedic, Brahmanical and Upaniṣadic background to the Bhakti world of Epic literature. Her first and most fundamental interest is to explain this phenomenon.

Biardeau approaches the issue by an ahistorical, symbolic analysis of key texts. By tracing names, etymologies, ideas and symbols from the Purāṇas back to the Vedas, Brāhmaṇas and Upaniṣads, she is able not only to resolve many of the apparent contradictions and inconsistencies that plague these works, but also to develop an overall theory regarding the structuring of the Bhakti tradition as a whole. She finds, for example, that the Purāṇas are not the product of a Dravidian indigenous tradition, but the work of the Aryan Brahmins themselves, worldly men (not renunciates) dissatisfied with the traditional sacrificial system.

This conclusion follows from detailed analysis of the laws of transformation, in myth, ritual or cultic practice. For instance, what began as an individual quest in the Upaniṣads becomes a collective adventure in the Purāṇas, symbolized by Brahmā, the perpetually transmigrating cosmic Person whose Life is the existence of the cosmos itself. Brahmā himself is a transformation, being the mythical personification of brahman, the sacrificial power of the Brahmin priest. In his function as destroyer (the Brahmā-Nārāyaṇa of the cosmic absorption or pralāya), Brahmā is a transformation of the Upaniṣadic Absolute. In general, the Purāṇic Brahmā symbolizes orthodox religion. This includes pravṛtti — with its Vedas and its sacrificial system together with the key Upaniṣadic notion of ahaṃkāra (ego) — which serves to mark off the higher worlds of renunciation and release from the trailokya, the three lower worlds of attachment and bondage. By contrast, the Upaniṣadic alternative, turning away from the world and its values (nivṛtti), is projected beyond the cosmic play of time and space in the figure of *Puruṣa*, another Purāṇic transformation with venerable antecedents, stemming, via the *Śatapatha Brāhmaṇa* and the *Praśna Upaniṣad*, from the Puruṣasūkta of *Ṛgveda* X. 90.

Such observations suggest that the Purāṇic vision is a transposition to the macrocosmic plane of the yogic process described in the *Kaṭha Upaniṣad*, supplemented by material drawn, and suitably adapted, from other orthodox works:

> In particular, the Purāṇic cosmogonies arose from the collective reflections centering on three Upaniṣads, the *Kaṭha* of the Black Yajurveda furnishing the ladder of mystical ascent required of any yogi on the path of liberation, while the *Muṇḍaka* and the *Praśna*, which teach the ātman-brahman identity rather than the path of yoga, provided the comparisons and the symbols destined to transform the individual yogic model of the *Kaṭha* into a cosmic adventure (*Études* 55, 75).

It is important to note that the periodic awakening of the Puruṣa to a new Creation, being necessarily a movement in the direction of sense experience, takes a direction opposed to the process followed by the yogi in the *Kaṭha Upaniṣad*. What better symbol, Biardeau asks, for the dramatic reversal of ideas and values that is found in the Bhakti tradition?

Although the Bhakti valuation of renunciation remains supreme (as it indeed was in orthodox Smārta as well as in Upaniṣadic circles), the deliverance it brings has been put on indefinite hold, so to speak:

> We are thus placed at the centre of a Universe where the ideal of the renunciant is projected onto the yogic God, where everything is undertaken in the interests of liberation, but where all things are organized to ensure that the world is kept forever turning (*Études* 55, 105).

The devotee (bhakta) may be willing to abandon his or her empirical ego (ahaṃkāra), but hardly attachment to the Lord. In Bhakti, even the sacrificial cult itself becomes a method of worship (sādhana).

Biardeau is able to find in these Purāṇas the mythical expression of a single coherent vision, comprehensive enough to incorporate orthodox perspectives and practices by transcending them and projecting them in the form of a macrocosmic hierarchy of time and space. The remarkable structural unity of the Purāṇic texts is evinced by various correspondences established between the destiny of the world hierarchy and its inhabitants according to the cycles of time and the different roles and levels of manifestation of the Deity, each with its own role. For example, the bhakta's valuation of the old Vedic gods is demonstrated by their position in heaven (svarga), which is lower than the heaven of the supreme deity. Their lives are measured in divine years of 360 human years. The avatāra, the Supreme Deity at work in this world to restore the dharma (particularly the Bhakti-sanctioned social order), descends at critical junctures in a cycle of time known as yuga, the full complement of four (a mahāyuga) being 12,000 divine years or 4,320,000 human years. Brahmā, the Bhakti symbol for secular orthodoxy, is a somewhat higher form of the Puruṣa as part of a triumvirate (trimūrti) who creates (Brahmā), sustains (Viṣṇu) and finally destroys (Śiva) the three worlds. His day is a kalpa, the duration of a secondary cycle of creation/destruction lasting a respectable 1,000 mahāyugas or 4,320,000,000 human years. His life of 36,000 kalpa (100 years of 360 days) is the complete span of the primary cycle. However, this represents but a moment (nimeṣa) in the Divine Consciousness, symbolizing the supreme value of Viṣṇu in his highest form as Yogi of yogis, beginning and end (prābhavāpyayau).

The Purāṇic hierarchization is nowhere more evident than in the structuring of the stages of creation (sarga) and absorption (pralāya), both of which are twofold according to the daily rhythms and eternal transmigrations of Brahmā respectively. There are two creation stories: (1) the prakṛtasarga or primary creation of Brahmā himself in the form of the Brahmāṇḍa or Cosmic Egg; and (2) the pratisarga or secondary creation of the three worlds (trailokya; which begins with Nārāyaṇa asleep on the cosmic ocean on the serpent Seṣa and ends with the rescue of the earth by Varāha, the sacrificial boar). Their discontinuity is related to the need to subordinate the values of orthodox ritualism (pravṛtti-dharma) to the Bhakti ideal of renunciation. That is to say, the ideal of renunciation *in* action is preferred to the Upaniṣadic ideal of renunciation *of* action. The primary creation is a yogic act in reverse as we have seen; the second is a cosmic rescue of the sacrificial system. Varāha, the boar, is "clearly identified with the Veda (vanmayaṃ vedasammitam) and with the sacrifice (yajñavarāhaḥ)" (*Études* 55, 66).

The two stages of absorption are related to the Purāṇic process of liberation in the form of a mystical ascent of the worlds (loka) made possible (at least in part) by a radical transformation of the concept of yoga. The mystical ascent is initiated during the intermediate destruction of the three worlds (naimittikapralāya), although as a prelude to its ultimate renewal. It is concluded only on the occasion of the mahāpralāya, the final death of Brahmā, when all the worlds and their inhabitants are once again re-absorbed by the return of the Supreme Yogi to his most profound, formless concentration (nirvikalpasamādhi).

The true significance of the naimittikapralāya is revealed in its dual character, the negative, destructive aspect simply masking its true purpose. This is not a day of wrath but the dawn of deliverance for those with the necessary merit (puṇya), and the promise of a new beginning in a new cosmos for the remainder. It is the cosmic expression of the familiar death-rebirth theme symbolized by a conflagration signaling the need for purification (the burning up of ego, ignorance, etc.) followed by a deluge symbolizing the primal fecundity that heralds the re-emergence of the three worlds at the beginning of a new Day of Brahmā.

This drama in two acts is produced under the direction of Śiva and Viṣṇu respectively. The responsibility of Śiva, as Kāla, Rudra or Kālāgnirudra, for the destructive, incendiary phase stems from his associations with death and sacrifice and with acts of violence (hiṃsā) in general, all of which carry overtones of impurity in brahmanical circles. As lord of the animals, Śiva is associated with all that is destructive in sacrifice, particularly the slaughter of animal victims. However, as an ascetic and a yogi, He is beyond all mundane notions of pure and impure and acts for the benefit of all. By contrast, the deluge, with its promise of renewal, is staged under the aegis of Viṣṇu, who symbolizes the prosperity and production of the eventual fruits of the Vedic sacrifice. In the form of Nārāyaṇa, Viṣṇu preserves the inchoate remainder of the three worlds during his cosmic sleep (yoganidrā), symbolized by the serpent Seṣa. Both events are modelled after Vedic sacrifice, the absorption like a gigantic cosmic funeral, and the creation like the sacrificial system by which the universe is maintained.

A major factor in preparing the aspirant for the mystical ascent is a set of proper social attitudes and practices collectively subsumed under the term yoga, originally an orthodox technical term but now radically transformed. In the Upaniṣads and in the *Yogasūtras* of Patañjali, the term was often used in opposition to saṃnyāsa, the abandonment of all activity, including yoga. In Purāṇic and Epic literature, the practice of yoga and the meaning of saṃnyāsa are broadened to reconcile the ideals of both the pravṛtti- and the nivṛtti-dharma in the ideal of acting without attachment for the welfare of the world. This involves abandonment of the fruits of the action rather than abandonment of the action itself. The best way of developing such an attitude is to have "faith in an ontological relation with God, the only way to transcend the egocentricity of one's empirical self and to invest one's action with a truly spiritual dimension having the support of grace" (*Études* 58, 64). In this manner, the devotee is able to imitate the way God himself acts in the world and to become his instrument. Such a yoga becomes an act of worship, a way of acting in this world that ensures a favourable rebirth and the possibility of moving to higher worlds at the end of the kalpa.

Two further benefits are realized as a result of the Purāṇic hierarchization and transformation. They are able to defer the final stage of deliverance almost indefinitely (a key Bhakti reversal of values, as already noted), and a place can be found for a provisional Upaniṣadic stage of deliverance in Brahmaloka, the spatial analogue of the Brahman of the Vedāntic Upaniṣads. Once again, this enables the authors to incorporate their own brahmanical heritage within the much broader and more popular framework of their new-found Bhakti universalism.

We pass from macrocosmic to socio-cosmic time in moving from: (1) the primary cycle of the universe (mahākalpa), the life of Brahmā which is brought to an end by the concentration without form (nirvikalpitasamādhi) of the Supreme Puruṣa; to (2) the secondary cycle (kalpa), the Day of Brahmā, which is brought to an end by his savikalpitasamādhi or concentration with form, in (the form of Nārāyaṇa); to (3) the system of yugas. We also pass from the two higher forms of the Divinity (as Supreme and as the forms of the trimūrti) to his more individual expression as the avatāra who descends (avatṛ) to "protect the good, destroy the evil-doers and to restore the dharma" (cf. *BG*. IV. 18). At this point Biardeau moves to the socio-cosmic stage of Epic literature, in which the human drama is played out. From an account of the life and yogic activity of the Cosmic Person, we turn to the play of individual destinies.

With the appearance of the avatāra, a number of cracks develop in the structural integrity of the Purāṇic cosmogony and eschatology, prompting a major line of enquiry for Biardeau. She asks: "How and why do we pass from a divinity dedicated to a perpetual yoga to a militant form of the divinity? And what is the practical result of this for the global image offered by Hinduism to the observer" (*Études* 63, 118). Biardeau treats this topic in the second chapter of her *Études*, "Bhakti and Avatāra," but finds it necessary to process so much detail and to raise so many side-issues along the way that no final word is evident in her more than three hundred pages of analysis. Yet she does provide a partial answer in the form of a detailed hypothesis about the nature of the Epic and what the authors had in mind for it.

In Biardeau's view, the *Mahābhārata* is "a teaching given to kings where the ideal sovereign appears indissolubly linked to the avatāra for whom he is a substitute" (*Études* 63, 173). The curriculum is designed by orthodox Brahmins, represented in the Epic by Droṇa, the Brahmin guru of all the protagonists. They intended, according to Biardeau, to legitimize and to incorporate new conditions and values hitherto ignored by the Dharmaśāstras. Although the problem of the impurity associated with the use of force (hiṃsā) in the ritual killing of animals had already been solved (cf. *Manusmṛti* V. 39b), the Brahmin priesthood still faced the more mundane issue of the royal killing of human beings in defence of the social order (dharma) and in support of the human goals (puruṣārtha) of all classes (varṇa) in society. Somehow, a religious sanction had to be found for the exercise of daṇḍanīti, the duties incumbent upon the king in the administration of justice.

As usual, the interests of Bhakti universalism are promoted by means of a hierarchization and transformation of values, beliefs and practices. This restructuring process is pictured as a new dispensation of the avatāra consequent upon the progressive moral decline of the third-level cycle of the yugas. In this way, the Epic manages to find a place not only for the kṣatriyadharma but also for the dharmas of all classes of society, including women and śudras. The gates of ultimate salvation are thrown open to all, based on the *Bhagavadgītā*'s notion that all action is a sacrifice, provided it is undertaken in a spirit of yoga, namely with an attitude of non-attachment to the fruits, ready to lose all, even life itself. In the case of the warrior (kṣatriya), the proper means of sacrifice is war, ultimately including ātmayajña, the sacrifice of death on the battlefield.

It is clear that the form which the epic teaching for the king must take is that of a sacrifice, in this case a sacrifice of total war. And because the king looks to the avatāra for his model of conduct, the epic structure necessarily mirrors the structure of the avatāric myths. Whatever the historical truth behind these events, the account of them must be given in the form of these myths. Not history but a "mythical necessity" is at work behind the epic narrative. This important factor is revealed by the yuga symbolism and highlighted by the manner in which the epic poets seek to dramatize the action by transposing it to a stage of cosmic dimensions. It is no ordinary war but one in which the family, social and international sources of the conflict are only part of a much larger set of relations concerning the three worlds as a whole. A reversal or perversion of the natural order is threatened. This is represented in the mundane sphere by a breakdown in the right order of the varṇas, more particularly of the sacerdotal and royal powers (brahman and the kṣatra). The breakdown is symbolized in cosmic terms by another episode in the perennial attempt of the demons to usurp the rightful place of the gods in heaven, to enjoy the immortal nectar of the gods and to use the sacrificial offerings for their own benefit, this time with the earth itself as the battleground.

Biardeau interprets the revolt of the demons (asuras) in Bhakti terms, as the continual refusal of brahmanical orthodoxy to submit to a new dharmic order integrated into the Bhakti hierarchy under the Supreme Deity, Viṣṇu. Whatever the merits of this argument, the forces of adharma are clearly on the ascendent, poised to sweep all before them. And it is at just such a critical juncture, the end of the yuga, that the descent of the avatāra to turn back evil is heralded.

Of course, Biardeau's initial hypothesis is not formulated with the kind of precision to be found in the scientific realm. It is rather a thesis revealed little by little after much clearing of underbrush. Such an approach is a fruitful but inherently messy business. Biardeau goes about her task energetically, in accordance with her own methodological dictum that "every important theme, by being repetitive and central to certain key notions, has a meaning for the totality of which it is a part" (*Études* 63, 156).

The broad outlines of her thesis emerge from her attempt to understand the avatāric myths and, in particular, to understand why they appear in the epic literature and elsewhere as transformations of the Purāṇic cosmogonic themes already discussed. For there is little doubt that the relation between avatāra and yuga repeats the Purāṇic model that related (1) the *Mahāyogin*, the highest form of the divinity, to the mahākalpa; and (2) the trimūrti, the intermediate level of the divinity, to the kalpa. And since it was on the basis of this macrocosmic structuring that the Purāṇic authors were able to incorporate the brahmanical orthodoxy within a new Bhakti universe of values, it is only natural to expect that the epic authors had something similar in mind when they introduced a third-level avatāra/yuga structure. What puzzles Biardeau are certain apparent inconsistencies between the Epic and the Purāṇic accounts of time. As well, the relation of avatāra and yuga is not entirely a happy one.

First, the yuga reflects a progressive decline in social conduct (dharma) that bears no clear-cut relation to the avatāra, who acts somewhat like a *deus ex machina*. Rather, it is governed by daiva, symbolized by four throws of a die. This raises questions about the role of karma and how the destiny of the individual may be reconciled with the fate (daiva) of the group. The positive Bhakti evaluation of the Kali Yuga offered by Vyāsa in the *Viṣṇu Purāṇa* also poses a problem. In addition, the process of decline is a linear one that does not fit into the cyclic form of the kalpa.

Biardeau's major concern is to explain the epic practice of characterizing the destructiveness of the times as a 'mini' pralāya. "When the epic talks of a yugānta, what is involved is all the symbolism of the pralāya" (*Études* 63, 135). The descent of the avatāra probably has little in common with the yogic activity of Nārāyaṇa at the end of the kalpa. Furthermore, one would expect the divine activity (as an act of last resort) to become manifest at the point of no return at the end of a Kali Yuga. But this is not typical of the Purāṇic and Epic accounts, including that of the *Mahābhārata*. The latter dates the avatāric activity at the junction of the Dvāpara and Kali Yugas, incarnating these yugas in the form of Śakuṇi and Duryodhana.

In Biardeau's view, these problems can only be resolved by standing logic on its head, so to speak. Faithful to her methodological postulate that "if incoherence is widespread, it can mean only that it is no barrier to understanding the whole" (*Études* 63, 151), she finds in this apparent confusion of symbols not an abuse of systematization but a "mythic necessity." It can be related only to the didactic intent of the story which, in Biardeau's reading, is to secure a place of honour for the dharma of the king (daṇḍanīti) with all that this implies for the transformation of orthodox notions of sacrifice (yajña), renunciation (saṃnyāsa) and yoga. After all, if hiṃsā must be justified, what better legitimacy than the example of the avatāra who destroys in order to create anew? And if war must be a sacrifice, what better dramatization than a sacrifice of the whole earth to make the point? Most importantly, what better symbol than the funeral sacrifice of the pralāya to heighten the drama of almost total destruction? Hence the fires of war at the end of the yuga are assimilated to the world-destroying fire at the end of the kalpa, the only difference being that on this occasion it is Viṣṇu, representing the purity and prosperity of the sacrifice, rather than Śiva, associated with the impurity of the killing of sacrificial animals, who plays the leading role. In this manner:

> the end of the yuga is essentially what unifies the symbolism employed by the authors and characters of the epic, and this unity is that of a socio-cosmic catastrophe in which the spheres governed by the dharma are implicated (*Études* 63, 135).

Yet there is no ready explanation of why the mythical date of the *Mahābhārata* has been placed at the end of the Dvāpara rather than at the end of the Kali Yuga. It is not clear that this can be explained in terms of the responsibilities of the king. What is clear, however, is that it is the king, or rather the quality of his administration, his royal actions, that determines the quality of the time, not the other way around[2] (cf. *MBh*. XII. 92.6; *Manu* IX 301-2). The king is thus key to the dharma, which extends to all three worlds. A rāja-kali is a prince who abdicates his responsibilities, either by his egoistic pursuit of power or by renunciation in the sense of retiring to the forest, which is forbidden to *Kṣatriyas* in the epic literature. Yudhiṣṭhira is warned to avoid the forest life on this account (*MBh*. XII. 12. 28-32), but it is only Śakuni and Duryodhana who are represented as actual incarnations of Dvāpara and Kali respectively. From the twofold use of the yuga symbolism as socio-cosmic time and as bad kings, Biardeau concludes that:

> it is not enough to say that the conflict is a reflection of the end of a yuga. Rather, the conflict is the symbolic transformation of the term, its use at another level. It is this level—the level at which the yugas become demon princes and the cosmic conflagration becomes war—that defines the Epic (*Études* 63, 172).

Having outlined the key role of Epic symbolism, Biardeau is able to return to the main path of her enquiry, namely, to understand the nature and social cultic role of the avatāra, particularly his relationship to the ideal king portrayed in the *Mahābhārata*. Before analysing this relationship in detail, she looks at the general structure of the avatāra and his myths taken from the Purāṇic and Epic accounts of Paraśurāma, Rāma Dāsarāthi, Narasiṃha and Vāmana:

> In this manner we seek to bring some order into this heterogeneous data by approaching it from two angles: we first of all separate out the characteristics that appear relevant to us owing to the fact that they are recurrent but which, as often as not, could also have been deduced from the general notion of the avatāra with which we began. These traits will be presented in abstract fashion, then illustrated from the available data .... Secondly, we will attempt to document the stability of a scenario concerning the avatāra with the help of three accounts briefly annotated in tabular form (*Études* 63, 176).

Biardeau shows that the avatāra is a "periodic accident in the biography of Viṣṇu," galvanized into action by the refusal of a brahmanical orthodoxy to accept the supremacy of Viṣṇu, symbolized in the accounts as an abuse of royal prerogatives. As a result, one can invariably trace the source of the extraordinary powers of evil human kings or of demons (asuras), who come from the nether world and perhaps are incarnated as human kings, to orthodox symbols of some kind. These may be sacrifices performed *ad infinitum* or some favour granted by Brahmā or a powerful Brahmin as a result of asceticism (tapas) or of services rendered. The kings or asuras are invariably ambiguous figures who act in dharmic fashion according to a dharma that leads not to ultimate salvation, granted only by Viṣṇu, but to the prospect of divine status achieved by egoistic self-aggrandizement, usually by taking the gates of heaven by storm.

The avatāra, too, is an ambiguous figure since He represents the true values of a Bhakti hierarchy that must be created anew from the ashes (or the remainder) of the old world order. He is the embodiment of Viṣṇu as destroyer (terrible but also pure) as well as creator; of the power of the warrior (kṣatriya) as well as that of the Brahmin. By mythic necessity He is shown to combine all these qualities. If He is born a Kṣatriya He has Brahmin antecedents, if born a Brahmin He is portrayed as a warrior Brahmin. Significantly, He must also incarnate the sacrifice associated with the sacrificial funeral pyre of the pralāya and the Vedic sacrifice of world creation, both expressed in the imagery of the end of the yuga. However, in its actual performance, this sacrifice has been completely transformed by the notion of performing all actions for the welfare of the world, sacrificing the fruits in an attitude of nonattachment.

The essential structure of the myths themselves may be outlined according to the tabular, comparative approach described by Claude Lévi-Strauss in his *Anthropologie structurale*. The structure includes four main components: (1) the initial crisis leading to a call from the gods for the intervention of Viṣṇu; (2) the actual descent or incarnation into terrestrial (usually human) form; (3) his divine activities leading to a symbolic pralāya; and (4) the inception of a Golden Age in which the values of the sacrificial system are superseded, being transformed into the new world of Bhakti in which even the asura or evil king is offered the prospect of ultimate salvation.

Although the transformations involved in passing from the Purāṇic cosmogonies to the avatāric myths are instructive in revealing the symbolic significance of the Epic accounts in general, there remains the task of explaining the rationale for the symbiotic relationship between the avatāra and the ideal king. The story of the Bhāratas[3] is clearly staged to replicate the structure of the avatāric myths, but the traditional role of the avatāra is almost completely delegated to the king, represented by the five Pāṇḍava princes, of whom Arjuna is chosen as lead actor:

> It is certainly an avatāric myth: a destruction is in prospect to the detriment of the asuras and for the welfare of the worlds, but the avatāra in the strict sense, Kṛṣṇa, the incarnation of Viṣṇu (and Vyāsa, his Brahmanic counterpart) is no longer at centre stage (*Études* 63, 204).

This task is now undertaken, based on the:

> hypothesis which remains to be substantiated, and will be revealed only by degrees as we proceed, according to which the Epic myth is designed to establish the avatāra as the model of the ideal king. But the objective of the present section, after a preliminary summary of the account as a whole, will be to deal with two major difficulties, the first concerning the person of the king, the second dealing with that of the avatāra (*Études* 63, 203).

There are three main sections in what remains of Chapter 2: a structural analysis of the main events and detailed analyses of the king (the issue of why Arjuna?) and of Kṛṣṇa.

The shift of focus from avatāra to king is clearly seen if the structure of the *Mahābhārata* is compared with the four-part structure of the avatāric myths, particularly the myth of Paraśurāma from which the great Epic takes its rise. Although the preparatory events of Book I provide all the ingredients typically associated with the traditional accounts of conflict between gods (devas) and demons (asuras) in stage 1, the incarnation of Kṛṣṇa in stage 2 is hardly mentioned. Instead, the birth and early years of the king, the five Pāṇḍavas, are described in great detail. Significantly, the mix of brahman and kṣatra essential to the avatāra is shown to be a quality of the king, provided we accept Biardeau's interpretation of the svayamvara of Draupadī, in which the princes are disguised as Brahmins. As for stage 3, the direct intervention of the avatāra, Kṛṣṇa is portrayed as a non-combatant even though the deciding factor is as councilor and guide of the Pāṇḍavas. By contrast, the conflict is symbolized as a sacrifice of the king for which the period of exile in the forest is the dīkṣa or ritual preparation. The final holocaust is reached during a cosmic night, when Aśvatthāman almost succeeds in annihilating the lunar dynasty. However, when the survival of the remainder in the form of Parikṣit is threatened in the brahmaśiras episode, at stage 4 Kṛṣṇa steps in to ensure the birth of a new order:

> In terms of the Purāṇic pralāya, we pass from the conflagration to the deluge and to the recreation. Between the nocturnal carnage and the resurrection of Parikṣit (in Book XIV), there takes place this magical killing of an embryo in the womb of a woman: the waters of the deluge that cover the residue of the conflagration are like the fertile womb which will give birth to the three worlds. Inversely, we might here regard the womb of Uttarā ... as the symbolic equivalent of the ocean of the deluge (*Études* 63, 213).

The episodic schema is framed by the two great royal sacrifices performed by Yudhiṣṭhira, which marks the beginning and the end of the conflict, respectively. The rājasūya or royal coronation and the horse sacrifice (aśvamedha) or ritual re-affirmation of the sovereignty are finally restored to the Pāṇḍava lineage. Though the symbolism of the royal coronation is obscure, that of the horse sacrifice seeks to highlight the inherent fecundity of the catastrophe. In agreeing to its performance, Yudhiṣṭhira is not out to consolidate only his own power, but also that of his posterity. Moreover, he enjoins Arjuna to spare the lives of all the foreign princes encountered while tracking the sacrificial horse.

In addition to the disorder on the cosmic plane, symbolized by the conflict of gods and demons, the Epic also takes account of a more mundane source of trouble. This includes the breakdown in the right relationship between the *Brahman* and the *Kṣatra*, symbolized by the fierce enmity between the Brahmin Droṇa and his former friend and companion, Drupāda, royal father of both Dhṛṣṭadyumna and Draupadī. By mythic necessity they end up in opposing camps. Yet because of his role as military instructor of both parties and by the example of his death:

> it is Bṛhaspati-Droṇa who engineers the mutation that is accomplished — illustrated by the Epic myth — in the notion of sacrifice .... In order to guarantee him (the Kṣatriya) his share of salvation, the Bhakti tradition henceforth expresses his own proper activities, principally the activities of war, in terms of sacrifice (*Études* 63, 253).

Through the sacrifice of a bird during his archery lesson, for example, Arjuna has not only a preliminary exercise for his own later sacrifice of war but also the attitude that goes with it. This is yogic concentration (ekāgra), the detachment and single-minded devotion to the task he is called upon by Kṛṣṇa to accomplish. In this way, the sacrifice of war becomes a yogic act, a self-sacrifice (ātmayajña), exemplified by the death of Droṇa himself who is ritually beheaded by Dhṛṣṭadyumna on the battlefield.

In Biardeau's view, the most significant result to emerge from a preliminary structural analysis of the Epic is the discovery of an inherent duality of the storyline, whereby the avatāra is cast in the secondary role of model and guide for a king who bears the brunt of the action. Biardeau is reminded of the two birds of the *Muṇḍaka Upaniṣad*, one that looks on while the other eats. From this she concludes that the *Mahābhārata* is not strictly a myth of the avatāra but a royal myth modelled on it. This dual perspective has the additional merit, in her view, of clearing up unresolved difficulties with respect to the yuga symbolism and the individual responsibility of the king. Thus, "the presence of the avatāra makes it necessary to date the Epic between the Dvāpara and Kali Yugas, while the transposition of his intervention into a royal myth of similar form translates into the incarnation of the asuras Dvāpara and Kali in two of the protagonists" (*Études* 65, 87). Why this necessarily follows is not clear. In any case, there is the duality of a double causality at work according to the point of view taken. From the divine perspective, the course of events is completely predetermined. However:

> if in contrast, we place ourselves at the point of view of the king who, by his action, brings about the reign of this or that yuga, thus imposing a human causality on the course of time, fate (daiva) may be overcome, and the role of the king is to turn this to the advantage of his kingdom (*Études* 65, 88).

The question must now be posed: who exactly is this king in the *Mahābhārata*? At first sight it is Yudhiṣṭhira, eldest of the Pāṇḍavas and the one who is actually consecrated king. "However, the Epic account is not for one moment based on the pair Kṛṣṇa-Yudhiṣṭhira ..., nothing that is comparable to the unity of Kṛṣṇa and Arjuna" (*Études* 65, 88). These two are not only incarnations of the Highest Divinity and the king of the Vedic gods (Indra) but also of the great sages Nārāyaṇa and Nara respectively:

> It remains to grasp the rationale for this creation, and the hypothesis I advance is that it is designed to make of the king the representative of the avatāra on earth and his substitute as sacrificial victim par excellence .... But the avatāra has become two, and everything that Kṛṣṇa says of himself in the *Bhagavadgītā* is found in the rest of the Epic in dual form in order to bring Arjuna into association with him. There is, therefore, no doubt that Arjuna shares the role of avatāra, that he is himself avatāra (*Études* 65, 92-3).

The truth of her hypothesis is revealed in two parts: the first dealing with the relation of the two older brothers to the issue of kingship (the twins not being included in this analysis), and the second with Arjuna in his role as ideal king and avatāra.

The elder Pāṇḍavas are, of course, also kings, but only in the sense that they represent what, in effect, are the two orders of value to which the ideal king must subscribe. The first looks away from the world towards the goal of ultimate salvation (mokṣa). The second represents the sensual (kāma) and materialistic (artha) values that keep this world in being. Thus, Yudhiṣṭhira represents not only the dharmic order in its totality but also the divine yoga, the intervention of fate (daiva) and the destructive forces of death that bring the promise of a new age. The association of Yudhiṣṭhira with Yama (who shares his title of Dharmarāja) finally reveals the true significance of the rājasūya as the coronation of Yama, king of death, leading to the temporary eclipse, or banishment, of dharma under the influence of daiva (via the dice-game). This suggests that the royalty of Yudhiṣṭhira is a royalty of death in contrast to that of Bhīma, which is a royalty of life through his associations with the life force (prāṇa), and with desire (kāma), since he is an incarnation of Vāyu.

Arjuna is formally subordinated to his two older brothers only because he serves the values they represent. In reality he is the ideal king, son of Indra, who is ontologically identical to the avatāra, as Nara. Should this second hypothesis be correct:

> one would expect to find in the terrestrial king, in one form or another, a combination of the kṣatra and brahman which gives him absolute dominion over the inhabitants of the three worlds, desiring at the same time to place his power at the service of the true Brahmanic values (revised and corrected by bhakti). At another level, and more particularly at a time of crisis where much is to be destroyed, we must clearly be able to recognize his Rudraic and Viṣṇuite components. In particular, his activities will bear a sacrificial character, but these sacrifices will be that of a yogi who is at the same time perfectly concentrated on his task—the royal form of meditation—and detached from personal gain, the egoistic motivation for his acts giving way to a concern for the welfare of the worlds. We should be able to show in a systematic fashion that Arjuna expresses all these traits, both in terms of his training and by his exploits (*Études* 65, 111).

Biardeau sets out to accomplish her aim by following the significant episodes of Arjuna's career in the next major section of her analysis, beginning with his birth and early years. Of course, given that Yudhiṣṭhira is *de facto* the king, one would expect the royal destiny of Arjuna to be expressed not only in his own character and exploits but by the symbolic associations attached to them. For example, in predicting that "the hero, together with his brothers, will offer three sacrifices" (*MBh* I. 114.34, and often elsewhere), the voice from heaven at his birth establishes the sacrificial character of the task that awaits all five brothers and suggests that Arjuna is the principal sacrificer (yajamāna), officiating priest and victim, throughout. Again, during the archery lesson (which, in Biardeau's view, represents the actual consecration of Arjuna as ideal king), it is only Arjuna who exhibits the yogic qualities that allow him to officiate as symbolic Brahmin priest at the sacrifice of the bird. It is also Arjuna among the brothers who is chosen to perform the test of prowess that wins Draupadī, after which Karṇa refers to him as crowned (kirīṭin). Furthermore, while the collective marriage of Draupadī is a symbol of the distribution of royalty over all five princes, Arjuna is finally revealed to be her favourite (*MBh* XVII. 2).

His terrestrial relationship to the avatāra, symbolic of his ontological identity, is cemented by his second marriage to Subhadrā, whereby he becomes the brother-in-law of Kṛṣṇa. Thus, Subhadrā becomes his counterpart as the ideal queen who places herself at the service of Śrī, the prosperity of the Earth represented by Draupadī. These are but a few of the many examples of symbolic correspondence that may be mentioned from the nearly hundred pages of detailed analysis in Biardeau's work.

The sacrificial and royal character of the Epic and of Arjuna's life and destiny in particular is evident both in terms of individual events and in terms of Arjuna's career. His three sacrifices are recognized:

> without too much difficulty as the rājasūya of Yudhiṣṭhira in Book II, the non-ritual but very royal sacrifice of the war and finally the aśvamedha with which the war is concluded and by which Yudhiṣṭhira is re-instated as the dharmarāja in Book XIV (*Études* 65, 114).

In each case, Arjuna acts with his brothers, but in each case he emerges as the principal yajamāna as well as officiating priest. The meaning of the war is obvious. Although Arjuna has no official position (Dhṛṣṭadyumna being general-in-chief), "the only one who can change the spiritual meaning of the war and restore the crumbling moral order is Arjuna, and his strength is derived from his close association with Kṛṣṇa" (*Études* 65, 118). This will be discussed in more detail below. In addition, Biardeau suggests that even in the rājasūya and in the aśvamedha, both of which are expressly related to Yudhiṣṭhira, Arjuna is the principal sacrificial agent. With respect to the rājasūya, the preliminary rite (dīgvijāya) of submission of the kings from all the four quarters is begun by Arjuna. During the ritual itself, although it is not described in detail in the text, the king is identified with Indra, who is referred to by name as Arjuna or Phālguna according to the ritual version. "If the king of the rājasūya accepts for himself the names of Indra, the temptation is strong to attribute the real investiture to Arjuna" (*Études* 65, 116). The rite of unction is also accompanied by twelve oblations bearing the name Pārtha. Similar symbolic attributions are also apparent in the case of the aśvamedha, in which Arjuna accompanies the sacrificial horse.

Like these three sacrifices, Arjuna's career may be likened to the ritual activities associated with a Vedic sacrifice. Biardeau sees in his early training, periodic brahmacārya, exile in the forest, and the various labours to which he is subjected, all the marks of a symbolic initiation (dīkṣa). These include the traditional fasting, purification, etc. required of the yajamāna prior to the ritual act itself. In his case, of course, this leads to a radical transformation of the original orthodox connotations by infusion of the new ego-transcending values of yoga and asceticism, based on actions undertaken with single-minded concentration and devotion to the task at hand in a spirit of true renunciation, abandoning one's own interest in favour of the welfare of the world (lokasaṃgraha). The emergence of some of these yogic qualities on the occasion of Arjuna's early training in sacrificial slaying has already been noted.

The theme of initiation is also evident in the brahmacārya that Arjuna is called upon to observe on several occasions. Biardeau shows how the meaning of this word shifts in the case of Arjuna as he moves from student of the Veda to renunciate in the sense of an ascetic life spent as a dweller in the forest or vānaprasthin. In common with all forms of tapas, the practice of asceticism and sexual abstinence is a way to self-conquest. This leads to the acquisition of the spiritual powers (siddhi) required for him to conquer the external world as well, symbolically setting it ablaze with his tejas. By a fusion of symbols, it is also associated with the power of the Brahman required to perform the sacrificial act of war. By the power of the Brahman, charged with the fires of tapas and saṃnyāsa, he is also able to assert control over his divine weaponry.

The link of brahmacārya with forest life is a way of distinguishing the life of renunciation from that of the worldly values associated with the town or village. The two periods of twelve years that Arjuna must spend in exile are assimilated to the notion of a dīkṣa in preparation for the sacrificial slaughter to come. The first is the result of an infraction of the agreement between the brothers regarding their common wife. Arjuna is obliged to interrupt his eldest brother at an inopportune moment in order to assist a Brahmin to recover his stolen cows. As a result, he leaves the well-ordered life of Indraprastha for a life of brahmacārya in the forest, which, paradoxically, nets him three additional wives, including Subhadrā. The second occasion is, of course, the time spent in forest exile with his brothers after the disastrous game of dice. Shortly after they had left, Duḥśāsana remarks that "the sons of Pṛthā (Kuntī), defeated, ritually prepared (dīkṣitā) as they were to live in the forest, each took with them the skin of a black antelope as an outer garment" (*MBh* II. 68.1-3a). The association of the black antelope with the Vedic sacrifice is well-attested in the orthodox literature, as is seen in the story of Prajāpati, the personification of the sacrifice, who changes into a black antelope to escape from Śiva (cf. *Aitareya Br.* III. 33; *Śatapatha Br.* VI. 4,1,6; *Manu* II. 23).

A dīkṣa related to a forest of a slightly different order is also suggested by the account of the burning of the Khāṇḍava forest. In this case, the forest is a symbolic microcosm of the three worlds, whose destruction is ordained by the sickness of Agni, the sacrificial fire being transformed into the fires of the pralāya, as a result of the deviation of King Śvetaki from his prescribed social role as a Kṣatriya (i.e., he acts like a Brahmin):

> The burning of the Khāṇḍava forest is thus presented as a sacrifice that is ungoverned as opposed to the regular sacrifices governed by dharma, and at the same time as a funeral sacrifice: the wood that burns is the funeral pyre of the creatures that inhabit it" (*Études* 65, 145-6).

The event is important not only as a dress rehearsal for the actual war, but also for the symbolism that marks Arjuna as a prospective avatāra capable of vanquishing the devas, in the figure of his own father, and destroying the world — always excepting a small remainder to provide the basis for a new creation. Here the remainder includes the serpent Takṣaka, symbol of creative chaos, and the asura Maya, master of illusion, who in all probability is the Epic analogue of the five-fold ignorance (avidyā) of the secondary creation (pratisarga).

In order to be dīkṣitā for the major sacrifice of his career, Arjuna must also be worthy of receiving and handling an arsenal of divine weapons from a variety of sources. Agni has already given him the bow Gāṇḍīva, two inexhaustible quivers, and a chariot with the Hanuman banner, which gave him victory over the devas at Khāṇḍava, with the help of Kṛṣṇa. However, an avatāra is also required to conquer the demons, now rampant in all three worlds — heaven, earth and beneath the sea — a much more difficult task since evil is always more powerful than the good. Śiva alone is able to help him secure what he needs in terms of weaponry and the necessary passport to enter heaven. It is no easy initiation because it involves not only a long journey and the rigours of extreme tapas, but also an encounter with Śiva and an asuric boar, which leaves him "in a state of piṇḍa, a shapeless mass or a small ball of rice reminiscent of an oblation. The sacrificial connotations of the whole account are clear. Arjuna is the victim who is smothered to death, and this takes the form of an oblation" (*Études* 65, 150). The episode is worthy to be regarded as a new initiation in its own right in the sense that:

> the dīkṣa is that phase of the sacrifice during which the performer offers himself as the victim in the form of the various ascetic practices of continence, fasting etc.: but in this respect the dīkṣa should be regarded as the sacrifice itself, given the fact that it is another victim that is finally substituted for the person of the sacrificer (Études 65, 156).

In effect, the *dīkṣa* itself becomes an *ātmayajña*, a self-sacrifice, a sacrifice in which Arjuna (the animal, *paśu*) offers himself as an oblation. "Mahādeva induces Arjuna to perform *ātmayajña*, to experience *ātmayajña*, the essential dimension of what should in fact be called the spirituality of the warrior, if war must be a sacrifice" (*Études* 65, 157). When he finally recovers, Arjuna offers a garland before a small mound of earth, marking his total devotion to Lord Śiva whom he had not previously recognized. Unlike the asuric boar Mūka (mute), Arjuna becomes the symbolic equivalent of the sacrificial boar who saves the world.

After receiving the brahmaśiras[4] from Śiva and other assorted weaponry from the gods of the four quarters, Arjuna is allowed to proceed to the heavenly domain of Indra where he receives all manner of royal honours, including the conch Devadatta and the royal diadem (kiraṭā). He concludes his heavenly education by learning the arts of music and dance (gāndharva veda) from Citrasena, arts symbolizing the divine līlā as it is played out in the events of the world. Henceforth Arjuna is also symbolically master of the divine play, the realm of māyā which, transposed into royal terms, implies the administration of the state (rājanīti or daṇḍanīti).

In contrast to the twelve-year exile in the forest during the reign of Duryodhana — which, for Biardeau, is "a sort of symbolic dīkṣa but with cosmic and ideological dimensions" — the thirteenth year at the court of Virāṭa, king of Matsya (fish), is the immediate preparation for war. Here "the value of the dīkṣa is characterized symbolically by a period of concealment: they [i.e. the Pāṇḍavas] are hidden like embryos in the womb of their mother, and they offer themselves as sacrificial victims according to their individual character" (*Études* 65, 188). In Arjuna's case, the enforced brahmacārya as the eunuch Bṛhannatā stands in sharp contrast to the emphasis laid on his royal status and character during his sojourn at the heavenly court of Indra. Given the key role of Uttarā as mother of Parikṣit, and Arjuna's daughter-in-law, this must be interpreted not only in terms of his attitude to the lady herself but also to what she represents for the future of the dynasty. In other words, he prepares to fight not for himself or even for his brothers but for the new order that is to emerge in the form of his grandson. In effect, he is prepared (dīkṣita) to fight like an avatāra in a spirit of detachment for the welfare of the world.

The royal, avatāric and sacrificial functions of Arjuna during the war is revealed in a number of ways. First, although he has no official military command, he is clearly in complete command of events and of the dreaded brahmaśiras weapon. Furthermore, it is evident from the discourse of Yama (*MBh* III. 42.24, just before his ascent to svarga) that Arjuna is the chosen instrument to wield the daṇḍa. "With Viṣṇu you must relieve the Earth. Take this weapon, my daṇḍa, which bears no obstacle. With this you will do a great karma." Among those specifically marked to die through his actions are Bhiṣma, Droṇa and Karṇa, with assorted dānavas and rakṣasas presently incarnated on earth, in short, all the kings responsible for the social disruption resulting from their misuse of the powers of the brahman and the kṣatra respectively. Finally, Biardeau selects for analysis three events that take place during the battle which serve to further highlight the royal nature of Arjuna. Two are related to the death of Bhiṣma: the creation of his bed of arrows and the enchanted arrow that pierces the earth to create a spring of drinking water. A third, the creation of a magical lake to water the horses in the midst of the battle, is an example of his mastery of māyā.

Biardeau also examines the problem of Kṛṣṇa, specifically the problem of reconciling the martial Kṛṣṇa of the *Mahābhārata* with the cowherd Kṛṣṇa portrayed in the *Harivaṃśa* (*HV*). Biardeau starts from the assumption that what appears to be a contradiction here is a contradiction for us rather than for the mythographers themselves:

> On the contrary, it is necessary to maintain the duality, to take account of the fact that the HV is given as a supplement to the *MBh*, albeit belonging to the genre of the Purāṇas rather than to the Epics, and to try and understand why the biography of Kṛṣṇa is split in two, a childhood spent in the region of Mathurā among the cowherds ... and the life of a man centred, on the one hand, around the residence at Dvārakā, on the other, around the exploits of the Pāṇḍava heroes .... One way of approaching the problem would be to ask whether the *Kṣatriya* of the *MBh.* completely excludes the cowherd of Mathurā and, in reciprocal fashion, whether the cowherd of Gokula is anything other than a Kṣatriya in disguise. If we are able to accommodate these two characterizations in this manner, we will then be justified in asking the reason for this duality ...." (*Études* 65, 205).

Her approach is always to seek in the *MBh* the reason for this or that detail in the *Harivaṃśa*, based on the assumption that it is the *MBh* that wishes to introduce the avatāra into the epic account.

As usual, she chooses the symbolic route. In order to test her first hypothesis, that there is a mythic linkage between the two Kṛṣṇas, she conducts a detailed examination of the respective texts, this time in sequence rather than in parallel. Biardeau finds her work rewarded in the form of symbolic connections that may be established largely in the Govardhana story but also in two earlier childhood episodes, which reveal Kṛṣṇa as avatāra through being saviour and protector of the cows, symbol of the dharma. The notion of cowherd is assimilated to the idea of one who wields the staff (daṇḍa) as royal protector of the dharma. It turns out, once again, that these early years are an initiation for the avataric mission that he undertakes in the killing of Kaṃsa, the mission being an active one in the case of the *Harivaṃśa*, whereas in the *Mahābhārata* the omnipresence and activity of Kṛṣṇa are delegated to Arjuna and to his cowherd warriors in the service of Duryodhana. The killing of Kaṃsa leads to the main episodic link between the two parts of Kṛṣṇa's life: the hostility of his father-in-law (Jarāsandha) who undertakes eighteen campaigns against the Yādavas, evoking the eighteen days of the *Mahābhārata* war, and is finally killed in his turn by Bhīma. A comparative, tabular analysis of texts reveals that:

> there are therefore two exploits in parallel. The first crowns the pastoral career of Kṛṣṇa and fully qualifies him as avatāra, since the death of Kaṃsa makes way for the restoration of the dharmic kingdom. The other leads to the rājasūya of Yudhiṣṭhira and initiates the great crisis of the *Mahābhārata* (*Études* 65, 225).

Having established to her satisfaction that the two Kṛṣṇas are one and the same, Biardeau must then explain the rationale for this apparent incongruity. Once again she looks for the solution to it in the *Mahābhārata*, specifically in the Jarāsandha episode, which clears the way for the rājasūya of Yudhiṣṭhira:

> The hypothesis is the following: it was necessary to introduce Jarāsandha as a sort of double of Kaṃsa to justify the presence of the Pāṇḍavas with respect to Kṛṣṇa and the exploits of the Epic, together with the incarnation of Nara in Arjuna at the side of Nārāyaṇa-Kṛṣṇa. Since Kṛṣṇa does not function as the avatāra in the Epic itself, it must be assumed that he had previously been engaged in a mission as avatāra and that this work, remaining unfulfilled, must be accomplished with the help of Arjuna surrounded by his brothers and under the overall direction of Kṛṣṇa himself (*Études* 65, 221).

Jarāsandha serves as a convenient heuristic device of mythographers wishing to shift the emphasis in the Epic from the avatāra to the role of the ideal king whose actions must be guided by his divine prototype.

Two effects may be noted. It relegates Kṛṣṇa to a secondary role, and it makes of Jarāsandha and his two lieutenants, Haṃsa and Ḍimbhaka, a negative counterpart to the triad of Kṛṣṇa, Arjuna and Yudhiṣṭhira:

> Arjuna and Kṛṣṇa, incarnations of Nara and Nārāyaṇa, make up with Yudhiṣṭhira the victorious triad for which Haṃsa, Ḍimbhaka and Jarāsandha are but the abortive counterpart. In the distinction between these two groups of heroes we find introjected the whole philosophy of the Epic or, even more precisely, an expression of the Epic transposition of the Upaniṣadic vision of the world. The crisis presided over by the dharmarāja, managed by the avatāra and successfully executed by Arjuna, is the prospect of salvation for the warriors who fall on the field of battle. Just as the conflagration that inaugurated the cosmic night between two kalpas is the opening for all the residents of svarga to obtain a definite deliverance, similarly the sacrifice of the battle as taught by Kṛṣṇa is the promise of salvation .... But this avataric role, linked to world crisis, is, in fact, the permanent task of the earthly king. Of the two birds of the *Muṇḍaka*, one remains inactive because he is the witness, the Supreme Puruṣa, the great yogi, whereas the other engages untiringly in empirical activities, which is the case with Arjuna because he knows he is supported by his inseparable friend. In contrast, Jarāsandha, the sacrificer of kings, would avoid world crisis in favour of the eternal return of old age (jarā) and death (*Études* 65, 233-4).

L'Hindouisme: anthropologie d'une civilisation

The remarkable odyssey in search of the symbolic keys to the transformation of values that took place at the very heart of brahmanical orthodoxy is, as yet, far from complete. A comprehensive vision of Hinduism would embrace a good deal more than the world of Purāṇic and Epic literature. As a result, if Biardeau's central thesis is to be accepted, she must find in orthodox Brahmanism the permanent heart not only of Bhakti but also of the various sectarian traditions and of the Hindu Tantra. Is this possible? Indeed it is, according to *L'Hindouisme: anthropologie d'une civilization*:

> It is true that the transition from the virgin goddess (the Kālī of the *Harivaṃśa*, the Devī of the *Devī Māhātmya*, the numerous territorial protectresses etc.) to the sexual partner of Śiva (the active prakṛti vs. the inactive puruṣa) involves a break in the unified framework that we have considered up to now. Let us not be surprised to rediscover, furnished with the opposite sign, the great themes of Hindu Bhakti and, beyond this, of Brahmanic renunciation. The Tantra invents nothing. In reinterpreting the Tradition in an esoteric manner it simply inverts the commonly accepted values (*L'Hindouisme* 164).

The process of inversion is almost entirely centred on attitudes towards egocentricity and the problem of desire (kāma) The latter is a legitimate goal of life (puruṣārtha) in orthodox circles but traditionally opposed to the goal of liberation (mokṣa), even in the classical Bhakti tradition which, as we have seen, attempted to solve the problem by cutting the link between action and its fruit. Renunciation became not renunciation *of* action but renunciation *in* action by renouncing only the results dedicated to egocentric purposes. Action is henceforth dedicated to the Lord in the form of the avatāra who acts for the welfare of the worlds and is responsible for all fruits. For the tāntrika, however, it is not so much the act itself but the rasa, the quality of the emotion that accompanies it, that is the focus of attention. From this perspective there can no longer be opposition between desire and liberation. Rather, desire, suitably transformed, becomes the salvific vehicle that transports one to the promised land:

> It is around the notion of kāma— in the comprehensive sense given to it by the renunciant — and of all the connotations associated with it, that the speculations on a truly universal salvation are constellated. Bhakti looks for a solution to the abolition of the kāma at the very heart of the ordinary activities of man. In other words it will try and introduce the ideal of the saṃnyāsin into secular life. In contrast, what by too vague a term has been called Tantrism will be the attempt to place kāma (in all senses of the term) and the values associated with it at the service of deliverance" (*L'Hindouisme* 97).

This new emphasis on the salvific benefits of affect, whereby the ego and all its desires are dissolved in an emotional flood of ecstasy (rāga), has a number of implications. First, it changes the very notion of divinity which, in its extreme forms (e.g. Sahajiyā in Bengal and in Śaktism), replaces the male with the female as supreme principle. It also broadens the notion of love by opposing a higher — a selfless form of love (prema) — to the kāma of ordinary human relationships. This is evident both in the emotional Bhakti of Rādhā-cults such as the Gosvāmin and in the sexual practices of the left-handed Tantra, which are ascetic rather than libertine in nature. In both cases this leads to the union of the devotee (bhakta) with the object of his or her love. The difference is that in Bhakti emotionalism — which must be distinguished from the classical Bhakti of the *Bhagavadgītā* and of Rāmānūja — the union of Rādha and Kṛṣṇa is dependent on God's grace, whereas in Tantric circles the sādhaka finds a way to the cosmic union of prakṛti and puruṣa within him- or herself through yoga.

Perhaps the most important implication of this inversion of attitudes to love lies in the field of private and public ritual practices. What the Upaniṣadic renunciant would abandon is reintroduced by the emotional cults in the form of a plethora of religious practices of all kinds, evocative of the importance given in traditional brahmanical circles to the power of the well- executed ritual formula. The focus in the private daily practice of yoga is on the body, based on the presumed correspondence between the microcosm of the subtle body and the macrocosm as a whole. This often takes the form of a ritual offered to the divinity in oneself. However, Biardeau makes particular mention of the yoga techniques associated with the raising of the sexual energy in the form of kuṇḍalinī, the serpent power reminiscent of the serpent Seṣa, the repose of Viṣṇu-Nārāyaṇa asleep on the waters of the deluge. The temple spectaculars, too, are all steeped in an elaborate symbolism in which "every ingredient, every formula, every movement in space has its symbolic significance, which only the initiate is able to understand" (*L'Hindouisme* 164-5).

Conclusion

Although Biardeau's quest is by no means over, we conclude by joining her in inquiring, as she does in the conclusion of *L'Hindouisme: anthropologie d'une civilisation*: "Have we kept to the kind of wager put forward at the beginning, to rediscover an underlying unity beneath the infinite diversity exhibited by Hinduism at first glance?" (*L'Hindouisme* 173). We note first of all that the unity she finds is not a unity of composition or of doctrine, but consists of a coherent symbolic structure of values that may be traced to orthodox antecedents in the Vedas and the Upaniṣads. The structural elements of this are primarily the Vedic sacrifice with all that this implies about the pure and the impure and the functional relationship between the brahmin and the kṣatriya, and the Upaniṣadic concept of renunciation.

Through the medium of a complex multi-dimensional symbolism the Brahmin authors of the epic, the Purāṇic and also the Tantric texts, were able to transform and hierachize these principles in the form of mythical stories set against the backdrop of a cosmic panorama of space and time. In this respect, Biardeau's argument about the brahmanical heart of modern Hinduism is a persuasive one. On the other hand, her characterization of the *Mahābhārata* — the "founding charter" of Bhakti — as a strategy for opening a path to salvation for kings, does not square with the facts of the narrative. The kings involved all end up in the same heaven from which they came, without a trace of final beatitude for any of them. Presumably countless lives of selfless service and devotion will be needed before this lofty goal is achieved.

Furthermore, Biardeau's insistence that a historical approach has no place in the Hindu world is extreme. Surely the very term itihāsa suggests a modicum of historical consciousness in the Indian psyche. And do not her own synchronic methods of structural analysis lead to a "historical" view to the extent that they enable her to trace a chronology of brahmanical continuity leading from Vedic orthodoxy, through a "universe of Bhakti," to the very different world of Hindu Tantra? We must remember, too, that the structural approach is itself of Western origin and thus not fully consonant with her attempt to work entirely within the traditional Indian framework. In addition, it is highly unlikely that the Bhrahmin authors of the text drew exclusively from a closed Vedic system of symbols and myth. One must allow for the possibility of cross-fertilization among the various cultural groups that are known to have co-existed in the Indian sub-continent.

It is nevertheless difficult not to be moved by Biardeau's enthusiasm for every detail that holds promise of further insight, by her readiness to try new approaches when others fail, and above all, by her evident humility in the face of the immensity of her task. In spite of her disagreements with some of her Western and Indian colleagues, Biardeau is willing to admit that "at the point where we are in epic research, my conviction is that there is a place for radically different approaches, with no initial connection between them, but which should tend to a long-term convergence" (*Études* 63, 218).

NOTES

1. All quotations from the French original have been translated by the author of this paper.

2. The episode of the dice game also reveals an element of daiva at work here.

3. Biardeau deliberately restricts her analysis to the *Mahābhārata* which, in contrast to the *Rāmāyana*, separates the two figures of avatāra and king.

4. The "head of Brahmā," symbol of the "power" residing in the sacrificial offering, here is affiliated with the Pāśuspata weapon, symbol of the "power" located in the sacrificial axe.

BIBLIOGRAPHY

Biardeau, Madeleine. 1968-1978. *Études de mythologie hindou.* Parts I-V, published in the *Bulletin de l'Ecole Française de l'Extrème Orient.* Vols. 54 (Part I), 55 (Part II), 58 (Part III), 63 (Part IV) and 65 (Part V). Paris.

—. 1981. *L'Hindouisme: anthropologie d'une civilisation.* Paris: Editions Flammarion, Collection Champs.

THE TAMILIZING OF A SACRED SANSKRIT TEXT: THE DEVOTIONAL MOOD OF RĀMĀNUJA'S BHAGAVADGĪTĀ-BHĀṢYA AND ĀḺVĀR SPIRITUALITY

Nancy Ann Nayar

Among the multitude of sacred Hindu texts, perhaps none has been treated with greater reverence or accorded more attention than the *Bhagavadgītā*. The profusion of commentaries written to expound its meaning testifies to this fact. One of the most important of these is the *Bhagavadgītā-bhāṣya* of Rāmānuja [*RGB*]. Rāmānuja (d. 1137) is best known as the founder-expounder of one of the major schools of Indian philosophy — Viśiṣṭādvaita Vedānta. He is revered within his own Tamil-based community of Śrīvaiṣṇavas not only as a philosopher, but also as a paradigmatic devotee of Viṣṇu and a leading preceptor-teacher (Ācārya) within a guru-lineage that extends to the present day. Detailed analysis of portions of his outstanding commentary — when viewed in the light of the spirituality of the Tamilian Āḻvār poems — demonstrates how Rāmānuja "Tamilized" portions of this sacred Sanskrit text through the incorporation of a concept of God and notions of a highly-charged emotional devotion from the Āḻvār side of his Śrīvaiṣṇava tradition.

As the inheritors of ubhaya-vedānta, the "dual" Vedānta, Śrīvaiṣṇavas give equal scriptural status to both the Sanskrit Veda and the "Tamil Veda" — a collection of the sacred Tamil poems (*Divyaprabandham*) of twelve poets known as the Āḻvārs ("those immersed in God") who lived approximately between the 6th and 9th centuries (Hardy 1983, 269). Because Rāmānuja nowhere in his philosophical writings explicitly refers to the Āḻvārs or their poems, there has been a widespread assumption among modern scholars that his thought as expounded in his philosophical treatises has remained uninfluenced by these Tamil Vaiṣṇava poets. On the other hand, some have noted the unique devotional "mood" of Rāmānuja's commentary on the *Bhagavadgītā*, contrasting it with his other philosophical works (for example, Van Buitenen 1974, 18, 28 and Carman [1974] 1981, 61). They have, however, not attempted either to develop or explain this aspect of Rāmānuja's work. This article, therefore, explores the unique "mood" of the commentary, tracing it to certain notions and phraseology contained in the Tamil poems of the Āḻvārs.

In this study, I examine in detail two frequently reiterated statements by which Rāmānuja establishes the different "mood" of his commentary on the *Bhagavadgītā*. One sets forth the concept of God's untaintedness (nirmalatvam/amalatvam), followed by a declaration of his auspicious qualities; the other describes the inability of the devotee to find sustenance for the soul in separation from God. In both of these case studies, the influence of Āḻvār spirituality can be discerned, and I have pinpointed some relevant passages from the *Divyaprabandham*. From this perspective, the *RGB* is recognized as an important text linking the spirituality of the Āḻvārs to the later tradition of the Ācāryas.

The implications of this finding are brought to bear upon the current understanding of the Śrīvaiṣṇava tradition regarding: (1) the general reliability and historicity of the hagiographical stories, in this case those that connect Rāmānuja with the Āḻvārs; and (2) the continuity or discontinuity between the Āḻvārs and the Ācāryas within the Śrīvaiṣṇava sampradāya with special reference to Rāmānuja's position therein.[1]

I. Rāmānuja's Relation to the Āḻvārs: The Traditional View and its Modern Critique

All extant Śrīvaiṣṇava literary sources— including poems in praise of Rāmānuja, independent eulogistic verses (taṉiyaṉs) by or about Rāmānuja, the three major Śrīvaiṣṇava hagiographical texts, and several major temple chronicles — are in unanimous agreement that not only was Rāmānuja a Vedāntic philosopher par excellence, but that he was deeply imbued with Āḻvār spirituality as well.

The *Irāmānucanūṟṟantāti*, a 108 verse Tamil poem in praise of Rāmānuja, contains what is probably the most compelling evidence of the link between Rāmānuja and the Āḻvārs. Reputedly composed by Tiruvaraṅkattamutaṉār (Amutaṉār), an immediate disciple of Rāmānuja, the *Irāmānucanūṟṟantāti* is an authoritative text (from the viewpoint of Śrīvaiṣṇava self-understanding) in that its inclusion as part of the *Divyaprabandham* confers upon it a special status among works of its kind. According to a story common to all the Śrīvaiṣṇava hagiographical texts, it was during the actual lifetime of Rāmānuja that the *Irāmānucanūṟṟantāti* came to be recited in the inner sanctum of the Śrīraṅgam temple immediately following the *Iyarpā*[2] recitation. Known as the prapanna gāyatrī, it was to be chanted daily by all Śrīvaiṣṇavas.[3]

Regardless of the historicity of this story, at some point in time — at least by the beginning of the 13th century C.E. — the *Irāmānucanūṟṟantāti* was included as a part of the *Divyaprabandham.* Its inclusion forms for Śrīvaiṣṇavas a substantive link between Rāmānuja and that corpus. The *Irāmānucanūṟṟantāti* contains what are probably the earliest explicit references connecting Rāmānuja with the Āḻvārs. John Carman has noted that "it may well be the only genuine contemporary work specifically about Rāmānuja ([1974] 1981, 36). This makes it an important text not only for the more traditionally-minded but for those involved in modern historical research as well.[4]

The poem contains a total of nine verses that directly connect Rāmānuja with Nammāḻvār, the most important Āḻvār, who wrote 1,000 hymns.[5] Rāmānuja is said to have mastered the Veda of Nammāḻvār (māṟaṉ maṟai) (v.46); he made the whole expansive earth to understand the pure Tamil Veda (centamiḻ āraṇam) (v. 19); and he made us understand deeply "the thousand hymns (*Tiruvāymoḻi*)" (v.18). Rāmānuja is said to have been intoxicated by the *Tiruvāymoḻi* [*TVM*] and is compared to an elephant from which flows the beautiful Tamil of Nammāḻvār (Caṭakōpaṉ) (v.64). Verses 54 and 60 link the Ācārya Rāmānuja, the Sanskrit Veda, the Tamil Veda and Rāmānuja's philosophical school. Rāmānuja, referred to as "the great one of our family or clan" (eṅ kula), is said to be present both in the yoga of the great wise ones (jñānīs) and in the fragrance of the *TVM* wherever it spreads in this world (v.60).[6]

The second most important source from the point of view of modern historical research are three Tamil taṉiyaṉs[7] that link Rāmānuja with Āḻvār spirituality. Because taṉiyaṉs are single verses in praise of an author or a sacred text, their authorship is almost impossible to verify. I think that the best method is to approach the question negatively. Are there any reasons why the taṉiyaṉ would appear not to have been composed by its presumed author either on grounds of content, language or the author's contemporaneity with the development of the taṉiyaṉ tradition? We know for certain that taṉiyaṉs were being composed at least by the time of Yāmuna, Rāmānuja's predecessor in the Ācārya line; the first dateable taṉiyaṉ was composed by Yāmuna in praise of his grandfather and predecessor in the guruparamparā, Nāthamuni.[8] We also know for certain — from the stotras of Kūreśa and Parāśarabhaṭṭar — that the tradition was flourishing by Rāmānuja's time.

Two taṉiyaṉs in praise of specific poems in the *Divyaprabandham* are said to have been composed by Rāmānuja himself. In the first, attached to Nammāḻvār's *Periyatiruvantāti*, the author "encourages his heart to recite the name of Māṟaṉ (i.e. Nammāḻvār)" (Hardy 1978, 78). A second taṉiyaṉ attributed to Rāmānuja praises Tirumaṅkaiyāḻvār's *Tiruveḻukkūṟṟirukkai*, which is said to contain the entire meaning of the Vedas:

> I bow down to the feet—
> which are our refuge—
> of the one who has given
> the entire meaning of the Vedas
> in the form of the *Tiruveḻukkūṟṟirukkai*
> which is composed in good Tamil (centamiḻ)
> for the uplift of the world.
> It is a great [poem],
> [it] is the ambrosia that never satiates.[9]

The other two taṉiyaṉs of interest here are both in praise of the *TVM*. The first is reputed to have been composed by Rāmānuja's immediate disciple, Anantāḻvāṉ; the second is by Parāśarabhaṭṭar (the son of Rāmānuja's favourite disciple, Kūreśa). That by Anantāḻvāṉ reads as follows:

> I praise the flower-feet (malarppātam)
> of Rāmānuja — of great glory—
> in order to acquire a heart
> which rests in the pure Tamil Veda
> (centamiḻvētam)
> born from Nammāḻvār (Caṭakōpaṉ),
> the repository of all auspicious qualities
> (cīrār).[10]

The *TVM* taṉiyaṉ attributed to Parāśarabhaṭṭar is an interesting one. It suggests not only that Rāmānuja was knowledgeable in the *Divyaprabvandham*, but that he was involved in its propagation as well. In it, Nammāḻvār is compared to the "first," that is the "biological," mother (mutaltāy) who is said to have given birth to the Tamil Veda (tamiḻ maṟai), while Rāmānuja is described as the "delightful foster-mother" (vaḷartta itattāy) who caused that Veda to flourish. I can find no reason to doubt the authenticity of Parāśarabhaṭṭar's authorship of this taṉiyaṉ.[11]

Following the *Irāmānucanūṟṟantāti* and the taṉiyaṉs, the three major hagiographical texts — *Āṟāyirappaṭi Guruparamparāprabhāvam* (a 13th century hagiographical text in Maṇipravāḷa), *Divyasūricaritam* (a 16th century Sanskrit kāvya), and *Prapannāmṛtam* (a 17th century Sanskrit kāvya) depict Rāmānuja as well-versed in the *Divyaprabandham* and devoted to its Āḻvār authors.[12] All three texts agree that the Āḻvār corpus was not a part of Rāmānuja's early spiritual training before his initiation into the sampradāya.[13] But after his arrival in Śrīraṅgam, Rāmānuja is said to have studied under five different gurus (all disciples of Yāmuna). From one of these five gurus — Mālādhara — he is said to have obtained "the meaning of the Drāviḍa Veda;" he learned the correct ordering of the hymns from Śrī Raṅgigāyaka, the same Araiyar[14] from the Śrīraṅgam temple who is said to have fetched Rāmānuja from Kāñcipuram and brought him to Śrīraṅgam at the behest of Yāmuna (18:76-78). Rāmānuja's expertise in the hymns of the Āḻvārs is expressed in the *Divyasūricaritam* story of his argument with his teacher Mālādhara over the interpretation of certain verses by Nammāḻvār (*Śaṭhāri*). After expressing anger towards his disciple for contradicting his interpretation, Mālādhara is said to have finally agreed to Rāmānuja's views (18:66).

Another theme in the hagiographies connecting Rāmānuja with the Āḻvārs is that of his famous pilgrimage to the holy places of South India. He is reported to have visited many "Cōḻa holy places." Special attention is given to his stay in Kurukūr, the birthplace of Nammāḻvār and Śrīvilliputūr, "where he recited verses from Āṇṭāḷ's (Godā's) poetry" (18:36-37 and 41-42).[15]

The third theme that connects Rāmānuja with the Āḻvārs is that of his famous temple reform and reorganization, especially that of the great Śrīraṅgam temple. While the reform itself is detailed in the *Divyasūricaritam*, specific reference to his institution of the recitation of the *Divyaprabandham* in the Śrīraṅgam temple is mentioned only in that temple's chronicle, entitled *Kōyil Oḻuku*. Rāmānuja is said to have made arrangements for its daily recitation within the inner sanctum during the pūjā hours along with a number of other Vedic and Purāṇic texts (Rao 1961, 49). The historicity of Rāmānuja's temple reform is questionable since there is no epigraphical evidence to substantiate the assertions of *Kōyil Oḻuku*. While there is no inscriptional evidence affirming Rāmānuja's actual involvement in temple reorganization, we do know from a stotra composed by his disciple Kūreśa that Rāmānuja must have been deeply involved in temple affairs in Śrīraṅgam. In his *Sundarabāhu Stava*, Kūreśa bemoans his separation from his Ācarya Rāmānuja and implies that the cause of the enforced separation is trouble in the Śrīraṅgam temple.[16] A further indication of Rāmānuja's close involvement with the temple milieu is the rapid appearance of Rāmānuja shrines after his death. For example, an inscription in Kāñci's Varadarājaswāmī temple indicates that his icon had been installed there within fifty years of the traditional date of his demise.[17]

The profuse commentarial literature acknowledging Yāmuna's and Rāmānuja's interpretations of the *Tiruvāymoḻi* is another source that substantiates the claim of the link between Rāmānuja and the Āḻvārs. These interpretations, originally an oral tradition, were handed down and recorded a few generations later. Venkatachari notes that:

> From these accounts we can conclude that the early Ācāryas acknowledged the ubhayavedānta, knew the hymns of the Āḻvārs themselves, and orally transmitted their interpretations — e.g. Yāmuna to Tirumālaiyāṇṭāṉ to

Rāmānuja to Piḷḷāṉ, who finally wrote a commentary. Recorded examples of how Rāmānuja's interpretation differs from Yāmuna's substantiates even further this line of reasoning (Venkatachari 1978, 18).

In the later literature, the panegyric quality of the *Irāmānucanūṟṟantāti* is fused with the biographical information related in the hagiographical texts to establish a new type of stotra: a praise of the Ācārya Rāmānuja through a reiteration of the events of his life. Two stotras are especially relevant to this discussion: *Rāmānujāṣṭottaraśatanāmastotram* by Āndhrapūrṇa[18] and *Yatirājaviṃśati* by Varavaramuni (also known as Maṇavāḷamāmuni, the late 14th to early 15th century Ācārya). In both of these stotras a number of poetic epithets are applied to Rāmānuja that continue the well-established tradition affirming his deep devotion to Āḻvār spirituality. Āndhrapūrṇa, to relate a single example, describes Rāmānuja as:

> ... He whose mind [comprehended]
> the truth of the Tamil Veda
> (drāviḍa-āmnāya-tattva)
> made well-known [to him]
> by Māladharārya. (v. 10)

Likewise, Varavaramuni praises Yatirāja (Rāmānuja) by means of such poetic epithets as:

> ... the friend of the lotus-faces
> of Śrī Bhaṭṭanātha (Periyāḻvār) and Parakāla (Tirumaṅkaiyāḻvār) ...
> [and]
> ... the large black bee
> [which hovers around]
> the lotus feet of
> Parāṅkuśa (Nammāḻvār) ... (v. 2)

The literary genres of praise and hagiography are necessarily suspect in terms of the historicity both of the events and the biographical images that they depict. Because hagiographers are neither historians nor biographers in the ordinary sense of the words, it is difficult to discern to what extent the figure reflected in their works is a real historical person or the creation of myth, legend, or social ideology.

Recently scholars have questioned Rāmānuja's relation to his supposed Āḻvār heritage. In the absence of only minimal corroborative evidence, one common procedure employed to verify the specifics of the hagiographical tradition on a famous author involves the comparison of the authentic works of that author with the stories and legends about him. This comparison may reveal either a discordance or a resonance among the various literary genres. With specific reference to Rāmānuja, the fact remains that nowhere in his works does Rāmānuja make any explicit references to his Āḻvār heritage generally or to the *Divyaprabandham* specifically. Could it be that the stories connecting him with the Āḻvārs are completely unhistorical legends? The current understanding of the relationship between the Āḻvārs and the Ācāryas contains two widely divergent views of the subject. According to the first view, there has been an effort on the part of the Śrīvaiṣṇava sampradāya to gain legitimation through the co-opting of Rāmānuja as part of a process of the "Sanskritization" of a Tamil-based temple tradition. Robert Lester, for example, states that:

> Basing our estimate of Rāmānuja's place in the Indian tradition on his writings, as it seems we must, there is little if any reason to conclude that he seeks to accommodate the Vedic perspective to popular bhakti developments or popular Vaiṣṇavism in particular.... It would appear that Rāmānuja was appropriated by popular Vaiṣṇava development.... We cannot dispute the tradition's association of Rāmānuja, Yāmuna and Nāthamuni, but the affirmation that any of these three figures considered themselves ācāryas of Śrī Vaiṣṇavism is highly problematic.[19]

Lester further writes: "Is it that 'Śrī-Vaiṣṇavism' adopts Rāmānuja?"[20]

The opposite point of view has been articulated by Friedhelm Hardy, who suggests that it was the Brahmin followers of Vedāntic spirituality who co-opted the Tamil Vaiṣṇavism of the Āḻvārs (could we call this "Tamilization"?). They then quickly did away with the emotional bhakti of the Tamil poets by reinstating the "normative Upaniṣadic ideology" including its negative attitude towards "the whole empirical personality" (Hardy 1983, 16-17). Both Lester and Hardy, in contradictory ways, imply that the deep connections between Rāmānuja and Āḻvār piety as described in the poems of praise, taṉiyaṉs, and hagiographies of Rāmānuja are without any historical foundation whatsoever.

More recently, Vasudha Narayanan (1987) has affirmed the authenticity of Rāmānuja's authorship of the *Gadyatraya* as well as his central role in the early development of Śrīvaiṣṇavism. She argues her case on the grounds of the Śrīvaiṣṇava sampradāya's self-understanding that it is founded on ubhayavedānta, the "dual Vedānta" based on the Sanskrit Vedas and the Tamil *Divyaprabandham* often referred to as the Drāviḍa Veda. She distinguishes between Rāmānuja's "theological treatises and polemical writings" and his *Gadyas*, which she calls "devotional and confessional pieces" representative of the tradition's stotra (hymn of praise) tradition. Narayanan's persuasive thesis is supportive both of Rāmānuja's key position within the tradition and of his authorship of the *Gadyas* (1987, 88-91). I am in basic agreement with Narayanan's thesis; however, in this study I go beyond it to suggest that not only was Rāmānuja influenced by the emotional spirituality of the Āḻvārs in his more sectarian and devotional works, but also that the influence of the Āḻvārs can be discerned in one "major" philosophical-cum-theological text, his *Bhagavadgītā-bhāṣya* (*RGB*).

II. The Untaintedness (nirmalatvam) and Auspicious Qualities of God: A Study in Continuity

The frequent reiteration of the concept of God expressed in the statement cited below is one factor responsible for the unique devotional mood of the *RGB* among Rāmānuja's philosophical commentaries: God, who is totally opposed to all that is defiling or impure (nikhila-heya-pratyanīka), is at the same time possessed of an "infinite number" of auspicious qualities (kalyāṇa-guṇa). The statement is repeated (in a variety of wordings) more than twenty times in the bhāṣya. A close analysis of its content reveals the direct influence of Āḻvār spirituality on Rāmānuja.

a. The Āḻvārs

The commonly used Tamil word in the *Divyaprabandham* for "auspicious qualities" is cīr (a Tamil form of śrī), which contains within its semantic field both the concept of auspiciousness and that of quality, trait, or characteristic.[21] Because the word and its synonyms are found throughout the *Divyaprabandham*, a few examples will suffice. The term is employed by Nammāḻvār in two phrases similar to those found in Rāmānuja's writings. In *Periyatiruvantāti* v. 69, Nammāḻvār describes Tirumāl [i.e. Viṣṇu] who dwells within the heart of the devotee as "an ocean of auspicious qualities" (çīrkkaṭalai). And *TVM* I.5.9 refers to the Lord's "limitless auspicious qualities" (ellai il cīr) in his transcendent, indwelling and worshipable icon forms.

With words even closer to those used by Rāmānuja, Toṇṭaraṭippoṭi, in his *Tirumālai*, v. 26, refers to the "auspicious qualities" of the Lord as tirukkuṇam. Tiru is Tamil for śrī or kalyāṇa (auspicious), and kuṇam is the Tamil equivalent of the Sanskrit term guṇa used by Rāmānuja.[22]

Like Rāmānuja after him, Nammāḻvār frequently joins the idea of the Lord's "auspicious qualities" with the idea of his "untaintedness/stainlessness/purity /blamelessness/faultlessness/sinlessness/without blemish, defilement or stain": the most commonly employed Tamil words for this concept are tītu-il and kuṟṟam-il.[23] As an example, the Lord of Tiruveṅkaṭam is described in *TVM* III.3.5 as being "without blemish/fault [and full of] auspicious qualities" (tītu-il cīrt tiruvēṅkaṭattāṉ). In *TVM* IX.1.7 the Lord is described as being possessed of "auspicious qualities without blemish/defilement/stain" (kuṟṟam-il cīr) and is presented to the reader as One to be meditated upon and enjoyed.[24]

The theme of untaintedness (without its immediate linkage with the term cīr) is a significant one in Āḻvār descriptions of the Lord. In *TVM* the Lord is praised as being "without stain or blemish" (kōtu-il in IV.2.4 and maṟu-il in IV.10.10). The familiar amala is used in *TVM* III.4.4-5 and IX.4.7, whereas the "stainless or blemishless Śrīman Nārāyaṇa" (navai-il tirunāraṇaṉ) is invoked in IX.8.3.

The idea of untaintedness is also present in a number of widely used epithets. What is most surprising to me is that although all of these names are of Sanskritic origin (amala, nirmala, niṉmala, vimala), not one of them appears in the popular *Śrīviṣṇusahasranāma* (which consists of a list of the thousand names of Viṣṇu contained in the *Mahābhārata*). In *TVM* IV.2.7, the epithet "immaculate/ untainted one" (niṉmalā!) is employed by Nammāḻvār in a teasing way. The gopīs, vexed with Kṛṣṇa for having taken their playthings, use this epithet to contrast his naughtiness with his reputed untaintedness! In *Periyāḻvār-Tirumoḻi* V.1.4., an emotional decade of entreaty, Periyāḻvār calls out to the Lord "O untainted one" (niṉmalā!). Other Āḻvārs also employ this and synonymous epithets. Āṇṭāḷ, the daughter of Periyāḻvār, refers to the Lord as "the untainted one" (vimalaṉ/vimalā) in *Nācciyār-Tirumoḻi* V.2 and XIV.9. and *Tiruppāvai* v. 20. Again, Tiruppāṇāḻvār in the first verse of his short poem of praise, *Amalaṉātippirāṉ*, calls the Lord of Śrīraṅgam "untainted one" in a series of synonymous epithets: amalaṉ, vimalaṉ, nirmalaṉ, niṉmalaṉ, and then again in v. 8 refers to "the untainted one of [Śrī] raṅgam (araṅkattamalaṉ)."

Two especially important references to the untainted/ stainless Lord are to be found in *Periyāḻvār-Tirumoḻi*, IV. 2 and 3. These two decades are devoted to the praise of the Lord of Tirumāliruñcolai, whose abode is a sacred mountain located near Madurai. (This mountain is the one described by Kūreśa in *Sundarabāhu Stava* vv. 7 and 68 cited below.) Verses IV.2.10 and IV.3.9 of *Periyāḻvār-Tirumoḻi* refer to the Lord of Tirumāliruñcolai as the untainted/ stainless one (vimalaṉ). Periyāḻvār calls the holy place "the mountain where the untainted one (vimalaṉ) is seated," and "the mountain where the untainted one (vimalaṉ) played." It is significant that this holy pilgrimage place — the mountain of Tirumāliruñcolai/Vanādri — has from ancient times been the site of both a Vaiṣṇava and a Śaiva temple. This is very likely one factor in the recurrent references by both Āḻvār and Ācārya to untaintedness with reference to that particular divyadeśa.

b. Rāmānuja

In several ways, Rāmānuja's use of various phrases regarding the untaintedness/stainlessness/purity (nirmalatvam) of God and God's unlimited auspicious qualities more closely resembles that of the Āḻvārs than the Upaniṣadic passages that he cites as proof texts for this idea. In Rāmānuja's writings: (1) the phrase about the nirmalatvam of the Lord is almost always followed directly by a statement on his auspicious qualities, a pattern found in Nammāḻvār's *Tiruvāymoḻi* [*TVM*]; (2) the reference to the untaintedness of God appears with considerable frequency, as in the Āḻvārs; (3) the phrases are employed in a devotional context, as in the *Divyaprabandham*; and (4) the employment of a variety of long phrases on God's nirmalatvam, rather than the use of a single word, creates an emotional tenor which the Āḻvārs already have by way of their literary genre, the prabandham.

Of central importance to Rāmānuja's conception of God is God's nirmalatvam or amalatvam (untaintedness). Rāmānuja does not express this idea in a single word; rather, he uses several longer descriptions that serve to highlight this quality of God in an exaggerated way. Rāmānuja employs a number of nearly synonymous phrases to express the nirmalatvam of the Lord. God is said to be:

(1) "[radically] opposed to everything defiling" (nikhila-heya-pratyanīka) (IX.34, X.3, XII.9, XIII.2);

(2) "[totally] free from all trace (lit. 'scent') of that which is defiling" (nirasta-samasta-heya gandha) (XVIII.54);

(3) "free from all trace (lit. 'scent') of imperfection or blemish" (nirasta-nikhila-doṣa-gandha); and

(4) "untouched by all imperfection or blemish without exception" (aspṛṣṭa-aśeṣa-doṣa) (VI.47).

Each of these nearly synonymous phrases is immediately followed by a lengthy and emotion-filled statement of the Lord's auspicious qualities, usually in the form of a compound such as "I am a treasure-house of multitudes of unlimited, abundant, innumerable auspicious qualities (anavadhika-atiśaya-asaṅkhyeya-kalyāṇa-guṇa-gaṇa-nidhi). A list of several of those qualities, usually beginning with knowledge (jñāna), sometimes follows.

In the *RGB*, Rāmānuja cites only three proof texts for the nirmalatvam of the Lord: (1) *Subalopaniṣad* VII: "... He is devoid of sin ..." (apahata-pāpma) as in his VII.7; (2) *Chāndogyopaniṣad* VIII.7.1: "The Self is devoid of sin" (ātma-apahata-pāpma) as in his introduction to Chapter III; and (3) *Śvetāśvataropaniṣad* VI.19: "blameless" (niravadyam) as in *RGB* X.4. He himself sometimes repeats these phrases in the body of his commentary, as in IV.6 in which the question of God's embodiment is discussed.

The importance that Rāmānuja gives to this quality of God — indicated by the number of times he refers to it — has been noted by John Carman ([1974] 1981, 104-107) in his book *The Theology of Rāmānuja*. He says that almost every description of Brahman by Rāmānuja, "however brief," includes and usually begins with one or another of the phrases indicating his untaintedness (nirmalatvam/ amalatvam). Carman believes that immateriality is only a negative and "more superficial definition of amalatva" ([1974] 1981, 104). He suggests three possible reasons why Rāmānuja gives such great importance to this particular doctrine: (1) Rāmānuja may desire to provide an alternative interpretation of a term commonly used by his most powerful philosophical opponent Śaṅkara to refer to the nirguṇa, or qualityless Brahman; (2) Rāmānuja may want to show that it is possible for Brahman to be "embodied in, and to be in contact with, imperfect and sinful beings, both material and spiritual, without detracting from or contradicting his perfection;" and (3) Rāmānuja held the fact of God's possessing a host of auspicious qualities of matchless excellence as a most important conviction.

A study of the way in which Rāmānuja uses the various terms that describe the Supreme Person's untaintedness indicates that the terms are used in a somewhat different way or for a somewhat different purpose in the *Śrībhāṣya* as compared to the *RGB*. Of course, this could partly be explained by the difference in the nature of the two works being commented upon. My reading of the *Śrībhāṣya*, however, indicates that Rāmānuja uses the term(s) in that commentary most often to distinguish Brahman from prakṛti (matter) and the jīva (individual soul) and in order to establish the fact that Brahman is indeed qualified (saguṇa) but untainted (e.g. *Śrībhāṣya* I.1.21, I.1.24, I.1.32).[25]

In the *RGB* the phrases sometimes appear in a context similar to that of the *Śrībhāṣya* (for example, for the purpose of establishing an argument against Śaṅkara in XIII.2). However, in the *RGB* the phrases appear most often in a devotional context. The emotional outpouring that verges on ecstatic poetry is either the devotee's praise of the Lord or self-praise by the Lord himself called ātma-stuti.[26] Rāmānuja himself acknowledges the legitimacy of the recitation of the qualities of God as a devotional exercise. In IX.14 he interprets the recitation of the names of God as the recitation of his qualities:

> [My devotees] remember and continually recite (kīrtayantāḥ) my names (mat nāmāni) that are expressive of particular qualities of Mine (mat-guṇa-viśeṣa-vācini) beginning with Nārāyaṇa, Kṛṣṇa, Vāsudeva.

It is in the context of praise and devotion that Rāmānuja directly links the untaintedness of God with a more *sectarian* Southern agenda, as in his commentary on XVIII.54.[27] Here Lord Kṛṣṇa praises himself as:

> ... the Lord of all, to Whom the creation, protection, and dissolution of all the worlds is [mere] sport, *Who am free of the [slightest] whiff of all that is impure*, (nirasta-samasta-heya-gandhe), Who am the sole ground of innumerable multitudes of auspicious qualities of unlimited excellence (anavadhika-atiśaya-asaṅkhyeya-kalyāṇa-guṇa-gaṇa-ekatāne), Who am an ambrosia-ocean of loveliness, *Who am always in association with Śrī*, Who has lotus-like eyes and Who am [the devotees'] own Lord. [italics added].[28]

c. *The Later Ācāryas*

The Ācāryas after Rāmānuja continued the tradition of giving great emphasis to the untaintedness (nirmalatvam) of the Lord. It persists both in the highly systematic philosophical treatises and Viśiṣṭādvaita handbooks of the later tradition and in the poetic tradition of the stotra literature.

For an example from the philosophical handbooks, Piḷḷailokācārya, in his *Tattvatraya*, explicates the three fundamental principles of Viśiṣṭādvaita philosophy (soul, cit; matter, acit; and God, īśvara). Following Rāmānuja, the chapter on Īśvara has the following as its opening statement:

> The essential nature (svarūpa) of the Lord is that
> He is radically opposed to all that is defiling (akhila-heya-pratyanīka)
> is infinite knowledge and bliss,
> [and] is full of all auspicious qualities (kalyāṇa-guṇa)
> beginning with knowledge and power (v. 66).

In the stotra tradition, the Lord's nirmalatvam and innumerable auspicious qualities are continual subjects of praise. Epithets are frequently based on terminology from Rāmānuja's *RGB* and *Gadyatraya*. One example is the epithet found in Kūreśa's *Śrīvaikuṇṭha Stava* v.31: "O Ocean of eternal, blemishless, spotless, changeless, auspicious, and good qualities (nitya-nirmala-nirañjana-nirvikāra-kalyāṇa-ṣaḍ-guṇa-nidhe)!" These phrases also frequently appear in the stotra literature in a mock dispute with the Lord over whether he obtains his auspiciousness from his qualities or whether his qualities are auspicious because of their association with him. The more common view is that the Lord's qualities are auspicious because of their association with him. For example, in *Śrīvaikuṇṭha Stava* v. 48 the Lord's qualities are said to "gain their auspiciousness from their association with [him]." The contrary view is taken by Parāśarabhaṭṭar, in v. 27 of *Śrīraṅgarāja Stava*, Part II:

> O Lord of Raṅgam!
>
> [Your] six qualities—
> knowledge, dominion, power,

valour, strength, and lustre—
which yield a flood of
countless and excellent
auspicious qualities
untouched by stain, limiting adjunct,
limitation, or number
(doṣa-upādha-avadhi-sama-atiśaya-
asaṅkhya-nirlepa-maṅgala-guṇa-ogha)

make You invaluable just like a
jewel is made priceless by its lustre.

III. Emotionalism (Separation and Union), a Study in Continuity

Another characteristic that appears repeatedly (indeed, eighteen times) in Rāmānuja's *Gītā* commentary is the description of the religious experience of a single-minded devotee of Viṣṇu. The primary feature of Viṣṇu's devotees is their inability to find support or sustenance in anything other than the worship of God on account of God's exceeding dearness (atipriyatva) and, for that same reason, an inability to endure separation (viyoga) from him for even a single moment. This idea, in part, both accounts for the bhāṣya's emotional mood and creates an opening for the legitimation of the kind of emotionalism contained in many poems of the Āḻvārs.

a. The Āḻvārs

The unique emotionalism in the poetry of the Āḻvārs has been meticulously documented by Hardy (1983). Their emotional spirituality, as expressed in a variety of ecstatic symptoms revealing their inability to live in separation from the Lord, appears to have been a major influence on certain sections of *RGB*.

The theme of the "inability to find support for his soul apart from Lord" and the "unbearableness" of the experience of separation from him is a central one in Nammāḻvār's poetry. While any number of examples could be given, *Tiruvāymoḻi*, IX.9.2-5 contains a series of relevant phrases. Several verses of this poem in which Nammāḻvār speaks in the role of the nāyakī (the female beloved) describe the frustration experienced as evening approaches and still the beloved (Kṛṣṇa) has not returned:

The cowherd ... still is not coming.
How can I preserve my life now?
(eṉ uyir kākkum āṟu eṉ?)....
My Māyoṉ, is not coming,
that cheat Kaṇṇaṉ (Kṛṣṇa)!

He made love to me ...
[but] now he has gone away
and left me in pain ...
How can I care for my life any more
(iṉi iruntu, eṉ uyir kākkum āṟu eṉ)? ...
My heart gives me no support
(neñcamum tuṇai aṉṟu),
my life is not bearable.

My heart gives me no support
(neñcamum tunai aṉṟu)....
How can I save my life
(uyir kākkum āṟu eṉ)? [29]

Another especially relevant *Divyaprabandham* passage is Āṇṭāḷ's *Nācciyār-Tirumoḻi* XII.1-10. In these ten verses Āṇṭāḷ expresses her inability to find sustenance for her soul, her inability to "live" in separation from the Lord, as she begs to be taken to Mathurā to be with him. The ten verses are replete with expressions such as: "If you want me to live, then just take me and leave me on the outskirts of Mathurā city..." (XII.1); "I cannot live here anymore [in separation from Kṛṣṇa] — leave me on the Yamunā bank ..." (XII.4). The importance given to the experience of permanent union with the Lord is revealed in the phala-śruti of the final verse. *Nācciyār-Tirumoḻi* XIV.10 promises that those who treasure these words of Āṇṭāḷ will never be parted from the Lord:

Those who would treasure as a balm
These words of Viṭṭucittaṉ's Kōtai (Āṇṭāḷ) ...
Will reach the sacred feet of the Lord
Never to be parted from them![30]

b. Rāmānuja

That much of Āḻvār spirituality contains emotionalism and the theme of separation and union needs hardly be stated. Hardy's book *Viraha-bhakti* has the separation motif as its central theme. Hardy himself, however, regards the experience of separation as foreign to yoga, even to the spiritual discipline of bhakti-yoga:

> There is no agony in yoga (including bhakti-yoga), because there is no emotive prefiguration of kaivalya which would entail the painful awareness of not yet having realized it, because senses and emotions are factors that are eliminated right at the start of the exercise (Hardy 1983, 3).

In contradiction to Hardy, I suggest that this theme of separation and union, found repeatedly in passages of the *RGB*, has been influenced more by Āḻvār spirituality than by "normative Vedāntic ideology."

Rāmānuja's frequent reiteration of this motif and his statements regarding the inability of the devotee "to find sustenance for the mind, self, and external organs of sense" apart from the Lord (IX.13) describe a devotee who is in a state of confusion and agony in separation from the Lord. This closely corresponds to the state of soul described by many of the Āḻvārs, especially Nammāḻvār and Āṇṭāḷ.[31]

Hardy distinguishes the intellectual bhakti of the *Bhagavadgītā* from the emotional bhakti of the Āḻvārs with its more ecstatic colourings. Concerning the bhakti of the *Bhagavadgītā* he writes:

> Bhakti thus seems to appear in the same slot as yoga/manas/cetas.... The emotionally minimal semantic field expressed here [in a number of *Gītā* verses] by bhakti, bhāj, and the verb bhaj appear to be *hardly* different from that established in Pāṇini ... [meaning] 'belonging to, liking for, being loyal to, and concentrating all one's mental faculties on him' (Hardy 1983, 27).

He further notes that "a careful analysis of Rāmānuja's bhakti would in fact reveal that it is very similar to the 'intellectual' bhakti of the *Gītā*" (Hardy 1983, 37).

If one were to confine oneself to a detailed study of Rāmānuja's understanding of the technical term bhakti-yoga, then Hardy's conclusion might be upheld. However, Rāmānuja creates an opening for emotional and ecstatic devotion in another way. One of Rāmānuja's standard descriptions (based on Yāmuna's *Gītārthasaṅgraha*)[32] is repeated eighteen times in almost identical wording throughout his bhāṣya:[33]

> [My, i.e., the Lord's devotees] ... on account of my exceeding dearness ... are unable to find sustenance (or support) for their souls (ātma-dhāraṇam-alabhamanāḥ) for even the atomic fraction of a second (kṣaṇa-aṇu-mātre-api) ... and are for the same reason unable to endure separation from me even for a moment (kṣaṇa-mātra-viśleṣa-asahatayāḥ).

In fact, the very rationale for the Lord's incarnation is declared by Rāmānuja to be in order for the Lord to show his worshipable form (ārādhya-svarūpa-pradarśanena). This is necessary because his devotees cannot find support for their souls without seeing him, and deprived of the sight of him become weakened in all their limbs.[34] Phrases identical to or similar to those cited above are thus used variously to refer to devotees less advanced along the spiritual path (as in IV.8) as well as to refer to devotees of the highest order: yogis (as in

VIII.14), and mahātmas (as in VIII.15, IX.13 and 22). While the description is sometimes used by Rāmānuja in the context of meditation and the directing of the inner self to the Lord (e.g. VI.47), it is always within the more devotional context of taking refuge (śaraṇam) with the Lord and one-pointed worship. Furthermore, Rāmānuja makes explicit reference to the fact that it is the whole empirical person who is involved, for the devotee is described as being impelled by the inability to otherwise "find support or sustenance for the mind, self, and external sense organs" (manaśca-ātmanśca-bāhya-karaṇānāmca in IX.13).

The passages that describe the inability of devotees to sustain themselves (that is, their souls) in separation from the Lord may be interpreted as an expression of Rāmānuja's key doctrine of the ontological dependence of the entire universe on God. This doctrine is termed śarīra-śarīri-bhāva or the "body-soul relationship." It holds that the relationship between the Supreme Self (Īśvara) and the individual soul (jīva), the latter being utterly dependent on the former, is the same as that which exists between the individual soul (jīva) and the physical body.[35] The basic postulate is that God is ādhāra, the supporter or substratum of the entire universe.

At another level of interpretation, however, it becomes clear that Rāmānuja is referring to more than the ontology implied in these doctrines so central to his theology of God and the universe. Rāmānuja moves from the ontological to the experiential level and in doing so he incorporates Āḻvār emotionalism into his bhāṣya in the following four ways:

(1) by his consistent preference for the term priyatva rather than a derivative of the term bhaj (being beloved) which would be more acceptable to "normative ideology;"

(2) through his emphasis on the inability of the devotee to *endure* or *bear* separation from the Lord for *even a fraction of a second*;

(3) by his clear association of the devotee's experience of the inability to find support or sustenance for the soul (ātma-dhāraṇa) with physical ecstatic symptoms; and

(4) through the employment of passages describing the "reversal of relationship" which takes place between the Lord and his devotees.

Rāmānuja consistently uses the word priyatva in the *RGB*, preferring it to derivatives of the more familiar bhaj. He repeatedly employs the phrase tipriyatvena, "on account of exceeding dearness," as the reason why devotees cannot sustain themselves (that is, their souls) or endure separation from the Lord for even the fraction of a second. Derived from the verbal root prī,[36] priyatva carries emotional associations that are alien to the character of Hardy's category of "intellectual bhakti" and, in fact, take us far beyond the more familiar bhaj/ bhakti. Unlike the word bhakti, prīti and priyatva carry the association of love between equals. Their semantic field is closer to that of the Tamil word aṉpu[37] (love), a term preferred by the Āḻvārs over bhakti's Tamil orthographic equivalent patti.

Aṉpu is a word frequently used by the Āḻvārs. Several examples indicating the content and flavour of its usage will suffice:

> With love (aṉpu) as the bowl,
> ardor as the fuel,
> thoughts that drip passion
> as the wick,
> I lit, with a melting [heart],
> the flaming lamp of wisdom
> to Nāraṇa—
> I who know the wisdom of Tamil.[38]
> (*Iraṇṭam Tiruvantāti*, v.1)

TVM 10.10.7 contains the word aṉpu used as a vocative, "O my Beloved One!" while in 5.8.1 Nammāḻvār says: "On account of love (aṉpeyō) for You, my body is melting just like water."

Because of the great love that they have for the Lord, devotees are described by Rāmānuja as being "... unable to find sustenance or support for their souls (ātma-dhāraṇam alabhama) for even the atomic fraction of a second (kṣaṇa-aṇu mātre api)" (e.g. IX.14). They are also said to be unable to endure separation [from the Lord] for even a moment because He is so exceedingly dear to them (e.g. VI.47). The opposites (dvandva) of pleasure and pain (sukha-duḥkha) are defined with reference to the jñānī, whom Rāmānuja describes as one who "feels happiness or misery solely on account of union with (saṃśleṣa) or separation from (viyoga)" the Lord (VII.27 and XI.55).

Furthermore, Rāmānuja's *RGB* links the experience of union with and separation from God with certain physical, ecstatic symptoms. Stating that "'ecstatic emotional bhakti' lies on the whole outside the awareness of the Ācāryas," Hardy has noted that:

> ... in the poetry of Nammāḻvār ecstasy may denote both the ecstatic bliss of union and the agony of separation, [and that] the description of the psychological symptoms of ecstasy does not differentiate the bliss and the agony elements (Hardy 1983, 433; 365).

Rāmānuja does not go into detail regarding the *psychological* state of the devotee, yet he does recognize that "inability to obtain support (dhṛtim/dhāraṇam) for the soul" is an experience that results in physical symptoms of ecstasy such as a weakening of the limbs of the body. In Rāmānuja's thought this weakening of the limbs is a symptom both of the experience of the intense sight of/union with God (XI.24) as well as of separation from him (IV.8). In *Bhagavadgītā* XI.24, Arjuna speaks of his agitation at the revelation of Viṣṇu's form with the following words:

> Seeing You... I am extremely agitated in my inmost soul (pravathita-antara-ātma) and do not obtain support (dhṛtim na vindāmi) ...

Rāmānuja directly links these spiritual symptoms (agitation of the inmost soul and the experience of the lack of support) with physical ones in a manner similar to that which we find in the ecstatic descriptions of the Ālvārs. According to Rāmānuja's commentary, at the vision of Lord Kṛṣṇa, Arjuna says:

> I am unable to obtain support for the body (dahasya dhāraṇam na labhe) ... and having seen You my senses are confused and all my limbs loose and weak (praśithila-sarva-avayavāḥ).

Compare this passage with the description of devotees who are *deprived* of the sight (darśana) of the Lord in Rāmānuja's commentary on *Bhagavadgītā* IV.8. This verse gives the rationale for the Lord's incarnations ("for the protection of the good, for the destruction of the evil-doers and for the firm establishment of dharma"). Rāmānuja adds to the above purposes given by the *Bhagavadgītā* another one: that of showing the Lord's worshipable form (ārādhya-svarūpa-pradarśana). His commentary includes the Lord's description of his devotees when *separated* from the Lord. In this passage (as in many others), "separation," according to Rāmānuja, means "without the sight of Me" (mat-darśanena vina). Note that for Rāmānuja, the Lord's availability to the "sight" of the devotees is inclusive of all their senses.[39] In IV.8 Rāmānuja writes that the Lord's devotees are:

> unable to obtain support, sustenance, etc. for their souls (svātma-dhāraṇa-poṣaṇa-ādikam) without the sight of me [the Lord] (mat-darśanena vina), and [in separation from me] even a single moment of time [seems as if] a thousand kalpas, because [their] every limb will be loose and weak (praśithila-sarva-gātrāḥ) [without me], [therefore] I am born ....[40]

This idea of the inability to find sustenance or support for the soul is most dramatically developed in Rāmānuja's commentary on *Bhagavadgītā* IX.14. The verse itself reads:

> Those [who wish to be] in constant union [with me], worship me with devotion (mām bhaktya ... upāsate), always singing my praises (satataṃ

> kīrtayantaḥ), making efforts [to serve me] with steadfast resolution, and bowing to me (namasyantaḥ).

Rāmānuja adds an element of emotionalism to each specific phrase of this verse, including two significant glosses that describe actual physical ecstatic symptoms. The *Bhagavadgītā* phrase satataṃ kīrtayantaḥ ("always singing [my] praises") is glossed by Rāmānuja with the words:

> ... remembering my names which are expressive of my particular qualities, they continually murmur Nārāyaṇa, Kṛṣṇa, and Vāsudeva, etc. ... with each and every one of their limbs experiencing horripilation (pula) ....

Furthermore, the devotees who stammer the names of God are described as having "throats choked with joy" (harṣa-gadgada-kaṇṭhāḥ).

Horripilation of the body is such an obvious ecstatic symptom that it hardly requires comment. The constant uttering of the names of God does, however, require some elaboration.[41] In one of the "girl poems" of Tirumaṅkaiyāḻvār (*Periyatirumoḻi* v. 5),[42] we are given a detailed description of the emotional state of the "girl." Two among the several symptoms listed there are found in Rāmānuja's description of the devotee quoted above: (1) that she continually repeats the names of the Lord (v. 6) and (2) that she speaks in a "choking voice" (v. 1). Thus, the continual recitation of the names of God in a "choking/stammering voice" is listed as one of the signs of the devotee's intense ecstatic-emotional state: "Without ever forgetting all the time she says 'Māyavaṉ! Mātavaṉ!'" (Hardy 1983, 384).

Similarly, in the *TVM* the continual recitation of the names of God is taken as a sign of ecstatic union between the "girl" and the Lord: "She murmurs only the names of the wondrous Lord ..." (VIII.9.1); "This jewelled woman constantly repeats the names (pēr) of the Lord ..." (VIII.9.4); "What shall I tell you ... of this woman? She utters only the names (pēr) of the Lord ..." (VIII.9.8).

Returning now to *Bhagavadgītā* IX.14, we find that the simple phrase "bowing to me" (mām namasyantaḥ) is elaborately glossed by Rāmānuja thus:

> The eight organs — the manas, the buddhi, the ahaṅkāra, the two feet, the two hands and the head — [all] having been made to bend down by the weight of loving devotion (bhakti-bhāra-avanāmata), fall prostrate onto the earth itself (dharāle) just like a stick (daṇḍavat), not caring for the dirt, wet mud, pebbles or the like.

This description of what is essentially "ecstatic prostration" appears to be based on Kulacēkarāḻvār's *Perumāḷ-Tirumoḻi* 1.9 in which a devotee is described as "tumbling over or rolling (puraḷum) on the earth (pūtalattil)." The verbal root puraḷ carries the additional meaning "to become besmeared, soiled, dirty" (*MTL*

V: 2771), a condition suggested by Rāmānuja's phrase "not caring for the dirt, wet mud, pebbles...."

And last but not least, Rāmānuja puts the entire passage into a temple context. He glosses the *Bhagavadgītā's* words "making efforts [to serve Me, the Lord] with steadfast resolution" with the following:

> In the very same manner [that is, because I am exceedingly dear to them and they cannot find sustenance for their souls ... without serving me] they make efforts [to serve me] (yatantaḥ) in works done for my sake, such as worship and in other activities ... such as the making of temples and [their attached] gardens.

The emotionalism of Rāmānuja's thought attains its height in those verses in which he describes the reversal of relationship that takes place between the Lord and his devotee. Here what Rāmānuja describes is not the devotee's inability to bear separation from God; rather, he describes the Lord's inability to endure separation from his devotee.[43] In this context, Rāmānuja expresses reversal of relationship in his commentary on four different verses (VII.18, VIII.14, IX.29, and XVIII.65).

It is significant that this reversal, involving God's dependence on his devotees, is expressed by Rāmānuja in exactly the same words as the devotees' dependence on God. In his commentary on VII.18, Rāmānuja glosses the *Bhagavadgītā* phrase "The man of wisdom (jñānī) is [my] very Self (ātma-eva)." Rāmānuja asks how this can be so and answers with the following statement of reversed relationship in which he uses the same phrase to describe the devotee's relation to God as he does God's to the devotee. Lord Kṛṣṇa speaks:

> I regard myself as depending on [the jñānī] for my support and sustenance. How is this so? Because this person considers me to be the highest goal, finding it impossible to support himself without me (mayā vinā ātma-dhāraṇa-asambhavanaya). Likewise it is impossible for me to maintain myself without him (ataḥ tena vinā mama-api-ātma-dhāraṇam na sambhavati). Thus he is indeed my very self.

The inability of the Lord to endure separation from his devotees is also expressed in VIII.14 and XVIII.65. In XVIII.65 Rāmānuja states that when the love of the devotee for God is very great, God's love for the devotee also becomes very great and He is therefore unable to bear their separation from him. The Lord says: tat-viyogam asahamānaḥ aham. His inability to endure separation from the devotees is also expressed in the very same words in VIII.14. Furthermore, Rāmānuja clearly states that the relationship of love that exists between the Lord and his devotees is not the special prerogative of the higher castes. The Lord speaks:

> But those who ... on account of [my] exceeding dearness are unable to find support for their souls without worshipping me whether of high birth or low ... remain with me at ease if they were of qualities equal to mine (mat-samāna-guṇavat). I also remain with them as if with my superiors! (IX.29)

"Reversal of relationship" — the ultimate expression of the Lord's radical accessibility — is found in the *Divyaprabandham* in a variety of manifestations.[44] At the devotional level, *TVM* contains numerous expressions in which the love and need of the Lord for the devotee is even more intense than that of the devotee for God. The suggestion has been made that the single most important fact for Nammāḻvār is that "God loves the human self and longs for its presence in a way which corresponds to and transcends the longing of the self for God" (Kaylor and Venkatachari 1981, 51). A few examples of this kind of reversal imagery from Nammāḻvār's *TVM* will suffice:

> Is there any wonder that I became his
> slave, that he has become my life?
> I was hungering for him, ready to devour
> him if I should see him, but his desire
> preceded mine! He came and entered my
> heart and ate me up to the last morsel.
> He is so much quicker than I![45]

An even clearer example of reversal of relationship with a direct reference to the inability of the Lord to bear separation from his devotees is that found in *TVM* I.7.7:

> ... I have not thought of keeping him
> out of my mind. He himself, out of love,
> conquered my mind, willful though it is,
> and has entered into me residing in my
> body and has inseparably united with it.
> Such a Person, *can He bear to be*
> *separated from me*? [emphasis added][46]

c. The Later Ācāryas

Following the Āḻvārs and Rāmānuja, the expression of a sensual approach to God and the emotionalism that it entails continues in the stotra literature. Emotionalism, including the description of a variety of physical ecstatic symptoms, is contained in a multitude of stotra verses.[47] On the other hand, the idea of reversal of relationship is expressed both in poetry and philosophical discourse. The great need of the Lord for the presence of his devotees and his joy at being accessible to them is a major theme in the hymns of praise. The stotras of Rāmānuja's immediate disciple Kūreśa are replete with reversal imagery, both mythological and devotional. Kūreśa's favourite image of the Lord is undoubtedly that of the child Kṛṣṇa in his acts of stealing butter and being punished by his mother Yaśodā by being tied down to the mortar.[48]

Doctrinally the most significant verse is that composed by Parāśarabhaṭṭar — Kūreśa's son who, according to the hagiographical literature, inherits Rāmānuja's role as the intellectual head of the tradition. He writes in *Śrī raṅgarāja Stava* Part II 74, a praise-hymn spoken directly to the main icon in the Śrīraṅgam temple:

> ... You experience delight
> at being worshipped here in this world
> in temples, homes, and hermitages.
>
> [As arcāvatāra] you bear all
> and are completely dependent
> upon the temple priests (arcakas)
> [who serve you].
>
> Good-hearted folk are stunned
> at this character [of yours]!

As the tradition became more conceptual, this idea was captured doctrinally in the notion of reversal of relationship.[49] Both Viśiṣṭādvaita handbooks written by the great 14th century Teṅkalai Ācārya Piḷḷailokācārya contain references to the doctrine in their sections on arcāvatāra (the incarnation as image/statue). In *Artha-pañcaka* 19, he says that as arcāvatāra the Lord assumes the form that is agreeable to his devotees, and:

> ... although He is all-knowing, He is as if wanting in knowledge; although all-powerful; He is as if powerless; although He has every desire fulfilled, He is as if needy; although He is the protector of all, He is as if needing protection. Having reversed the relationship between the owner and the owned (sva-svāmi-bhāvam viparītam kṛtvā) He is accessible to all by becoming an object of visual perception [and] dwells in the temples and homes [of his devotees].[50]

Conclusion

By the time of Rāmānuja, there was a movement toward a more conceptual understanding of the Vaiṣṇava faith. In order to establish themselves as a respectable philosophical school within the Vedāntic fold, it was important for

Śrīvaiṣṇavas to have a firm and clear doctrine of God to distinguish themselves from the Advaitins, on the one hand, and the Śaivas of various hues, on the other. One of Rāmānuja's central tasks, therefore, was to develop a concept of *who God is and who He is not.* Rāmānuja undoubtedly had a philosophical and theological purpose in his employment of the phrases descriptive of the untaintedness (nirmalatvam) of the Lord who possesses infinite auspicious qualities. Yet the frequency with which he repeats the statement, the emotional nature of his wording, the linkage he establishes between the "untaintedness" of the Lord with his auspicious qualities and the phrases he employs in the context of praise all seem to indicate that he was as much or more influenced by the Āḻvārs (especially Nammāḻvār) as he was by the Upaniṣadic proof texts which he cites.

Likewise, Rāmānuja frequently reiterates (in a variety of contexts) the inability of the Lord's devotees to find support for their souls without worshipping him or to bear separation from him for even the "atomic fraction of a second." My detailed analysis of *RGB*'s description of this spiritual state and its connection with specific physical ecstatic symptoms documents the influence of Āḻvār religiosity. If Rāmānuja was so well-versed in the *Divyaprabandham* as to have been directly influenced by it, even to the point of incorporating from it details such as descriptions of ecstatic symptoms into his *RGB*, then two questions automatically arise: (1) Why does Rāmānuja never cite the hymns of the Āḻvārs in his commentaries? and (2) Why did he not choose to compose a commentary on the *Divyaprabandham*, so central to the sampradāya?

A general answer to the first question has been suggested by Venkatachari:

> Yāmuna's and Rāmānujua's scholastic energies were directed towards establishing the authority of Viśiṣṭādvaita among the contending schools. It was necessary for them to use the Saṃskṛt language and Saṃskṛt texts for this task, as the other philosophic traditions were based on Saṃskṛt śruti and smṛti texts.... Indeed, we might conclude that the authority for ubhayavedānta was established in two ways: its Saṃskṛtic basis of śruti and smṛti texts was asserted to establish its legitimacy outside the community, while its Tamil basis remained more an assumption within the Śrīvaiṣṇava community (Venkatachari 1978, 18).

Two detailed studies[51] have proposed that the *RGB* may in several respects function as a bridge between the tradition of Sanskritic Vedānta and the mood and doctrines of Tamilian Vaiṣṇavism. They argue that Rāmānuja's major purpose was the establishment of a Vedāntic philosophical foundation for bhakti-yoga and that his audience was the larger Brahmanical community. At the same time, in the *RGB* he subtly creates the scope for a religiosity closer to the hearts of the members of his own Śrīvaiṣṇava community.

Although not logically dependent on the findings of either of the aforementioned works, my present study does confirm their conclusions. Through the analysis of a variety of *RGB* passages, it shows how Rāmānuja, while citing only proof texts that are acceptable to the larger Brahmanical community, remains true to the original *Bhagavadgītā* text and avoids explicit reference to the Āḻvārs. In this way, Rāmānuja is able to provide a sound Vedāntic foundation for bhakti-yoga and, at the same time, implicitly incorporate some major themes of Āḻvār spirituality (including emotionalism) into his bhāṣya.

In her study of Rāmānuja's commentary on *Bhagavadgītā* 4:7-11, Katherine K. Young argues not only that Rāmānuja was not *against* image-worship but that indeed his "blueprint" for the concept of arcā is a major contribution to the development of Śrīvaiṣṇava theology (Young 1978, 154). She substantiates her claim by a detailed analysis of Rāmānuja's bhāṣya. One of her conclusions is that *RGB* 4:11 represents the first attempt to bring together the prevailing thoughts on the 'image-form' of God hitherto appearing implicitly in the form of poetry (Āḻvārs) (see Young 1978, 145-84). Following the lead of Young, my study of prapatti in Rāmānuja's thought contains an analysis of his commentary on *RGB* IX:26-34, which demonstrates that Rāmānuja incorporated many ideas central to the concept of prapatti in this important section of his bhāṣya. Drawing on the intense "mood" of surrender found in the *Divyaprabandham*, Rāmānuja created the scope for the later and fuller development of the doctrine of prapatti as an independent means to mokṣa.[52]

The second question asks why, if Rāmānuja were so well-versed in the hymns of the Āḻvārs and so committed to Āḻvār spirituality, he himself did not write a commentary on the *Divyaprabandham*, so very central to his sampradāya. One persuasive answer to this question is derived from the tradition's own understanding of the nature of commentarial literature. According to Śrīvaiṣṇavas, Sanskritic śruti may have only one correct interpretation, but the *Divyaprabandham*, known as an anubhava-grantha (a book to be enjoyed),[53] may have more than one interpretation. Rāmānuja, it is said, did not want to write a commentary on the *Divyaprabandham* because of his unique status within the sampradāya. He feared that a commentary by him would be regarded as the final authoritative word on the corpus, and thus succeeding generations would be denied the great enjoyment that comes from the varied interpretations that may be put upon that work.[54]

Another possibility is that there was a "division of labour" (Young 1978) among the Ācāryas in the development of the theology of Śrīvaiṣṇavism. According to hagiographical tradition, Tirukkurukaippirāṉpiḷḷāṉ (Piḷḷāṉ) was appointed by his Ācārya Rāmānuja to write the first commentary on the *TVM*. The fact that Piḷḷāṉ has incorporated into that commentary (called *Āṟāyirappaṭi*, literally "The Six-thousand [granthas]") words and whole phrases from Rāmānuja's writings would appear to substantiate their close association.[55]

My analysis of key passages in the *RGB* suggests that the opposing interpretations of Lester (that Rāmānuja was "adopted" by later Śrīvaiṣṇavas to legitimize their tradition) and Hardy (that Rāmānuja reinstituted the "normative ideology" of the anti-sensual Upaniṣadic spirituality) are both too extreme. Rather, my findings substantiate the thrust of the poetic, hagiographical and commentarial literature beginning with the *Irāmānucanūṟṟantāti* and the taṉiyaṉs that Rāmānuja was both well-versed in and influenced by the *Divyaprabandham*. That Rāmānuja's function within the Śrīvaiṣṇava sampradāya as the one to establish a sound Vedāntic philosophical basis for bhakti-yoga with its ultimate aim the legitimation of that sampradāya vis-à-vis the larger Brahmanical community and other competing schools is, I think, beyond doubt. He was not "adopted" (Lester) by that community; rather, legitimation was a conscious effort on his part. Nor was his aim to re-establish "normative anti-sensual Upaniṣadic ideology" (Hardy) within the sampradāya itself; instead, in his commentary on the *Bhagavadgītā*, Rāmānuja has a dual agenda. He interprets the *BG* according to the hermeneutical principles of the Vedic establishment, and in doing so provides a sound philosophical foundation for bhakti-yoga acceptable to the wider Brahmanical community. At the same time, he subtly includes a great deal of Āḻvār spirituality in his commentary on this widely respected sacred text and in doing so creates and sustains his commentary's unique devotional mood. His own disciples Kūreśa and Piḷḷāṉ, working alongside of him, carried out the task of a more explicit integration of Āḻvār and Vedāntic spirituality.[56]

NOTES

1. I wish to express my gratitude to Professor K.K.A. Venkatachari of the University of Bombay and the Ananthacharya Indological Research Institute who, during a stay in Montreal (May 1988), assisted me with the translations from the Tamil and gave generously of his time in order to discuss connections between Rāmānuja and the Āḻvārs.

2. Iyaṟpā is the name of the third section (the third thousand) of the *Divyaprabandham*, and consists of verses in short metre. While most of the works in the collection are in the form of songs, Book III consists of "literary and abstract pieces" (See Hardy 1983, 247-8).

3. For the complete story see Rao 1961, 55-56. The 16th century Sanskṛit hagiographical work *Divyasūricaritam* relates the story of the composition of *Śrī Rāmānuja Nūtrandādi* which made manifest "the glory of Yatirāja (Rāmānuja) in the Drāviḍa language" in 18:51-52.

4. Carman also notes that "unfortunately for the historian, this poem gives almost no biographical information about Rāmānuja.... According to tradition, the original

version contained much more about Rāmānuja's qualities and deeds, but Rāmānuja disapproved of these verses because they made too little reference to the Āḻvārs. Whatever the explanation, this ode gives very little information of the kind that would have been helpful in lending Rāmānuja's support to positions taken by either of the later schools [Teṅkalai and Vaṭakalai]. This seems to me to increase considerably the possibility of its genuineness (Carman [1974] 1981, 36).

5. The verses connecting Rāmānuja with Nammāḻvār are vs. 1, 18-20, 29, 46, 54, 60, 64. In addition, v. 13 notes that Rāmānuja considered Toṇṭaraṭippoṭi's works concerning Śrīraṅgam to be very great, and v. 16 links Rāmānuja with Āṇṭāḷ (Godā), stating that when the Vedas declined in status and the Kali Yuga was in power all over the world, Rāmānuja saved the world through the grace of "the one who gave her garland to Raṅganātha," i.e. Āṇṭāḷ.

6. The translations both from the Tamil and from the Sanskrit here and elsewhere in the text are my own unless otherwise indicated.

7. The word taṉiyaṉ means "a stray verse in praise of an author or a work; stray verse in salutation to a guru," and is derived from taṉi, which means "to be alone, single, solitary, to be separate, detached from company, to have no equal or match." (*Tamil Lexicon*, III, 1816 and 1818). Taṉiyaṉs are used in two different ways: they may be attached to a particular composition, and are then faithfully chanted before the recitation of that work (as is the case with the three taṉiyaṉs referred to here). Again, the taṉiyaṉs of all the Ācāryas are strung together for daily recitation by every Śrīvaiṣṇava. For a history of the development of the taṉiyaṉ tradition see Venkatachari 1978, 9-11.

8. See Yāmuna, "Stotraratna," in *Stotramālā*, 1969, v. 1.

9. This translation is by Venkatachari. Several minor revisions and the insertion of appropriate Tamil words are mine (Venkatachari 1978, 17).

10. The translation is a revised version (with Tamil words inserted) of that found in *Tiruvāymoḻi English Glossary*, Vol. I, xxii-xxiii.

11. Regarding Parāśarabhaṭṭar's authorship of this taṉiyaṉ, the following arguments can be made. We do know that the taṉiyaṉ tradition was taking shape at the time of Yāmuna, Rāmānuja's predecessor, on the basis of his *Stotraratna* v. 1 which was to become the official guruparamparā taṉiyaṉ for Nāthamuni. On the basis of the stotras of Rāmānuja's immediate disciple Kūreśa and his son Parāśarabhaṭṭar, we can be sure that the taṉiyaṉ tradition was flourishing during his lifetime. Two other points may be made that give credence to Parāśarabhaṭṭar's authorship of the taṉiyaṉ under question: (1) on the basis of the stotra compositions of Parāśarabhaṭṭar and his father Kūreśa we may be sure that they were very familiar with both the Tamil language and the Āḻvār corpus, so a taṉiyaṉ composed in Tamil cannot be discounted as his composition on the basis of language; and (2) the images of mother and foster-mother found in the taṉiyaṉ is one current during his time, as his father Kūreśa

(following Āṇṭāḷ's *Tirupāvai*, v. 25) uses it in a similarly playful way with reference to Kṛṣṇa and his two mothers in *Sundarabāhu Stava*, v. 107.

12. The confused chronology of the three major hagiographical texts has been a major problem for scholars of the Śrīvaiṣṇava tradition. The dating of the *Divyasūricaritam* is a matter of dispute, and the discussion has revolved around the question as to why, if *Divyasūricaritam* was written long after the time of Rāmānuja, does it end without mentioning his demise. Hardy places the text in the 12th century, and his major argument is "that it ends abruptly with Rāmānuja, never mentioning his demise" (Hardy 1983, 243 and Hardy 1978, 78).

Ramanujam in his *History of Vaishnavism in South India* establishes (perhaps on sounder grounds than Hardy) a very different chronology. Arguing his case from a variety of perspectives, Ramanujam concludes that the chronological ordering of the texts is: *Āṟayirappaṭi Guruparamparāprabhāvam* (13th century), *Divyasūricaritam* (first half of the 16th century), and *Prapannāmṛtam* (last half of the 17th century) (Ramanujan, 1973, 13-59).

For a complete discussion of this disagreement as well as my own view on the subject see Nayar 1988.

13. In the basic matters discussed in this paper concerning the connection between Rāmānuja and the Āḻvārs, all three of the major hagiographical texts are in agreement. Because I have already translated the entire text on Rāmānuja from *Divyasūricaritam* for another project, it is the text most accessible to me right now. Therefore, the hagiographical references in the remainder of this paper are from *Divyasūricaritam*.

14. Araiyar means "priests in some Viṣṇu temples whose duty it is to chant the *Divya Prabandham*" *MTL*, 1:139.

15. For a full discussion of Rāmānuja's pilgrimage to various holy sites in the Tamil land based on both historic and literary evidence see Young 1978, 145-84.

16. O Lord of Vanagiri, please assent to my truthful request! May I [once again] be absolutely subject to Rāmānuja in one corner of Śrīraṅgam, just like before ... (v. 129).

> ... Hear my request! ... enhancing day-by-day the glory of Śrīraṅgam, and expressly destroying the request of [our] adversaries, accomplish [things] in such a manner that [life there] becomes ever enjoyable for your devotees. (v. 130)
>
> ... Setting aside all the worthless [ones] and forgiving in the twinkling of an eye all the misdeeds committed by good people, make the glory of Śrīraṅgam ever enjoyable to them! (v. 131)

17. An inscription recorded during the reign of Kulottuṅga III (dated C.E. 1191) notes that "an influential Coḻa chieftain named Ilaialvan Kalingarayan of Nettūr

consecrated an image of Emberumānār [Rāmānuja] and donated all the taxes accruing from two villages to meet expenses and offerings to the deity" (quoted in Raman 1975, 65).

18. Āndhrapūrṇa is the name of one of Rāmānuja's immediate disciples. However, due to the presence of the term "viśiṣṭādvaita" in v. 17 of this stotra, I would argue that it is more than likely that the composition dates from a later period. Some confusion as to authorship may result from persons having the same name or title. (The Śrīvaiṣṇava practice of naming the grandson after the grandfather may result in confusion as well.)

On the whole, the desire of the Śrīvaiṣṇava sampradāya to honour each and every Ācārya means that authorship is better established in this than in many other Hindu communities. Compare with the tradition of Śaṅkara that has attributed a multitude of works to him which are clearly by other later authors (see Carman [1974] 1981, 266). Compare also with the Northern bhakti tradition of Sūrdās, etc. where authorship is *suggested* by the inclusion of the name of the main personality of a tradition in order to give authority to a particular poem (see Hawley).

19. Lester, "Rāmānuja and Śrī-Vaiṣṇavism," esp. pp. 4-8 quoted in Carman [1974] 1981, 231.

20. Lester quoted in Narayanan 1987, 192. For a fuller discussion of this subject see Narayanan 1987, 4-6. The focus of Lester's argument centres on the ostensible doctrinal discrepancy between Rāmānuja's "major" or "larger" works and his "minor" and more devotional sectarian works, that is, the *Gadyatraya* ("Three Prose Poems") and *Nityagrantha* ("A Manual of Daily [Worship]").

21. (*MTL* III:1482 and Winslow, 469). Śrīvaiṣṇavas often translate pukaḻ as "auspicious qualities". While the semantic field makes that a possible translation of cīr, I do not think that the same is true for pukaḻ. Pukaḻ is better translated as "praise, panegyric, eulogy, fame, reknown, glory, celebrity, famous deed, exploit" (*MTL* V: 2741). I have therefore excluded it from this study.

22. The word kuṇam is not entirely absent from Nammāḻvār's compositions, although he does have a strong preference for cīr. According to Hardy's tentative chronology of the Āḻvārs, Toṇṭaraṭippoṭi is from the late Āḻvār period. Hardy writes: "The apotheosis of Śrīraṅgam, which Toṇṭaraṭippoṭi expresses, and the highly elaborate ritual song he wrote (TPal) favour the assumption of a late date for him, viz. perhaps the 9th or even early 10th century" (Hardy 1983, 268).

23. Kuṟṟam = "fault, moral or physical blemish, defect, flaw ... pain, distress, impurity, ceremonial or moral defilement, as cause of offence to the deity ..." (*MTL*, 2:1043).

Tītu = "evil, vice, fault, blemish, defect ..." a synonym of kuṟṟam. (*MTL*, 4:1940).

24. A slightly different wording can also be found in certain verses: e.g. in III.10.6 Kaṇṇaṉ, who has come down to live amidst the sorrow-stricken, is praised as "[full

of] auspicious qualities without affliction" (tuyaram-il cīrk kaṇṇaṉ), while in IV.5.1 and 3 the Lord is described as "the possessor of auspicious qualities without death" (vīvu-il cīr and vīvu il cīraṉ).

25. It is interesting to note that nowhere in *RGB* does Rāmānuja cite the *Viṣṇu Purāṇa* as a proof text for the nirmalatvam of God. In *Śrī-bhāṣya* I.1.1.1, however, he cites *Viṣṇu Purāṇa* V.5. 82-87. This explication of the term Vāsudeva refers to his being "separate from products, qualities and imperfections (doṣa) of prakṛti" (v. 83); v. 84 contains the phrase "He is the possessor of all auspicious qualities" (samasta-kalyāṇa-guṇa-ātmakaḥ) a phrase often used by Rāmānuja himself; v. 85 contains a description of the Supreme God as being the one "in Whom there are no afflictions."

26. In many *Gītā* verses, Lord Kṛṣṇa indulges in ātma-stuti, or self-praise. Lord Kṛṣṇa often waxes even more eloquent in describing his own qualities in Rāmānuja's gloss. Gonda writes on the Ṛgvedic concept of self-praise thus:

> The ancient authorities qualified some hymns or parts of hymns [of the Ṛgveda] as self-praise (ātma-stuti). That is to say, in a case such as 10, 48-50 Indra is not only the deity to whom the texts are addressed, but also their reputed seer or poet, and in 10, 48, 1-49, 10 he is represented as addressing the people of the Purus and the gods and as, unrestrained by modesty, singing his own praises (Gonda, 110).

27. In XVIII.73, Rāmānuja links "untaintedness" explicitly with Viṣṇu in a passage combining both polemic and praise. He writes that:

> ... knowledge of the Supreme Person, who is denotable by the expression Supreme Brahman, who is a great sea of multitudes of all auspicious qualities beginning with knowledge, strength, lordship, valour, power and lustre — unlimited and abundant — whose essential nature consists of auspiciousness alone, who is opposed to all imperfection (aśeṣa-doṣa-pratyanīka) ... is linked with the knowledge that you are Vāsudeva (vāsudevaḥ tvam iti jñānam).

28. For a discussion of the relation between sacred power and the brahmanical emphasis on the untaintedness of God in the compositions of Rāmānuja and his disciple Kūreśa, see Nayar 1992, 82-85.

29. This translation is by Kaylor and Venkatachari 1981, 80-81. I have made a few minor changes and inserted the original Tamil wording where appropriate.

30. The translations from Āṇṭāḷ's *Nācciyār-Tirumoḻi* are based on that of Sundaram except for minor changes. The Tamil words have been added by me.

31. Interestingly, beginning with the *Irāmānucanūṟṟantāti*, the hagiographical tradition attributes to Rāmānuja a special devotion to the works of both Nammāḻvār (as already quoted in the earlier part of this article) and Āṇṭāḷ.

According to the *Irāmānucanūrrantāti* v. 16, Āṇṭāḷ is said to have been an especially important figure for Rāmānuja whose "life is sustained (vaḻkinṟa)" by the grace (aruḷāl) of Āṇṭāḷ. Note the similarity of the phrase "whose life is sustained" to Rāmānuja's own references to "sustenance or support for the soul."

32. "The jñānī is a paramaikāntī; the life of his soul is dependent on him [i.e. the Lord] (tat-ayatta-ātma-jīvanaḥ); his happiness and sorrow [come] solely from [his] union with (saṁśleṣa) and separation from (viyoga) him." (*Gītārthasaṅgraha*, v. 29).

33. See Rāmānuja's commentary on verses IV.8, VI.15, 18, 27, 47; VIII. 14-15; IX. 13-14, 22, 26, 29-30 and 34; X.9; XI. 24, 55; and XVIII. 65.

34. For the way in which Rāmānuja creates an opening for arcāvatāra in his interpretation of *Bhagavadgītā* IV.8 and 11, see Young.

As Sampatkumaran notes in his translation of this passage, "the good," while not novices on the path of devotion, are at a lower stage than the devotees of the highest order whose experience Rāmānuja describes in such similar words as yogīs or jñānīs (see, e.g. VIII. 14-15, IX. 13, 22).

35. For a good discussion of śarīra-śarīri-bhāva see Carman [1974] 1981, 124-133.

36. Prī means among other things "to please, gladden, delight ... like, love." Its derivatives priyatva/prīti mean "being dear, being beloved, being fond of/and any pleasureable sensation, pleasure, joy, gladness ... favour, grace, affection love ..." (M-W 710-11).

37. Aṉpu means "love, attachment, affection, friendship." Aṉpu's definition as "devotion, piety," which makes it a synonym of pakti, appears to be a later development (*MTL* I:183).

38. This attractive translation is by Narayanan 1987, 50. I have inserted the Tamil words.

39. "They keep on experiencing with their own eyes and other organs of sense in all ways, that is, in every manner desired by them My form, that is, all My essential character, even though it is beyond the range of speech and thought of the yogins" (IV.11 in Sampatkumaran 1985, 108).

40. Note that Rāmānuja makes an explicit sectarian reference in his commentary on this verse. The Lord incarnates "for the protection of the good (sādhunām)." According to Rāmānuja's gloss, "the good" are those who are "devoted to dharma," "the foremost among the Vaiṣṇavas (vaiṣṇava-āgresarāḥ)" and "those who are devoted to taking refuge (samāśrayaṇe pravṛttāḥ)."

41. Prominent among ecstatic symptoms described in the Āḻvār poems are singing and especially ecstatic dancing. The Tamil term for ecstatic dancing resembling possession is aṇaṅkāṭutal. It is mentioned several places in *TVM* (see Narayanan 1987, 43).

The Tamil epic *Cilappatikāram*, which "probably has its roots in the third century A.D. and developed until the sixth century or even later" (Hardy 1983, 170), mentions Brahmins who, even though they wore the sacred thread, had lost their rank because they were addicted to music and dancing. Interestingly, Rāmānuja carefully avoids the mention of dancing among his descriptions of ecstatic symptoms.

Certain texts of the later tradition seem to suggest the acceptability of song and dance for Brahmins, as long as they have Viṣṇu as their subject. For example, Vātsyavarada Guru, Vedānta Deśika's Ācarya, says the following:

> Singing, dancing etc., which are enjoined by the special Āgama-śāstra — all these shall a Vaishnava do. Yama and Sounaka have thus declared:
>
> 'O the purest of men! except the singing of God, no other song of words should be sung by a Brahmin. Therefore (if other songs are sung) sin has been committed by you.'
>
> Singing of Vishnu, composing songs on Him and dancing, O Brahmin! ought to be specially done by those born of the Brahmin caste, like the obligatory karmas (Nitya Karma).
>
> The birds of great sins which inhabit the bodies of men who dance in the presence of God are scared away by the clapping of hands, etc. (Sri Nadadoor Ammal 1971, IX.5-8 [translator's name not cited]).

42. Hardy notes that in the poetry of Tirumaṅkaiyāḻvār the "girl" functions "as a symbol of himself in the state of ecstasy" (Hardy 1983, 377).

43. For a full discussion of reversal of relationship see Young 1978, 165-71, and Nayar 1992, 196-201.

44. At the level of mythology, one poignant expression of the vulnerability and neediness of the Lord is that found in *Periyāḻvār-Tirumoḻi*. "The founder of what is now called Bāla Kṛṣṇa poetry," Periyāḻvār never lets "the miraculous exploits of the Lord become the central focus of his poem; rather, he excites devotion through parental affection" (Ate 1978, 71). Kṛṣṇa in his infancy makes himself so vulnerable that he quite literally cannot sustain himself or bear separation from his devotee mother (see especially *Periyāḻvār-Tirumoḻi* I-III.6).

45. IX.6.10. The translation is by Kaylor and Venkatachari.

46. The translation, with modifications, is by Varadachari 1971, 182.

47. See Nayar 1992, 185-216.

48. Kūreśa loves to dwell on the accessibility of the Lord in his Kṛṣṇa incarnation. Images from *Viṣṇu Purāṇa* and *Harivaṃśa* — sometimes via the Āḻvārs — appear time and time again in Kūreśa's verses. See, for example, *Atimānuṣa Stava* vv. 35-42 in *Stotramālā*.

49. Sva-svāmi-bhāva means "the relation of possession and possessor" (M-W, 1277) or "the relation of the property and its proprietor, of the thing owned and its

owner" (*MTL*, VI:3901). Note that Piḷḷailokācārya uses the term along with the word viparītam kṛtvā, meaning "having reversed or turned around."

50. For a similar passage, also by Piḷḷailokācārya, see *Tattvatraya*, 12-14.

51. See Young 1978, 145-84 and Nayar 1990, 111-132.

52. Prapatti ([salvation by] surrender) is, according to later Śrīvaiṣṇava teaching, a direct and independent means to mokṣa. Unlike bhakti-yoga it is not limited to male members of the higher ("twice-born" dvija) castes. Its "six limbs" are: (1) complete conformity of the prapanna to the will of the Lord; (2) the renunciation of whatever is contrary to the Lord's will; (3) the virtue of "great faith" (mahāviśvāsa), consisting in a total trust in the saving power of God as well as faith in prapatti as a guarantee of mokṣa; (4) the experience of utter helplessness and unworthiness before God; (5) the prapanna must seek the mercy of the Lord as the sole hope for salvation; and (6) there must be a total giving of the Self to the Lord accompanied by a sense that such self-donation is itself made possible only through his grace. Interestingly enough, the very disqualifications for the adoption of bhakti-yoga are essential requirements for the aspirant to prapatti: inability to adopt the more rigorous paths of karma-, jñāna-, and bhakti-yoga, ignorance of the Śāstras, "inferior" birth by caste or sex, and the inability to await delay in the attainment of mokṣa and the Lord.

53. "Śrīvaiṣṇavism can be called a tradition of spiritual enjoyment. The basis of the tradition is the Āḻvārs' enjoyment (anubhava) of the Lord. Secondly, there is the commentators' enjoyment (anubhava) of the hymns of the Āḻvārs. Because the commentators did not consider their task of commenting a pedantic work, but rather the very embodiment of their own enjoyment, their commentaries in turn became a literature to be enjoyed by the subsequent generations. In the Śrīvaiṣṇava tradition direct enjoyment of the Lord can also be indirect enjoyment of Him through the hymns of the Āḻvārs and also the commentaries, which are testimonies of the spiritual experience of the community" (Venkatachari 1978, 94).

54. From an interview with Professor K.K.A. Venkatachari, April 1987 in Bombay. The following story from the *Guruparamparāprabhāvam* is related in Narayanan 1987, 213:

> Earlier, in the time of Uṭaiyavar [Rāmānuja], all the preceptors paid respect to Uṭaiyavar's spiritual son (mānasa-putra) Piḷḷāṉ and submitted their desire to him: 'Please request Uṭaiyavar to comment on the works of the Āḻvārs so that the inner meaning is made manifest.' When Uṭaiyavar was in a large assembly, Piḷḷāṉ bowed formally before him and with a prayerful attitude said, 'I have a request to make.' Uṭaiyavar graciously asked, 'What is it?' and Piḷḷāṉ submitted, 'You have graciously [composed] the Śrī-bhāṣya, and after a victorious expedition the philosophy (darśana) has been firmly established. Could you now comment on the *Tvm* and other divine works (divya-prabandham) of the Āḻvārs and thus protect them?' Uṭaiyavar thought about this and then commanded Piḷḷāṉ, 'If we do a commentary on the "graciously said words," those of dull intellect may think that there is only

this [limited] meaning. This is improper; the songs of the Āḻvārs will increase according to the understanding of each person. Therefore it may seem as if I have created a boundary for the "graciously said words." *You* do a commentary in the same manner [or in the same way] on the *Tvm.*' Tirukkurukaippirāṉ Piḷḷāṉ, with the permission of the King of Ascetics, graciously wrote the first and foremost [muntura muṉṉam; also 'earliest'] commentary on the *Tvm*, the *Āṟayirappaṭi* [*The Six Thousand Granthas*], like *Śrī Viṣṇu Purāṇa*. Bhaṭṭar also graciously and correctly transmitted *The Six Thousand* to Nanjīyar, following Piḷḷāṉ.

55. Venkatachari 1978, 61-64. See also Narayanan 1987, 113-130.

56. For a full-length study of the integration of Āḻvār and Vedāntic spirituality effected by Kūreśa and his son Parāśarabhaṭṭar, see Nayar 1992.

BIBLIOGRAPHY

Primary Sources

Amutaṉār. 1981. "Irāmānucanūṟṟantāti." In *Nālāyira Tivyap Pirapantam*. Ceṉṉai: Tiruveṅkaṭattāṉ Tirumaṉṟam.

Anantārya. 1983. *Prapannāmrutam*. Tirucci: Kṛṣṇasvāmi Ayyaṅkar.

Āndhrapūrṇa. 1969. "Rāmānujāṣṭottaraśatanāmastotram." In *Stotramālā*. Kancipuram: Granthamālākāryālayaḥ.

Āṇṭāḷ. 1981. "Nācciyar-Tirumoḻi." In *Nālāyira Tivviyap Pirapantam*. Ceṉṉai: Tiruveṅkaṭattāṉ Tirumaṉṟam.

Garuḍa Vāhana Paṇḍita. 1978. *Divyasūri Caritam*. Bombay: Ananthacharya Research Institute.

Hari Rao, V.N. 1961. *Kōil Oḻugu: The Chronicle of the Srirangam Temple with Historical Notes*. Madras: Rochouse and Sons.

Kulacēkarāḻvār. 1981. "Perumāḷ-Tirumoḻi." In *Nālāyira Tivviyap Pirapantam*. Ceṉṉai: Tiruveṅkaṭattāṉ Tirumaṉṟam.

Kūreśa. 1969. "Sundarabāhu Stava." In *Stotramālā*. Kāñcipuram: Granthamālākāryālayaḥ.

—. "Varadarāja Stava." In *Stotramālā*. Kāñcipuram: Granthamālākāryālayaḥ.

[Madras] *Tamil Lexicon* [*MTL*]. 1982. 6 Vols. Madras: University of Madras.

Monier-Williams, Monier. 1976. *A Sanskrit-English Dictionary*. Delhi: Motilal Banarsidass.

Nadadoor Amal. 1971. *Prapanna Parijāta*. Madras: Viśiṣhṭādvaitin Prachārini Sabhā.

Nālāyira Tivviyap Pirapantam. 1981. Ceṉṉai: Tiruveṅkaṭattāṉ Tirumaṉṟam.

Nammāḻvār. 1981a. "Periyatiruvantāti." In *Nālāyira Tivviyap Pirapantam*. Ceṉṉai: Tiruveṅkaṭattāṉ Tirumaṉṟam.

—. 1981b. "Tiruvāymoḻi." In *Nālāyira Tivviyap Pirapantam*. Ceṉṉai: Tiruveṅkaṭattāṉ Tirumaṉṟam.

—. 1981c. *Tiruvāymoḻi English Glossary*. Trans. S. Satyamurthi Ayyangar. Bombay: Ananthacharya Indological Research Institute.

Parāśarabhaṭṭar. 1969. "Śrīraṅgarāja Stava Part II." In *Stotramālā*. Kāñcipuram: Granthamālākāryālayaḥ.

Periyāḻvār. 1981. "Periyāḻvār-Tirumoḻi". In *Nālāyira Tivviyap Pirapantam*. Ceṉṉai: Tiruveṅkaṭattāṉ Tirumaṉṟam.

Piḷḷailokācārya. 1972. *Artha Pañcakam*. Bombay: Srinivasa Udyoga Pratisthan.

—. 1973. *Tattvatraya of Lokācārya: A Treatise on Viśiṣṭādvaita Vedānta*. Trans. B.M. Awasthi and C.K. Datta. New Delhi: Munshiram Manoharlal.

Piṉpaḻakiyaperumāḷjīyar. 1975. *Āṟāyirappaṭi Guruparamparāprapāvam*. Tirucci: Kṛṣṇasvāmi Ayyankar.

Rāmānuja. 1956. *Granthamālā*. Kāñcipuram: Granthamālā Office.

—. 1961. *The Vedānta-Sūtras with the Śrī Bhāshya of Rāmānujāchārya*. 3 vols. Trans. M. Rangacharya and M.B. Varadaraja. Nungambakkam, Madras: The Educational Publishing Co.

Sampatkumaran, M.R., trans. 1985. *The Gītābhāṣya of Rāmānuja* [BBh]. Bombay: Ananthacharya Indological Research Institute.

Śaṅkara. 1986. "Śivānandalaharī." In *The Hymns of Śaṅkara*. Trans. and ed. T.M.P. Mahadevan. Delhi: Motilal Banarsidass.

Shastri, J.L., ed. [n.d.] *Upaniṣatsaṅgrahaḥ*. Delhi: Motilal Banarsidass.

Stotramālā. 1969. Kāñcipuram: Granthamālākāryālayaḥ.

Sundaram, P.S., trans. 1987. *Andal: Tiruppavai Nachiyar Tirumozhi*. Bombay: Ananthacharya Indological Research Institute.

Tiruppāṇāḻvār. 1981. "Amalaṉātippirāṉ." In *Nālāyira Tivviyap Pirapantam*. Ceṉṉai: Tiruveṅkaṭattāṉ Tirumaṉṟam.

Van Buitenen, J.A.B. 1974. *Rāmānuja on the Bhagavadgītā: A Condensed Rendering of His Gītābhāṣya with Copious Notes and an Introduction*. Delhi: Motilal Banarsidass.

Varavaramuni. "Yatirājaviṃśati." In *Stotramālā*. Kāñcipuram: Granthamālā-kāryālayaḥ.

Wilson, H.H., trans. 1980. *ViṣṇuPurāṇa*. 2 vols. Delhi: Nag Publishers.

Winslow, M. 1984. *Winslow's A Comprehensive Tamil and English Dictionary*. New Delhi: Asian Educational Services.

Yāmuna. 1985. "Gītārthasaṅgraha." In *The Gītābhāṣya of Rāmānuja*. Trans. M.R. Sampatkumaran. Bombay: Ananthacharya Indological Institute.

Secondary Sources

Ate, Lynn Marie. 1978. *Periyāḻvār's "Tirumoḻi" — A Bāla Kṛṣṇa Text from the Devotional Period in Tamil Literature*. Ph.D. Dissertation. Madison, Wisconsin: The University of Wisconsin.

Carman, John Braisted. 1981. *The Theology of Rāmānuja: An Essay in Interreligious Understanding*. Bombay: Ananthacharya Indological Research Institute.

Gonda, Jan. 1975. *Vedic Literature*. Vol. 1, *A History of Indian Literature*. Weisbaden: Otto Harrassowitz.

Hardy, Friedhelm. 1983. *Viraha-Bhakti: An Early History of Kṛṣṇa Devotion in South India*. Delhi: Oxford University Press.

Hart, George. 1975. *The Poems of Ancient Tamil: Their Milieu and their Sanskrit Counterpart*. Berkeley: University of California Press.

Hawley, John Stratton. 1988. "Author and Authority in the Bhakti Poetry of North India." *Journal of Asian Studies* 47:269-90.

Ingalls, Daniel H.H. 1972. *Sanskrit Poetry: from Vidyakāra's "Treasury."* Cambridge, Massachusetts: The Belknap Press of Harvard University Press.

Kaylor, R.D. and K.K.A. Venkatachari. 1981. *God Far, God Near: An Interpretation of the Thought of Nammāḻvār*. Bombay: Ananthacharya Indological Research Institute.

Lester, Robert. 1976. *Rāmānuja on the Yoga*. Madras: The Adyar Library and Research Centre.

Lipner, Julius J. 1986. *The Face of Truth: A Study of Meaning and Metaphysics in the Vedāntic Theology of Rāmānuja*. Albany: State University of New York, Press.

Narayanan, Vasudha. 1987. *The Way and the Goal: Expressions of Devotion in the Early Śrī Vaiṣṇava Tradition*. Washington, D.C.: Institute for Vaishnava Studies.

Nayar, Nancy. 1988. "Methodology in the Study of Sacred Biography and Śrīvaiṣṇava Hagiography." Paper delivered at the Conference on Religion in South India at Research Triangle, North Carolina.

—. 1990. "The Concept of Prapatti in Rāmānuja's Gītā-bhāṣya." *Journal of South Asian Literature* 23:111-132.

—. 1992. *Poetry as Theology: The Śrīvaiṣṇava Stotra in the Age of Rāmānuja*. Wiesbaden: Otto Harrassowitz.

Raman, K.V. 1975. *Srī Varadarājaswāmi Temple-Kāñchi: A Study of Its History, Art and Architecture*. New Delhi: Abhinav Publications.

Ramanujam, B.V. 1973. *History of Vaishnavism in South India up to Rāmānuja*. Annamalainagar, Tamilnadu: Annamalai University.

Varadachari, K.C. 1970. *Āḻvārs of South India*. Bombay: Bharatiya Vidya Bhavan.

Venkatachari, K.K.A. 1978. *The Maṇipravāḷa Literature of the Śrīvaiṣṇava Ācāryas*. Bombay: Ananthacharya Research Institute.

Yokum, Glenn E. 1982. *Hymns to the Dancing Śiva: A Study of Māṇikkavācakar's Tiruvācakam*. New Delhi: Heritage Publishers.

Young, Katherine K. 1978. *Beloved Places (ukantaruḷi ṉanilaṅkaḷ): The Correlation of Topography and Theology in the Śrīvaiṣṇava Tradition of South India*. Ph.D. dissertation. Montreal: McGill University.

ETYMOLOGY AS A BRIDGE BETWEEN TEXT AND SECTARIAN CONTEXT: A CASE STUDY OF PARĀŚARABHAṬṬAR'S COMMENTARY ON ŚRĪVIṢṆUSAHASRANĀMA

Alaka Hejib
Katherine K. Young

Inspired by Western interest in hermeneutics, Indologists have begun to analyze the strategies of Sanskrit commentators in earnest. One of these strategies is the use of etymologies. The study of etymologies forms a branch of traditional learning called Nirukta. The word nirukta literally means saying or expressing something in such a manner that nothing is left behind — bringing out thoroughly. By extension it means the etymological interpretation of a word. The science (in the sense of *Wissenschaft*, in which the rules and maxims that comprise the system must be obeyed) of etymology began with Yāska (c. 8th-5th century B.C.E.) who systematized this branch of knowledge in a work called the *Nirukta*. It was further elucidated by Durga and Skandamaheśvara, who wrote commentaries on the *Nirukta*. In his introduction, Durga defined etymology as one of the subsidiary tools of Vedic interpretation: "now commences this subsidiary discipline (aṅga) of the Veda called nirukta (etymology) whose subject matter is the thorough understanding of the meaning of the Veda." Besides being a pedantic tool for supporting the overt semantics of a text, etymologies contribute to its interpretation. Later commentators discussed etymologies found in the grammatical analysis that generally concludes a commentarial unit, giving technical approval to the foregoing explanation.

This study will explore the hermeneutical role of the science of etymology by demonstrating how Parāśarabhaṭṭar uses etymology to bridge text and context in his commentary on the *Śrīviṣṇusahasranāma*. The *Śrīviṣṇusahasranāma*, which enumerates the thousand names of Lord Viṣṇu, is an extract from the epic *Mahābhārata* (Anuśāsana Parvan XIII.149, 6950-7056). These thousand names were a popular japa or name-chanting in the Bhakti tradition. They also inspired commentaries by Śaṅkara (9th century C.E.) and Parāśarabhaṭṭar (12th-13th century) who represent the schools of Advaita and Viśiṣṭādvaita, respectively. (The latter, according to tradition, wrote his work upon the personal request of Rāmānuja, his Ācārya). In his commentary, Parāśarabhaṭṭar seeks to connect the names of Viṣṇu with the theological concepts of Viśiṣṭādvaita. We shall present examples in which the commentator, by resorting to etymologies to bridge text and context, initiates discussion on two key concepts: (1) the consecrated image-form of God that presents his fullness (arcā-avatāra); and (2) the holy places (kṣetra) where He dwells.

Parāśarabhaṭṭar extracts the concept of arcā from Arcita, a name of Viṣṇu appearing in the *Śrīviṣṇusahasranāma* (Annaṅgarācārya 1964, 159, verse 68). First, we note that he deviates from the standard order; usually an etymology concludes a discussion, but here it begins the commentary. Second, he gives etymology a different function. Usually it is used for semantic clarification and substantiation (as in Sāyaṇa's commentary on the *Ṛg-Veda* and Mallinātha's on the *Raghuvaṃśa*), but here it provides linkage between text and context. Third, we expect the etymology of arcita to explain the customary meaning of the word as the "worshiped one/the worshipable one," since the word is the past passive participle from the verbal root arc, to worship. Parāśarabhaṭṭar, however, takes this occasion to introduce the Viśiṣṭādvaitic concept of arcā as the Lord's consecrated image-form that presents his ontological fullness. The word arcita has the general semantics of any deity (or object) that is worshipped. The word arcā is a technical term in Viśiṣṭādvaita; its meaning is philosophically restricted. Arcā refers not to *anyone* (or anything) that is worshipped but specifically to the presence of Viṣṇu as a consecrated image fit for worship. Accordingly, the author makes a commentarial leap from arcita to arcā. Because of the derivational kinship between arcita and arcā (both words are derived from the verbal root arc), the commentator has a grammatical footing. But it is apparent that he is preoccupied with the concept of arcā and uses the occasion of etymology for hermeneutical purposes. His maneuver may be labelled: the process of individuation of general meaning to technical specificity; or, technical specificity through semantic parochialization.

But is this process legitimate according to the Indian science of etymology? Authentication of the derivation depends on the correlation of phonetics, morphology, and semantics. A proper etymology commences with a phonetic analysis. Once this analysis is set forth, every ingredient must be verified to be a morpheme, a meaningful element. Subsequently, the juxtaposition of morphemes should yield a "chemically" unified meaning.

We must now analyze the relation between grammar and etymology as branches of learning. Yāska says that etymology is complementary to grammar (tadidam vidyāsthānam vyākaraṇasya kārtsnyam; *Nirukta* 1.5.15). Both etymology and grammar are subsidiary disciplines used for the interpretation of the Veda. The role of grammar in interpretation is manifold as grammar is said to include formation, enumeration, preservation, brevity and clarity. The science of etymology (nirukta) also performs these functions but goes one step further. It elucidates the semantics in addition to the mere presentation of words. Nirukta presupposes that all nouns are derived from verbal roots. It investigates semantics through verbal analysis.

Because both grammar and etymology analyze words (but with different emphases and orientation), and since word and meaning are interconnected, grammar and etymology are interdependent. Grammar depends on etymology for semantics. In fact, without etymology, argued the traditional Sanskrit etymologists, grammar cannot determine the meaning of words. Etymology is also assisted by grammar (Śarma 1966, 107-108). According to Durga's commentary on Yāska's *Nirukta* 1.3.12, verbal derivatives are those nouns, participial adjectives, etc., formed from a verbal root through the rules of grammar formulated by Pāṇini in his *Aṣṭādhyāyī*. It is difficult to recover the etymology of verbal derivatives whose meaning is unclear by following Pāṇini's rules. Nonetheless, they must be elucidated according to the etymologists (nairuktas), and a root located through creative analysis.

The word megha (cloud), for instance, is derived by Yāska from the verbal root mih, to sprinkle, shower: that which sprinkles (or showers) is the sprinkler (or showerer). Thus mih becomes meh (with guṇa modification of the vowel i) and then becomes megh (a guttural aspirate being substituted for h). Next this becomes megh + a (a in the sense of doer). The phonetic similarity between the root mih and its final derivation megha is elucidated. The morphology is smoothly explicable by *Aṣṭādyāyī* rules. And the semantics of mih and megha, with considerable morphological affectation, is consistent (see *Nirukta* 2.6.21). Therefore, the etymology is considered sound and scientific. The meaning or interpretation based on such an etymology is, in turn, accepted as valid, even though it may be totally unknown in common parlance. Similarly, Yāska in *Nirukta* 2.7.27 explains the word aśva (horse) by the etymology aśvaḥ kasmāt aśnute 'dhvānam mahāśano bhavatīti vā; that is to say, "that he covers, traverses, the path or that he eats a lot" makes him a horse. The first root aś is 5th class, the second 9th class. Yāska's suggestion is grammatically justified by traditional criteria but not known to ordinary speakers of the language.

At this point we shall examine the soundness of Parāśarabhaṭṭar's etymological method. His linkage of arcita and arcā, discussed above, is satisfactory from the perspective of grammar. We also observe that through this method he has accomplished his purpose of reading the theologically technical meaning of arcā into the word arcita. His assignment of a meaning, which is unknown to common parlance, is initially disturbing. We have no reason, however, to complain about his innovative semantics, for grammatical accuracy legitimizes both his method of interpretation and the interpretation itself in the eyes of the tradition. Thus, his originality invalidates neither his method nor its outcome. In fact, Parāśarabhaṭṭar should be given credit for his contribution to the use of etymology, given his method of technical specificity through semantic parochialization. The applicability of the etymological method for this purpose constitutes a hermeneutical technique, for it permits and even validates his sectarian agenda according to the traditional rules of Nirukta. Parāśarabhaṭṭar is original in his treatment of etymology. His use of etymology, in fact, is more like an art than a science.

We have noted that the creative potential of the science of etymology was already known to Sanskrit commentators prior to Parāśarabhaṭṭar. Now we shall look more closely at how the science provides scope for interpretation. Yāska's view of etymology is basically pedagogic, pedantic or heuristic, for etymology is perceived as a method that justifies and verifies the meaning of a word. But Yāska also notices that in some cases different etymologies can be given, since various origins of the word may be surmised.

For example, Yāska's etymology of the word puruṣa (man) in *Nirukta* 2.1.3 is:

> (1) puriṣādaḥ from pur (city; body) + sad (to sit), therefore, he who stays/sits in the body (or city); (2) puriśayaḥ from pur (city; body) + sī (to lay, sleep), therefore, he who sleeps in the body (or city); and (3) pūrayatervā from pṝ, therefore, he who fills, supports; and (4) pūrayati ... antarpuruṣam from pṝ, therefore, referring to he who completely fills or occupies the interior (i.e. heart).

Similarly, Yāska in *Nirukta* 2.5 derives the word payas (drink) from two different verbal roots: (1) pā (pib) to drink; and (2) pyai (to grow) following Pāṇini's *uṇādi sūtra*:189. Therefore, depending on the verbal origin, the word paya means: (1) any thirst-quenching drink; or (2) a nourishing drink in a special sense. In this manner, Yāska discusses cryptically whether a word can have only one origin or multiple origins. He also discusses whether a word retains one meaning irrespective of its multiple origins (e.g., payas means drink, even though it may be derived from two roots) or whether there is a one to one correspondence between the verbal origin and the semantic outcome. He arrives at different conclusions based on his analysis of the Vedic data. Durga summarizes Yāska's types of etymologies as being possible through: (1) addition; (2) metathesis; (3) syllabic alteration; (4) elision; and (5) determination of the root in accordance with semantics (Śarma 1966, 53-59). In other words, different explanations or etymologies of words can exist. This gives some hermeneutical scope to the commentator. Indeed, it is Yāska himself, the pioneer of the science of etymology, who contemplates the scope for originality inherent in the interpretive nature of this science. According to Durga, Yāska notes the possibility of explaining complex or ambiguous words in the Veda by resorting to the desired semantics:

> Those words — which bear the accent and grammatical operation that are consistent with [their] meaning and which are also in accordance with their verbal origin — should be derived accordingly. However, if the meaning is not consistent [with the verbal origin or the constituent morphemes] and if the grammatical operation [i.e. morphology] is not apparent, one must investigate the meaning on the basis of any kind of similarity [between the root and the word]. Even if such similarity is not found, one must explain it [literally, derive it] on the basis of syllabic similarity. But *one must not refuse to seek etymological explanation by some means.* One need not [always] respect the grammatical operations, for the [grammatical] word-formations are [by nature] ambiguous. *The verbal analysis is to be molded in accordance with the [desired] semantics [of words]* (Durga on *Nirukta* 2.1.1).

The Sanskrit word for explanation is nirvacana, derived from the root niḥ +vac. (The word nirukta is also derived from this root.) In other words, real explanation of a word involves etymological analysis in accordance with the desired semantics. Commenting on Yāska's concluding remarks, Durga states:

> Either the internal evidence [from Śruti texts] or logic should be employed to find the meaning of a word through the etymological method. More important than these two, however, is context. Unless the general context is determined, one must not proceed to the task of etymology (Śarma 1966, 1003).

Herein is the key to the hermeneutical scope granted by the science of etymology. Durga implies that the seeker of the meaning studies the context where the meaning of the word is to be discovered. Of course, the interpretation arising from the context must involve the congruence of phonetics, morphology and the final semantics, but that can be done with grammatical expertise. Contexts may differ according to the orientation of the commentator. Durga, in his discussion of Yāska's *Nirukta* 13.1.12, says that the ṛṣis (ancient sages endowed with spiritual intuition) can penetrate the meaning of the Vedic words. Others must become tapasvins (assiduous scholars with imaginative and creative intelligence). Scholars must use their devices in a scholastic manner in order to interpret difficult words. Those who are neither ṛṣis nor tapasvins cannot be competent interpreters. Thus, according to etymologists such as Yāska and Durga, creative freedom is granted to select individuals by the discipline of etymology. The science of etymology coupled with the science of grammar is to serve the hermeneutical enterprise.

Now we are in a position to better appreciate how Parāśarabhaṭṭar uses the scholastic freedom allowed by the science of etymology in order to bridge text (the *Śrīviṣṇusahasranāma*) and a particular sectarian context (Viśiṣṭādvaita, a school of theology and branch of Vedānta). His way of relating the names of Lord Viṣṇu to particular sectarian ideas by methods such as the one analysed above in the discussion of arcita-arcā — namely, technical specificity through semantic parochialization of the general meaning — is certainly legitimate according to the rules of the science of etymology as understood by Yāska and Durga.

But are there limits to this creative freedom? Let us examine several other etymologies provided by Parāśarabhaṭṭar. We take as our next example the name Kumbha, which immediately follows the name Arcita in the *Śrīviṣṇusahasranāma*. In common parlance, this word signifies "pot." Śaṅkara's theological interpretation of the name Kumbha complies with customary usage, for he comments: "As everything is contained in him as in a pot" (Anantakrishna Sastri 1955, 87). Parāśarabhaṭṭar, however, chooses to disregard completely the literal connotation of the word in order to preserve his commentarial scheme of treating theological topics. In the section of the text under consideration, for example, he relates one series of names to the concept of image-incarnation (arcā) and another to the concept of sacred place (kṣetra). He provides a transition from the topic of arcā to that of sacred place through an etymology of the name Kumbha.

The word kumbha is derived from the root kam, to desire. Kumbha as a name of Viṣṇu therefore means "He who is desired by them [i.e. the devotees] on account of his beauty which is familiar to them and belongs to the same category [as theirs]" (tatra taiḥ paricitasajātīyasaundaryādinā kāmyata iti kumbhaḥ) (Annaṅgarācārya 1964, 159). To justify this derivation of kumbha from kam, which initially seems to be inspired by mere phonetic resemblance, Parāśarabhaṭṭar offers some morphological adjustments. Two additional phonetic elements are required: *u* after the sound *k* and *bha* as the terminal sound. To introduce the required phonetic modifications, the commentator appears to employ Pāṇini's metalanguage. The discriminating eye, however, finds fault with his use of Pāṇini. The grammatical operations that are involved in the process of derivation of the word kumbha are to be mentioned in proper grammatical order. According to the Pāṇinian metalinguistic formula, the explanation should be as follows: (1) kam changes to kum; and (2) the affix bha is joined to kum. Parāśarabhaṭṭar, however, confuses the order and says: kameḥ kum ca, iti bhapratyayaḥ kumādeśaśca (instead of saying kameḥ kum ca iti kumādeśaḥ bhapratyayaśca). The syntagm "kameḥ kum ca" invokes the application of Pāṇini's maxims I.1.49 and I.1.52 for the grammatical operation of substitution, but the resulting modification would be kakum, not the desired kum. Parāśarabhaṭṭar may have insufficient knowledge of Pāṇini's method and hence makes this mistake. It is more likely, however, that his desire to make the transition in his commentary to the topic of sacred place is so strong that he fakes the grammatical operation and makes it appear Pāṇinian in order to give his etymology the semblance of technical rigour.

Parāśarabhaṭṭar gives a second etymology of kumbha: kau ... bhāti (He who shines on the land) (Annaṅgarācārya 1964, 159). In this derivation the formative components of the word seem to be ku (in the locative singular: kau) and bha (the modified form of the verbal root bhā, to shine). The intervening m sound in kumbha remains to be explained. To overcome this last difficulty, the commentator suggests that the compound may be regarded as an addition to one of Pāṇini's lists of irregularly formed compounds. It may be argued that because Pāṇini himself had to deal with grammatical irregularities by creating a list of exceptionally formulated words so, too, it is legitimate (or at least extremely clever) for Parāśarabhaṭṭar to use the same tactic and to claim that kumbha belongs to such a list.

The common meaning of the word kumbha (pot) is irrelevant to Parāśarabhaṭṭar's commentarial scheme devised for the theological context that he wishes to link to this text by means of his commentary. Consequently, he attempts two etymologies. The first serves to provide a thematic transition by relating the previous concept of the image-incarnation to the subsequent discussion of sacred place through the idea of "[He who is] desired by them [the devotees]" and the idea that "He shines on the land." In this manner the commentator provides a transition from the topic of arcā to kṣetra, which denotes land in general and connotes sacred place in particular. After the occasion is created by the etymology of the word kumbha for the transition, the definition of kṣetra as sacred place promptly appears. Then the commentator links the names to particular sacred places and relates the arcā in these places to such other forms of God as para, vyūha, and vibhava (atha kṣetraviśeṣeṣu pūrvokta-vyūha-vibhavānām sthitiviśeṣaḥ) (Annaṅgarācārya 1964, 160).

Once again a transition is mandatory. The names of Viṣṇu that follow in the text have no obvious connection to the commentator's intent. Parāśarabhaṭṭar accepts the challenge to provide a transition, which he accomplishes by introducing more etymologies. This new transition commences with the names Viśuddhātman and Viśodhana, two names of Viṣṇu that describe respectively "his spotlessness on account of the availability of his fullness to his devotees" and "his act of purifying his devotees who abandon their bodies in his kṣetra and thereby deserve to attain the Lord." These names are indicative of the presence of the image-incarnation (arcā) of Viṣṇu in the kṣetras. At this point, the commentator himself makes explicit to the reader his commentarial scheme by noting that he is going to relate the other forms such as para, vyūha, vibhava, etc., to particular sacred places.

Although we expect the commentator to resort to etymology yet again to provide a bridge between text and a new theological context, he does not do so in his commentary on the name Keśava, one of the names of Kṛṣṇa, the incarnation of the Lord in the form of a man, etc. (vibhava). Rather, Parāśarabhaṭṭar simply fits this name into the context of a particular sacred place by saying that "Keśava [is the one who] dwells in the kṣetra of Mathurā and also in Vārāṇasī" (Annaṅgarācārya 1964, 162). This tactic is only a descriptive analysis and not an etymological explanation of the name.

In all the etymologies considered in the foregoing discussion, it is obvious that employment of etymology is not merely pedantic — that is, to investigate the meaning of the word as such. Rather, it is to provide a creative interpretation and give it authority. The process of interpretation is not from word analysis to the determination of meaning. It is quite the opposite. Etymology is an avenue to novelty of interpretation. It is likely that our author resorts to etymology because the conventional meanings of Viṣṇu's names are too well-known to any reader of Sanskrit to require exegetical comment. And yet he wants to relate this popular text to a particular sectarian school of Vaiṣṇavism. It is also possible that Parāśarabhaṭṭar, as a Sanskrit scholar, wishes to follow the tradition of Sanskrit commentaries, in which etymologies are both an essential and a stylistic requirement. This is not an easy task. Parāśarabhaṭṭar strives hard to become tapasvin (an assiduous commentator) according to Durga's expectation. He realizes that the chasm is much too broad to be crossed without employing the device of etymology as a hermeneutical tool to bridge the gap and leap from the theologically barren text to the theologically rich sectarian context. He is in good company, for Yāska and Durga had already argued that words are to be explained in accordance with the *desired* meaning.

NOTES

1. All Sanskrit citations of the *Nirukta* are from Bhakshi ([1930], 1982) unless otherwise noted.

2. For example, the word nabhas is explained in *Nirukta* 2.4.2 as derived from the root nī, to take, lead, therefore netā bhāsām: the leader of the luminaries, that is, [the deity] Aditya. It may also be derived from the root bhan through metathesis; then it means: that which shines (therefore, sky) or from na (not) + bhā (to shine), therefore, na bhāti [iti na] (which indeed shines), that is, Dyaus.

BIBLIOGRAPHY

Annaṅgarācārya, P.B., ed. 1964. *Śrīviṣṇusahasranāmabhāṣyam* of Parāśarabhaṭṭārya. Madras: Ratham Press.

Bakshi, Mukund Jha. ed. [1930] 1982. *The Niruktam of Yāska Muni* [in the form of Nighaṇṭu Bhāṣya of Kaśyapa Prajāpati] with *The Niruktavivṛti [of Durga] and Exhaustive Notes*. New Delhi: Panini.

Monier-Williams, Monier. [1899] 1970. *A Sanskrit-English Dictionary*. Oxford: Clarendon Press.

Śarma (Ṛṣi) Umā Śaṅkara. 1966. *Hindī Nirukta*. Vārāṇasī: Chowkhambā Vidyā Bhavan.

Sastri, R. Anantakrishna, trans. 1955. *Viṣṇusahasrarāma with Śrī Śaṅkarācārya's Commentary*. Madras: The Vavilla Press.

SYNCRETISM ON THE MODEL OF THE FIGURE-GROUND: A STUDY OF PĪR SHAMS' BRAHMA PRAKĀŚA

Tazim R. Kassam

The term syncretism has commonly been used in a pejorative sense to indicate a tradition corrupted or contaminated by foreign elements. This interpretation is predicated upon a static, predefined view of purity of tradition. In his book *Comparative Religion*, Michael Pye defines syncretism more positively:

> Syncretism is the coherent yet somewhat uneasy coexistence of elements drawn from diverse religious contexts. Even when a smooth cohesion has been achieved the various elements often seem to maintain their potential for conveying independent meanings (Pye 1972, 146).

An excellent visual illustration of this kind of situation, I suggest, is the typical figure-ground image of a chalice and two faces (see Figure 1 below). It helps to demonstrate three basic aspects of syncretism: (1) the *coexistence* of diverse elements; (2) the *coherence* of their combined configuration; and (3) the retention of their respective *self-identities* whose prominence and recognition depend upon the viewer's perspective. Accordingly, syncretism may perform a dynamic role in initiating change between cultures in contact as well as enabling those cultures to make their transitions with relative ease and continuity.

It has been said of Islamic vernacular literatures in India that they are syncretistic. Into this category fall the gināns or devotional hymns of the Shīᶜā Ismāᶜīlī Nizārī Muslims, better known in the subcontinent as *Satpanthī Khojās*. I will focus on a ginān called *Brahma Prakāśa*, which means Divine Light or Illumination, for two reasons: (1) to ascertain, through an analysis of a few key terms and concepts in the text how the term syncretistic may be applied to it;

and (2) to determine, by examining its structure, how the text may have served to bridge two religious traditions, the Muslim and the Hindu.

As a missionary movement since the time of the first caliphs, the Ismā^{c}īlī sect had consciously cultivated a system of inviting outsiders to its path. Frequently forced underground during its turbulent history by the ill-disposition of other Muslim groups in power, it often preserved itself as a secret society and invented unique ways of furthering its cause, now political, now religious, and sometimes both. The central institution that oversaw these various activities was called the da^{c}wa, meaning both its system of operation through its dā^{c}īs or pīrs (preachers) as well as its religious doctrines and traditions (Nanji 1978). The gināns were composed by these preachers who were sent from centres of the Ismā^{c}īlī mission, located in Iran, to the Indian subcontinent between the ninth and seventeenth centuries C.E. The ginān tradition is regarded as one of the most creative and significant achievements of the da^{c}wa because of its contribution to the Ismā^{c}īlī movement's proselytizing activity. The gināns were not an accidental by-product of contact and change between two cultures mutually influencing each other but rather the result of a specific intention to create a certain kind of literature by the da^{c}wa. Since the purpose of the dā^{c}īs was to win converts, we should find in the gināns clues to their methods of effecting change. That is to say, the gināns should reflect techniques of transformation that facilitate conversion.

Allegedly the work of a twelfth century dā^{c}ī Pīr Shams, *Brahma Prakāśa* is a poem of a hundred and fifty couplets. It is written in simple Hindi with a style typical of Kabīr and Nānak and with a vocabulary drawn from sāḍhukaḍi bolī (a dialect of Hindi used by various saints and associated with Tantric meditative practice).[1] The central theme of the poem is the attainment of bliss (sukha) through the continuous repetition of the word (śabda) or name (nāma). It provides concrete prescriptions for developing concentration (e.g. repeat the śabda aloud for three months). It describes various spiritual experiences that follow concentration (e.g. after three months of repetition, something sweet is released in the mouth). It also makes statements about the efficacy of the word (śabda) and its essential nature. In addition, this composition contains both long sections devoted to a critique of false paths and a list of achievers of bliss (sukha).

On the basis of its language, style, and content, there is serious reason to question both its authorship and dating. Clearly, the text can be no earlier than the sixteenth century, assuming that the list of achievers is not an interpolation, since Nānak and Kabīr, who belong to the sixteenth century, are among them. Moreover, because *Brahma Prakāśa* appears on the surface to be distinctly Hindu both in terms of terminology and concept, it even calls into question the idea that the text was authored by an Ismā^{c}īlī.

Textual analysis may help to ascertain whether or not the text was composed by an Ismā^{c}īlī. If the text reflects minor alterations and insertions of Ismā^{c}īlī references that stand out like intruders, displaying no real integration with the other elements of the text, we would be justified in concluding that *Brahma Prakāśa* was merely appropriated and then clumsily edited by Ismā^{c}īlīs. On the other hand, if the text evinces (in its use of Hindu symbolism and allusions) the characteristics of a skilled, selective and intentional usage that provides scope for a coherent *shift* in perspective from Hindu to Ismā^{c}īlī, this would indicate Ismā^{c}īlī authorship. If the latter can be demonstrated, we may presume that the text reflects the deliberate, albeit subtle, technique of the da^{c}wa to instigate conversion through the use of local languages and religious idiom to convey its message. In this case, the text may have been attributed to Pīr Shams of the twelfth century, even though it was written much later, or it may have been written by another Pīr Shams of the sixteenth century.

Since *Brahma Prakāśa* is a fairly lengthy poetic work, I have decided, for the sake of brevity and focus, to approach it in terms of the network of connections it makes in relation to one pivotal equation presented in the opening verse: the equation between śabda (word) and guru. In order to do so, I have isolated key terms in the text and their equivalences or linkages, overt or covert, with these two terms. I shall deal first with the significance of these terms as they are developed in the text itself. Then I shall attempt to see how the clusters of meanings and associations shift in emphasis and focus depending upon the perspective from which they are viewed, Hindu or Ismā^{c}īlī. In short, I shall explore how a bridge is built by key terms whose amplified and ambiguous meanings connect concepts of Hinduism and Islam.

The text may be summarized as follows. Verses 1 to 5 give instructions on the method of attaining bliss, namely, by the continuous repetition of śabda. Verses 6 to 11 describe the inner state experienced after three months of continuous repetition, emphasizing its nature of love (prema), rapture (sukha) and trance-like ecstasy (matavālā). Verses 12 to 40 constitute a long section that criticizes the ways of those who are unrealized, as in:[2]

> They read aloud from leaves of bulky volumes;
> But they attain not the way to that happiness (12).
>
> They anoint themselves with ash but are hollow within;
> For not a speck of that happiness do they taste (14).
>
> They drink all kinds of mixtures and elixirs;
> But they know not the means to happiness (26).

This is immediately complemented by verses 40 to 60, which list names of Hindu deities, mythological figures, and historical people (notably Śiva,

Prahlāda, Kabīr, Nānak, Rohidās, Dādu and Gorakhnāth) who, according to the author, have attained sukha. Verses 61 to 77 explain the nature of spiritual states attained after concentration (dhyāna) has been anchored in the heart for six months, then in the navel for nine months, and finally ascends to the skull where the following spectacle is witnessed:

> Without storm, yet the sky rolls with thunder;
> Without palace, yet one sits on a terrace (65).
>
> Without clouds, yet there is rain;
> Without body, yet there dwells a man (66).

Subsequent verses explain how such a state is possible. Verses 77 to 93 focus on the nature of śabda as Indestructible (akhara), Immortal (amara) and so on, and how union with śabda gives liberation (mukti). Verses 93 to 105 elaborate on the latter. The next 12 verses describe the basis of the author's teaching as his own experience. He says:

> ... not from hearsay, but from experience do I speak (108);
>
> ... as I have reached [realization], so I have described it (109).

He goes on to state emphatically that the means of salvation is to focus upon the *name* of the Sāheb (master) who is the boat for crossing the ocean of life (111). Verses 118 to 140 introduce the idea of the four ages (yugas) and the idea that the form (rūpa) which the Absolute (nirguṇa, ḥaqq) takes in the fourth age (kaliyuga) is niṣkalaṅka (Impeccable; Gujerati nakalaṅkī), and none other than the Sāheb:

> During the kaliyuga, (the Formless took) the form of nakalaṅkī
> He is the Sāheb, the Lord of the earth (137).

Finally, the last 10 verses bear the author's name: Shams. Shams claims that he has revealed the secret of the true path (satmārga) to realization, namely, the worship of the guru who is the Sāheb (144).

The unifying element of the poetic work is the word śabda. Key relations are established in the first four verses in which an explicit equation is made between sat śabda and guru (verse 1). In the śabda = guru equation, the stress is on the śabda, the word to be repeated constantly. This is important to note, for later in the text the stress shifts to the word guru. This equation is followed by implicit equations in the next four verses between śabda and Pīr Shāh, Pīr Shāh and nāma, and nāma and Brahma. The term Pīr Shāh adds a twist to the situation because it has a double meaning. For the Hindu, it is only a *word* to be repeated constantly (japa) . But for the Ismā^{c}īlī, it is understood as the *name* or nāma of the guru, for Pīr Shāh is a term, like Sāheb and Mowlā, that refers to the Shī^{c}ite Imām. The Shī^{c}ā believe the Imām to be the legitimate successor to the Prophet, the key interpreter of the *Qur'ān*, and the true guide for each time. Pīr Shāh is the nāma, and this nāma is connected to Brahma, which provides a name (Sanskrit, Brahmā) familiar to Hindus. In fact, the whole text may appear to be a Hindu treatise to them because it contains terms such as sat panth, japa, śabda, and Brahma. For established Ismā^{c}īlīs, however, Pīr Shāh identifies the text as Ismā^{c}īlī.

After the second verse, the term śabda does not reappear until verse 76. Instead, the words nāma (name) and eka nāma (one name) are found. However, śabda is implicitly present in all those verses referring to the path or way to happiness that has been lost by the non-achievers of sukha, namely, the path of repeating the śabda. This link becomes explicit in verse 84, in which the Ineffable is made known by skill-in-means (jugatī), the skill of concentration on śabda.

In syllogistic form: if a=b and b=c, then a=c. Accordingly, all the other connections with śabda until it reappears in verse 76 are made through the words nāma or eka nāma. Therefore, it is necessary to examine the word nāma more closely. In verse 4, as noted above, it is identified with Pīr Shāh and Brahma and, if repeated, leads to prema prakāśa (divine love). It next appears after the section on non-achievers in verse 39 as eka nāma, where it is clearly stated that:

> Whether it be the ascetic or the householder;
> Without worshipping the one name,
> that happiness remains inaccessible (39).

This sense of the one name is reinforced in verses 60 and 63 by the enclitic hī in nāma hī, that name alone, as the means to sukha.

Nāma is not used in the next 50 verses, and śabda is reintroduced with a series of negative adjectives that underline its transcendent nature. For example, it is akhaṇḍa (Indivisible), ajara (Insoluble), akāla (Timeless), aḍola (Immovable), apāra (Boundless) and akhara (Indestructible). Of significance here is the equation made in verse 93 between śabda and niriñjan (Unblemished) and śabda and nirākara (Formless), which connects it to the term nirguṇa (Unqualified) used later in the text as its synonym. In effect, then, śabda is not just the mystical word or syllable as means, but also the Word as end, much as aum as mantra becomes aum as Brahman on another level. This emphasizes further the śabda side of the śabda = guru equation spoken of earlier. An anomaly was created, however, by the identification of śabda and Pīr Shāh, which retains simultaneously the senses of its being the word (śabda) and the actual guide (guru).

Curiously but significantly, śabda once again disappears after verse 93, this time permanently; nāma returns again in its place. However, this time nāma is accompanied by a co-referent: Sāheb. In verse 110, the author states that liberation cannot be attained without worship of the one name (eka nāma). In the next verse, this name is identified as that of the Sāheb, the saviour as indicated by the connection between Sāheb and boat. Following closely is verse 113, which says:

> Should he thus repeat "Sāheb, you and you alone" night and day;
> He will surely swim across the ocean of life (113).

In this verse the phrase to be repeated is sāheba tunhi tu (Sāheb, you and you alone). This immediately calls to mind verse 3, in which Pīr Shāh was the name exhorted to be repeated night and day. The striking parallelism suggests that there is a subtle but clear link between Pīr Shāh and Sāheb. The balance of the śabda = guru equation is hence restored as an equivalent of guru. Sāheb becomes the central focus in the latter half of the text through the following equations: guru = śabda = nāma = Pīr Shāh = Sāheb nāma (the preceptor is the word, which is the name, which is Pīr Shāh, which is the name of the Sāheb). We shall return to the term Sāheb. Suffice it to say at present that this term carries the same ambiguity as śabda in the earlier section. It connotes both the guide and the goal, as in guru with a small g and Guru with a capital G. So, for instance, the author states:

> He who concentrates on Sāheb's name;
> That devotee attains the Sāheb Himself (114).
>
> By repeating the name, the Named is attained;
> By effacing itself, in Self is the self merged (127).

Therefore, we have a very significant realignment or superimposition of teleology, in which śabda and its cognates lead not only to sukha and mukti but also to the owner and essence of the name, namely Pīr Shāh, or Sāheb. And the firmness with which it is asserted in verse 115 ("Without repeating the name, life is wasted") helps to establish the special position of the one name (eka nāma). The focus on the one name is further underlined in verse 120 and 129, where it is said that although the Sāheb has endless names and the One without qualities (nirguṇa) has numerous qualities (guṇas), they are, in fact, essentially one. Thus, on the one hand, the one name (eka nāma) includes all other names and, on the other hand, it is singled out as the essence of all names.

As pointed out earlier, the term śabda disappears after verse 93, with the terms nāma and Sāheb taking over its function. Clearly, after the term Sāheb is introduced, it becomes identified with nāma, the name. Further associations are made with Sāheb. In verse 96, Sāheb is He who is detached from all (sabahi se mugata), and He who is attained only by the few yogis who know the true skill in means (yugatī). In the preceding and following verses, Sāheb is kiratār, the Creator, and niriñjan, the Formless. Then, in verses 111 to 114, Sāheb is equated with eka nāma and is to be worshipped as tunhi tu (you and only you), which leads to Sāheb himself. He has numerous names, and those who abandon evil and worship them are saints (santa). Verse 121 is a key text, since it establishes the authority of Sāheb by appeal to sacred scripture. It reads:

> The Āgamas, the Nigamas, the Purāṇas and the Qur'ān
> All have variously explained the Sāheb's greatness (121).

Sāheb is then further connected with the term haka (Arabic ḥaqq: Absolute, Truth). Verse 130 says: haka arupī rūpa hoi āve, that is, "The Absolute is Formless, but assuming a form It comes," or, given the context that follows, it "descends." Verses 133 to 137 state that the Ḥaqq came in four forms (rūpa) during satyuga; Prahlād was among the five million It saved. It came in three forms during tretāyuga; Hariścandra was among the seven million It saved. It came in two forms in dvāparayuga; the Pāṇḍavas were among the nine million It saved. And finally:

> During kaliyuga, It took the form of Nakalaṅkī (the Sinless One)
> Who is the Sāheb, the Protector-Saviour of all souls (137).

Accordingly, Sāheb is the tenth form (rūpa). It should be noted that none of the other forms are identified and that the word avatār does not occur. The term rūpa (form) is used instead. This covert evocation of the avatār doctrine is carried further in verses 137, 138, and 140 that focus on the idea of Sāheb as khelāḍī, that is, as the divine player. However, when we look at the three verses carefully, it becomes apparent that khela (game) is used in a special sense. Immediately after the verse that proclaims Sāheb as the nakalaṅkī form, these two verses follow:

> One day, the Creator (khālaq) will play a game (khela)
> He will relieve the world of evil and tyranny (137).

> When the Imām Mahdī becomes king,
> Twelve million, nay countless souls will attain mokṣa (139).

In other words, Sāheb has now been implicitly identified as the Mahdī, the expected messiah who will both relieve the world from oppression and lead it to salvation.[3] But in terms of avatār as the saviour of the world from evil forces, the verses still appeal to the Hindu idiom and world view. The above idea of khela, however, has a rather different connotation from the līlā concept in Hinduism, even though the image of play conjures up the latter. The development of associations is not allowed to rest here:

> They will witness everywhere ᶜAlī's sport (vilāsa)
> (Those) who search for Brahma Prakāśa through dhyāna (140).

The Divine Player, who is in this case identified as ᶜAlī, evokes the figure of Viṣṇu, both in his transcendent aspect and in his immanent aspect as the incarnation Kṛṣṇa. However, there is no direct reference to the Hindu (Vaiṣṇava) concept of avatār, only an appeal through the imagery of play and Player. The absence of such a direct link leaves the stage empty for the figures of Imām Mahdī and ᶜAlī to assume pivotal roles not specifically identical to the notion of the avatār. The vagueness of the idea that the Formless takes form to save humanity permits the meanings associated with the names Imām Mahdī and ᶜAlī in their original context to continue to exist. Hence, the lack of an explicit reference to the avatār idea prevents any possible cognitive dissonance from an Ismāᶜīlī perspective. Nothing is clearly defined, and it is this very ambiguity that creates scope for multiple linkages and interpretations.

Finally, in the culminating verse of the text, Sāheb is identified as the gurunara (the man who is the guru):

> May the man who is guru (gurunara) fulfil the wishes of all;
> [So prays] he who has spoken about concentration on Brahma Prakāśa (150).

If we juxtapose this final verse with the text's opening one — "The true word is my guru. But the world does not recognise it" — the emphasis is no longer on śabda but on guru. The "it" is really "him," "the guru," and the true word (sat śabda) is none other than the guru's name. This shift of emphasis from śabda to guru in the śabda = guru equation, becomes virtually total by the end of the text. The transformation can hardly be detected, however, unless one follows, step by step, the connections made by repetition, paraphrase, substitution or parallelism.

To review the central associations in the text, I have sketched a diagram (see Figure 1) illustrating the primary associations among the cluster of terms. It shows how the central focus shifts, depending on whether a Hindu or Ismāᶜīlī were reading the text. On the left part of the diagram, śabda is at the centre of the circle. Ignoring the box at the extreme left margin, the associations could be clearly identified as Hindu, inclining towards Vedānta and Yoga but also having a flavour of Vaiṣṇava Bhakti. Excluding the box, there is nothing to indicate that

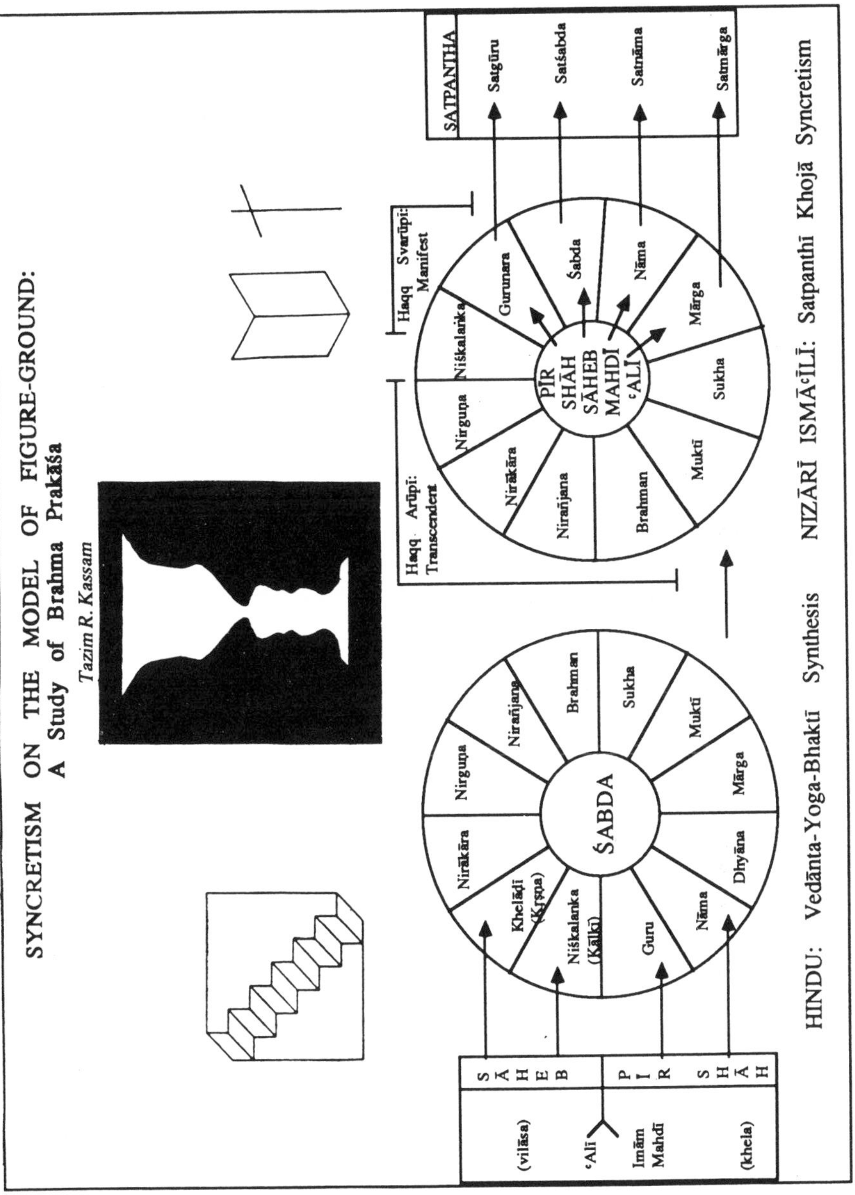
SYNCRETISM ON THE MODEL OF FIGURE-GROUND:
A Study of Brahma Prakāśa
Tazim R. Kassam
HINDU: Vedānta-Yoga-Bhaktī Synthesis
NIZĀRĪ ISMĀʿĪLĪ: Satpanthī Khojā Syncretism
ŚABDA
Nirākāra
Nirguṇa
Nirañjana
Brahman
Sukha
Muktī
Mārga
Dhyāna
Nāma
Guru
Niśkalanka (Kalki)
Kheladī (Kṛṣṇa)
PĪR SHĀH SĀHEB MAHDĪ ʿALĪ
Gurunara
Śabda
Nāma
Mārga
Sukha
Muktī
Brahman
Nirañjana
Nirākāra
Nirguṇa
Niśkalanka
Haqq Arūpī: Transcendent
Haqq Svarūpī: Manifest
SATPANTHA
Satgūru
Satśabda
Satnāma
Satmārga
SĀHEB
PIR
SHĀH
(vilāsa)
ʿAlī
Imām Mahdī
(khela)

the system is syncretistic. On the contrary, it appears to be a perfect synthesis of key Hindu philosophies. Why is it, however, that instead of using the terms bliss (ānanda) and mantra, the text uses happiness (sukha) and word (śabda)? Although this may be purely a matter of vernacular usage, it is possible that the author is purposely avoiding the former terms because of their Brahmanic or Yogic overtones, which would make them too Hindu from the perspective of Ismā^{c}īlism. Once again, as in the case of the Divine Player, the words śabda and sukha are used to create scope for redefinition, although appeal is made to familiar Hindu notions of the sacred word and the experience of bliss.

The principal technique used by the author to shift the focus of the primary system is exposed in the diagram. The diagram reveals a careful and subtle infiltration of the contents in the box into the definition of the terms nāma, guru and Niṣkalaṅka, without in any way disturbing the rest of the structure. Hence, by amplification, nāma comes to mean eka nāma, which is Pīr Shāh, which is the Sāheb's name, which is Imām Mahdī and ^{c}Alī. Guru comes to represent the gurunara who is, in fact, the form of the Formless, the Niṣkalaṅka Sāheb who will save all men. Even after introducing these foreign elements into the structure, śabda still retains the central place, only now śabda becomes the name of the Sāheb. What results is the transformation represented in the circle at the right of the diagram.

The transformation is subtle but pivotal. While previously śabda was the pivot of the terms mārga, sukha, mukti and so forth, now Sāheb occupies that central place and in doing so imparts a different meaning to these terms. So, for instance, guru, śabda, mārga and nāma are no longer *any* guide, word, path or name, but become the True Guide (satguru), the True Word (satśabda), the True Path (satmārga) and the True Name (satnāma). This transformation and development towards a singular identification is anticipated in the text's first verse, where the True Word (satśabda) is, in fact, the Guru. It is affirmed in the penultimate verse, where the True Path (satmārga) is the path of the Satguru. Such an interpretation would ring true for Indian Ismā^{c}īlīs who were known as Satpanthīs.

The principle of syncretism afforded such elasticity and amplification of meaning as to allow an effective bridging of two cultures. However, as was noted above in Pye's definition of syncretism, the coexistence of foreign elements remains uneasy. In *Brahma Prakāśa*, the terms Pīr Shāh, Sāheb, Imām Mahdī and ^{c}Alī may be identified by Hindus as alien elements, strangers in the text, although they were introduced unobtrusively and without elaboration of their Ismā^{c}īlī Muslim meanings. The terms do not, however, lose their separate identities. They do not dissolve and disappear to become inseparable from the primary structure in the left circle of the diagram. On the contrary, if they are taken seriously, if their presence in the text is acknowledged, they influence the text's primary structure in a fundamental way, as illustrated in the circle at the right.

With respect to the question of authorship, the artfulness by which this change is accomplished suggests that the mystical poem *Brahma Prakāśa* was composed by an Ismāᶜīlī. Further, the text reflects a typical method of the Ismāᶜīlī daᶜwa to achieve change without the sudden, dramatic and drastic shift in perspective so common to the idea of conversion.

Whereas the various elements in *Brahma Prakāśa* coexist coherently, the fact that they retain their potential to communicate meanings specific to different religious communities make it a syncretistic text. I would like to note, however, that this syncretism has a dynamic aspect. By creating tension, the coexistence of foreign elements demands resolution. The syncretistic effort in *Brahma Prakāśa* is less an amalgam resulting from a compromise reached between two different religious traditions than a conscious, clever and creative strategy to effect a smooth process of conversion. Like the figure-ground illustration, the text may be read from either Hindu or Ismāᶜīlī viewpoints while retaining the central meaning for each respectively. Syncretism, in this example, sustains a tolerable co-existence of separate identities. But if the Hindu accepts the central role assigned in the text to elements such as Pīr Shāh and Sāheb, a substantial shift of identity takes place so that the true path is no longer Hindu but Ismāᶜīlī. If the Hindu perspective is represented by the two faces and the Ismāᶜīlī by the chalice in the figure-ground model, this would mean that the chalice would become the more consistently recognized and identified view.

NOTES

1. In general, technical terms cited in this article remain faithful to the spellings of the vernacular text and have not been Sanskritized; e.g., Brahma instead of Brahman or Brahmā.

2. The verses of *Brahma Prakāśa* cited in this article have been translated by the author.

3. The inclusion of the name Mahdī raises another set of questions which we shall not attempt to address here. For instance, is this a direct reference to the first Ismāᶜīlī Fāṭimid Caliph, al-Mahdī, who took Cairo in 909 C.E.? Or is it related to the Twelver concept of the Mahdī, the hidden twelfth Imām who will return "at a time when oppression and inequity in the world reach their peak" (Madelung 1986, 261)?

BIBLIOGRAPHY

Esmail, A. and A. Nanji. 1970. "The Ismā^c^īlīs in History." In *Ismā^c^īlī Contributions to Islamic Culture*, ed. S.H. Nasr. Tehran: Imperial Iranian Academy.

Kassam, T. R. 1992. "Songs of Wisdom and Circles of Dance: An Anthology of Hymns of the Ismā^c^īlī Saint, Pīr Shams." Montreal: PhD Diss., McGill University.

Madelung, W. 1986. "Shiism." In *Encyclopedia of Religion*, volume 13. Ed. M. Eliade. New York: Macmillan.

Nanji, A. 1978. *The Nizārī Ismā^c^īlī Tradition in the Indo-Pakistan Subcontinent*. New York: Caravan Books.

Pye, M. 1972. *Comparative Religion*. New York: Harper and Row.

Shams, Pīr. 1921. *Brahma Prakāśa: An ancient treatise on the attainment of the experience of divine light (with explanations and commentary)*. [Gujerati text] Bombay: Lāljī Devrāj.